Mac® Application Development

FOR

DUMMIES®

by Karl G. Kowalski

WILEY

John Wiley & Sons, Inc.

Mac® Application Development For Dummies®

Published by
John Wiley & Sons, Inc.
111 River Street
Hoboken, NJ 07030-5774

www.wiley.com

Copyright © 2012 by John Wiley & Sons, Inc., Hoboken, New Jersey

Published by John Wiley & Sons, Inc., Hoboken, New Jersey

Published simultaneously in Canada

For general information on our other products and services, please contact our Customer Care Department within the U.S. at 877-762-2974, outside the U.S. at 317-572-3993, or fax 317-572-4002.

For technical support, please visit www.wiley.com/techsupport.

Wiley also publishes its books in a variety of electronic formats and by print-on-demand. Not all content that is available in standard print versions of this book may appear or be packaged in all book formats. If you have purchased a version of this book that did not include media that is referenced by or accompanies a standard print version, you may request this media by visiting http://booksupport. wiley.com. For more information about Wiley products, visit us www.wiley.com.

Library of Congress Control Number: 2011937927

ISBN: 978-1-118-03222-0 (pbk); ISBN: 978-1-118-15999-6 (ebk); ISBN: 978-1-118-16001-5 (ebk); ISBN: 978-1-118-16002-2 (ebk)

Manufactured in the United States of America

10 9 8 7 6 5 4 3 2 1

WILEY

About the Author

Karl Kowalski has traveled the world of computers and software development for far longer than he's willing to admit. He has written programs for airplanes, robots, games, and even particle accelerators, and he has developed software on platforms ranging from desktop computer to mainframes and all the way down to smartphones. He is also the author of BlackBerry Application Development For Dummies (John Wiley & Sons, Inc.). He lives near Boston and works for RSA, the Security Division of EMC, where he develops security solutions for mobile platforms such as BlackBerry and iPhone, and desktop operating systems such as Windows and Mac OS X. In his spare time, he develops software for smartphones as part of his startup, BlazingApps LLC (www.blazingapps.com). And if there are any spare seconds in the day, he does some voice-over work for one of his favorite journals, The Objective Standard.

Dedication

To my parents, Constance and Stanley Kowalski, who have always encouraged me to do the best and at every step helped me to become who I am today. Thanks, Mom, for making sure I eat right and especially enough.

To my family — Lee Anne, David, Rosemarie, Joseph, Candi, and Reese and Mason — who helped me to keep focused and moving forward. Thanks for letting me vent when things weren't always perfect.

Finally, to the members of the RSA Credentials Everywhere team, past and present: You have always been behind my efforts to express myself, 100 percent. Thank you for keeping me sane during the non-book-writing hours.

Author's Acknowledgments

I owe many thanks to Carole Jelen for her efforts to keep me writing. She is everything I want in an agent, and she has set the bar very high.

Acquisitions Editor Kyle Looper kept me on top of my progress and gave me more than a few ideas for things to think about and write about. Project Editor Pat O'Brien has earned tremendous thanks for all his efforts to move me above the level of apprentice-writer and for keeping me on track with all my chapters and rewrites. Senior Copy Editor Barry Childs-Helton helped me greatly by taking my letters and attempts at punctuation and polishing them into something readable. And Dennis Cohen was phenomenal at keeping my technical expertise sharpened and shiny.

Thanks to Daniel Bailey at EMC for his efforts to ensure that I maintained a distinct separation between my EMC efforts and my writing efforts.

And very special thanks to Irina Furman (irina@igrafica.com) for her work in creating a spectacular set of icons for DiabeticPad.

Lastly, I promised I would thank my supervisor, Jennifer Chong, who gave me enough time to perform my duties at RSA as well as write another book.

Publisher's Acknowledgments

We're proud of this book; please send us your comments at http://dummies.custhelp.com. For other comments, please contact our Customer Care Department within the U.S. at 877-762-2974, outside the U.S. at 317-572-3993, or fax 317-572-4002.

Some of the people who helped bring this book to market include the following:

Acquisitions, Editorial, and Vertical Websites

Project Editor: Pat O'Brien

Acquisitions Editor: Kyle Looper

Senior Copy Editor: Barry Childs-Helton

Technical Editor: Dennis Cohen

Editorial Manager: Kevin Kirschner

Vertical Websites Project Manager:
Laura Moss-Hollister

Vertical Websites Project Manager:
Jenny Swisher

Supervising Producer: Rich Graves

Vertical Websites Associate Producers:
Josh Frank, Marilyn Hummel, Douglas Kuhn,
and Shawn Patrick

Editorial Assistant: Amanda Graham

Sr. Editorial Assistant: Cherie Case

Cover Photo: © iStockphoto.com / Cary Westfall

Cartoons: Rich Tennant
(www.the5thwave.com)

Composition Services

Project Coordinator: Patrick Redmond

Layout and Graphics: Samantha K. Cherolis

Proofreaders: Melissa Cossell,
Christine Sabooni

Indexer: Potomac Indexing, LLC

Publishing and Editorial for Technology Dummies

    Richard Swadley, Vice President and Executive Group Publisher

    Andy Cummings, Vice President and Publisher

    Mary Bednarek, Executive Acquisitions Director

    Mary C. Corder, Editorial Director

Publishing for Consumer Dummies

    Kathy Nebenhaus, Vice President and Executive Publisher

Composition Services

    Debbie Stailey, Director of Composition Services

Contents at a Glance

Table of Contents

Introduction

. . . .

*T*he Apple Macintosh personal computer ushered in an age of powerful computer capabilities combined with elegant user experience. More than a quarter-century later, the Macintosh is still going strong, with even more powerful features and more usability, allowing all kinds of users to take advantage of their computers in new and productive ways. The engineers at Apple could not achieve this all by themselves, and so they created and put together tools and libraries of code to give independent software developers the ability to craft Macintosh apps beyond the basic software Apple ships with each Macintosh. And in January 2011, Apple went one step further: The Macintosh App Store opened its virtual doors, giving Macintosh developers a place to market, advertise, and sell their apps to Macintosh users all around the world.

Macintosh Application Development For Dummies shows you how to develop a Mac app from concept to completion, from coding to uploading to the Macintosh App Store where users can find it and buy it.

About This Book

Macintosh Application Development For Dummies is a guide to developing Macintosh applications for Apple's Mac OS X. This book will show you the paths through the basics of Mac app development so you can create apps that extend the features and functionality of your Macintosh beyond what Apple provides. No Macintosh development experience is required, but familiarity with a programming language such as C, C++, or Java is assumed. The libraries of code, also known as *frameworks*, that Apple supplies with every Macintosh were created to work with a programming language called *Objective-C*. Objective-C is an object-oriented language and is similar enough to C and C++ that you'll be able to pick it up fairly quickly if you've used either of those languages. If you're a Java programmer, you'll also find Objective-C to be relatively easy to understand, and you should have no difficulty figuring out the code examples.

Macintosh computers deliver powerful features to users who expect these features to be easy to use and simple to figure out. The collection of all the Apple-provided frameworks, known as the *Cocoa framework*, provides you with the code necessary to deliver a user experience for your app that Macintosh users have come to expect. And Apple provides tools to help you put your app's visual interface together in a way that adheres to the guidelines Apple has devised for how Macintosh apps should deliver a great user experience. Your app's display is its primary means of communication with your users, and you want your app to present itself to meet their expectations. This book will give you experience in putting together the visual interface for your apps, so that you understand how to support your users according to Apple's interface guidelines.

This book will help you get started with the resources of Macintosh development to show you only what's absolutely necessary to start developing Mac apps that are useful and rewarding for your users. And at the end, you'll see how to polish your apps to make them ready for submission and review at the Macintosh App Store, so your apps can find Mac users worldwide, and users can purchase and download your app with the click of their mouse.

Conventions Used in This Book

You're going to come across a lot of code examples in this book, because that's one of the best ways I know to learn how to write code. The code examples in this book appear in a monospace font so they will stand out from the surrounding descriptive text. A code block will look like this:

```
#import <Cocoa/Cocoa.h>

@interface MyAppDelegate : NSObject <NSApplicationDelegate>
{
}

@end
```

 Objective-C is a case-sensitive programming language, just like the C programming language it derives from. When you use code that appears in this book, type it *exactly* as it appears in the text. (You can find code samples for this book at www.dummies.com/go/macintoshappdev — download the code samples, and you won't have to type in long code blocks!)

All the URLs referenced in this book also appear in a monospace font as well; for example, www.apple.com.

Foolish Assumptions

In writing this book, I have to make certain assumptions about you, the reader. I assume you have the following basic components for Macintosh software development:

✔ An Apple Macintosh computer with an Intel CPU

✔ Version 10.6 or later of Mac OS X

✔ Version 4.0 or later of Xcode

I assume that you're comfortable and familiar with using a Macintosh computer. I'll cover what type of Mac hardware is useful in a later chapter, but for now you don't need to worry about the differences between an iMac, a MacBook, or a Mac Pro. Apple makes OS X behave identically on all Mac models, so your development efforts don't have to target one machine separate from another.

You'll need some skills in using a Macintosh computer. You should be familiar with the different aspects of working with Mac OS X as a user, including how to launch applications, open and save files, work with the Finder, and access online resources over the Internet. I also assume you have some kind of Internet access so you can download the resources you need and also so you can establish yourself at Apple online as a registered Macintosh developer. You'll definitely need this to upload your Mac apps to Apple so they can get onto a shelf at the App Store.

Lastly, I assume you have some programming knowledge and that you have at least a basic understanding of object-oriented programming (OOP), either in Java or C++. If you'd like a more comprehensive introduction to Objective-C, consider *Objective-C For Dummies* by Neal Goldstein. Apple also provides many helpful online tutorials for Objective-C and Macintosh development.

How This Book Is Organized

The chapters in Macintosh Application Development For Dummies are divided into five parts.

Part 1: Getting Started on Macintosh Apps

Part I opens and walks you through the door into the world of Macintosh application development. You'll discover what you need to know about Macintosh apps in general and how to get ready for developing Mac apps. Before the end of this part, you'll also create a very basic Macintosh app.

If you aren't a registered developer, Bonus Chapter 1 on the web site shows how to get registered and download Xcode, if you don't have it.

Part II: A View to an App

In Part II, you'll take the lid off of Mac programming and dive right into code. Not the deep end, but not exactly shallow, either. You'll learn the basics of Objective-C programming and how to use the code libraries that make up the Cocoa Framework. Then you'll find out how to create a Mac app's user interface so you can effectively communicate with your users and give them a top-notch experience when using your app.

Part III: Focus on the User

Part III gives you strategies and ideas for supporting users and their expectations about what your app is doing. You'll learn how to manage and store the information users will provide to your app, as well as how to print that information when users want a hard copy. In addition, you'll find out how to place certain operations your app performs into the background so they don't detract from the user's control over your app and their machine.

Part IV: Polishing and Supporting Your App

In Part IV I'll show you the basics of one of the most important tasks you will do while developing your app: hunting down and terminating the programming anomalies — also known as *bugs* — that always appear in apps.

When your app is ready to submit to Apple, Bonus Chapter 2 and Bonus Chapter 3 on the web site contain the steps you follow to organize all the files and data you need to upload your app to Apple's reviewers.

Part V: The Part of Tens

Part V provides some of the helpful tips and hints that you'd eventually discover on your own after you've developed many apps for the Macintosh — only you'll get them right at the start of your Mac app development path. You'll find ten of the sample apps that I've used to figure out how to get my Mac apps to do things, so you can learn from code written by Apple's engineers about the right way to achieve your app's goals. I've also included information about some tools and some general programming techniques to help make your Mac app development experience smoother and less challenging.

Icons Used in This Book

 When you see this icon, you're looking at a code example that is also available at the *For Dummies* website. You don't have to type in all the code in this book's examples; instead, you can go to www.dummes.com/go/ macintoshappdev and save your fingers some wear and tear.

 This icon indicates a useful pointer that you shouldn't skip. Tips make your development effort easier by showing a shortcut or letting you know the information provided gives you an easy approach to resolving a coding problem.

 This icon represents a friendly reminder so that you are aware that this section of a chapter contains important information you should keep in mind.

 You'll see this icon when the accompanying information may be helpful or even interesting, but is technical and is not required for your goal of understanding Mac application development. You can safely detour around these pieces without losing any valuable information.

 This icon alerts you to potential challenges you may encounter on the way. Read and obey these commentaries to avoid problems later on.

Where to Go from Here

You're ready to start your Macintosh app development adventure. You can turn the page and start your journey right at Chapter 1. If you're anxious to start doing some development, you can jump to Chapter 2 and get through the registration and downloads sections so you've got the latest tools and access to the online resources. If you have a particular question or problem, check the Index or Table of Contents to find the information you need.

If you have questions or comments about this book or about Macintosh app development in general, contact me at kgkfordummies@gmail.com. You can also find additional information about my Macintosh application, DiabeticPad, at www.diabeticpad.com. And you can find sample code for this book at www.dummies.com/go/macintoshappdev.

Good luck, and happy coding!

Part I
Getting Started on Macintosh Apps

The 5th Wave — By Rich Tennant

"The sensor in my running shoe is transmitting information and encouragements to my iPod. Right now, Lance Armstrong is encouraging me to stop running like a girl."

In this part . . .

Your objective is to develop an application that will run on the most innovative, creative, and captivating computer systems the world has ever seen — the Apple Macintosh. You've got a fantastic idea for an app that will astound and amaze everyone who runs it. So now what?

You start here. In this part, you'll learn how to start developing Macintosh apps, including what tools you need and how to use them.

Also in this part, you get a chance to learn about Xcode, the main weapon in your arsenal of Macintosh application development. You'll also discover Cocoa and all the code resources that Apple engineers have developed for your battles to deliver a great user experience with as little code as possible. Finally, you get to jump into coding a simple application that will let you get comfortable with Xcode and Cocoa and let you see just how easy it is to get a Mac app up and running.

If you aren't a registered developer, Bonus Chapter 1 on the web site shows how to get registered and download Xcode, if you don't have it.

Chapter 1

Gathering What You Need to Develop Mac Apps

In This Chapter

▶ Discovering Mac apps and why to develop them

▶ Collecting the right tools

▶ Sharpening the right skills

▶ Meeting the challenges of Mac app development

You've just awakened, gotten out of bed, and you want to check your stocks because one of those big high-tech companies made an announcement just after the market closed, and you want to see how the overnight trading of some of your favorite high-tech stocks has turned out. You look at your Mac laptop sitting on your dresser, and say, "Show me how Apple is doing today."

Your laptop speaks back at you: "Password."

"Adam Smith," is your response. The MacBook's monitor comes alive and shows the current pre-market trading trends for Apple stock. If you'd said the wrong thing, the laptop would have remained off, and you wouldn't know how Apple stock was doing.

Does that sound like a dream? Everything I've mentioned above is possible for a Mac application. A Mac application can hear you speak and analyze your voice — Mac laptops and iMacs come with built-in microphones, and a library of code to listen for and react to sounds. Saying specific words in your voice such that an app can identify you as *you* would be the most difficult part of the scenario just described, but there are companies that sell software that can understand what you say, so even that aspect would be possible.

Apple's Macintosh line of computers supports the needs of users by doing just about anything you can think of. Macintosh applications now span all the categories of apps that users have wanted to use on their Macs — and if the app isn't there today, it soon will be. Users now use their Macs for everything: e-mailing, web browsing, accounting, keeping track of dates, keeping track of contacts, listening to music, watching videos — the list is endless. And since today's laptop computers have become smaller, lighter, and more powerful, users now take them everywhere.

A Mac application is meant to be useful, fast, and responsive to its users, because that's what those users expect. Your app may not please all your users, but you can develop apps that do useful work and do that job well. Your app should provide the user with the kind of experience that standard Mac apps deliver, so that your app will fit right into the elite set of must-use apps, giving your users what they want and need.

In this chapter, I will show you what tools, skills, and ideas you need to gather and discover to start developing Macintosh applications.

On the web site, Bonus Chapter 1 shows how to become a Registered Apple Developer, sign on to the Mac Dev Center website, download the latest Xcode tools, and join the Mac Developer program.

Why Develop Macintosh Apps?

The Apple App Store now provides millions of Macintosh users with thousands of apps they can download, just like the App Store does for millions of iOS device users. Apple opened the store in January 2011, and although many apps are available there already, a great many apps of all different kinds have yet to be built. The Mac consumers are out there, and Apple has just created a marketplace that will bring your software to them. You don't need cardboard boxes, or shrink-wrap, or a machine to make millions of DVD-ROMs. All you need to make the next Killer App is your idea and a Mac to develop it with.

Apple takes care of the virtual shelf space your app sits on, and will accept users' payment for your app on your behalf, charging only 30 percent of the price you choose to sell. Your users can feel safe and secure — they're dealing with Apple, so they don't worry about handing credit card information to a stranger on the other end of a wire. Users also know that Apple cares about their experience, and will only allow well-behaved apps to be put up for sale. Your app will sit with the thousands of others at the App Store, available to everyone with a Macintosh and the latest version of OS X.

Here are a few other reasons why I see the Mac as a great development opportunity:

✔ **The Mac desktop App Store is new.** There are millions of Mac users out there, and until now they bought their software shrink-wrapped and packaged, or found an online site they trusted to provide a safe download. With the success of the iPhone App Store, Apple has brought the same ease-of-use to the desktop. There's still a lot of shelf space at the App Store.

✔ **Your app's life cycle is now made easier.** You no longer have to maintain your app via a website; when you make improvements to your app, your users will know about it via the App Store. Upgrades are easy, and you don't have to keep in contact with your users to tell them about the new things your app will do.

✔ **The tools are free.** You can do all your development on an Apple Macintosh, but the tools to create Mac apps are free to download from Apple. And your development machine also turns into your test machine, because Apple makes sure that all Macs running the same version of OS X provide your app with the same functionality. You can rest assured that if you develop the next 3-D chess app on your MacBook Air running OS X 10.7, it will work equally well on an iMac 21.5" with a 3GHz processor also running OS X 10.7.

✔ **There are millions of Mac users.** This is a huge marketplace, and the doors to the App Store have only just opened. This means only one thing: huge demand.

✔ **Apple provides the App Store for you to showcase and sell your app.** This venue takes care of the responsibility for credit card handling, hosting, downloading, and notifying your users of updates. The App Store has a variety of pricing tiers, including free and try-and-buy. Apple keeps 30 percent of your application price to cover some of its costs. You will have to pay a fee of $99 per year, but that's all the payment you have to make to Apple, no matter how many apps you put up for sale.

I love my Mac — it's the first computer I use every day, and it's the most usable of all the computers I've ever used. Apple has made it into a great machine, and now Apple has given developers a great way to deliver apps to consumers. This is A Great Thing, and it's a beautiful opportunity.

Discovering Apps Like a User

Apple introduced the Macintosh nearly three decades ago, and developers have been making apps for the Mac ever since. The Mac popularized the concept of a _graphical user interface_: Users were presented with "windows" that they could move on the screen, along with switches and buttons and all kinds of controls they could manipulate using a mouse. This was in stark contrast to the computer user's world before the Mac. And now, nearly all computer users expect to interact with their machines through the same approach, by maneuvering a cursor and clicking buttons to make their apps do what they need done.

Your app will have to live up to these expectations — you shouldn't feel confined to obeying the same look-and-feel as every other app out there, but you should understand what users want, and anticipate their needs. You want them to enjoy using your app so they'll use it again and again, and as a result you don't want them to learn a completely new way of doing the same thing.

If you're just starting to use a Mac, run some of the Apple apps available on every Macintosh so that you can get a good feel for how Apple sees its apps' users — and how you can exploit all the user experience expertise Apple has invested in its products.

The following apps all come with every Mac and are worthwhile to play with in order to get a feel for how users see and use Apple apps:

- **Safari.** Safari is Apple's web browser. It behaves like every other web browser by rendering HTML for display. I recommend Safari because you're undoubtedly experienced with the other browsers, and you can explore Safari while still retaining some familiarity with what it's supposed to be doing. Figure 1-1 shows the Dummies' main page, and you can see the different visual aspects of the Safari web browsing experience.

- **Mail.** Apple provides an e-mail app that users can set up to access their mail from anywhere they connect to the Internet. Mail provides a rich user experience for creating, reading, and searching their e-mail messages.

- **Address Book.** Address Book lets you store the contact information for all the important people in your life. The Address Book provides a great user experience — you don't have to save the changes you make, you simply make them and Address Book keeps track. Figure 1-2 shows you an entry in the Address Book.

- **iCal.** My Professional Organizer keeps my life organized — and she has introduced me to iCal. This calendar program syncs with my iPhone and keeps on top of all my scheduled appointments. This is another great app that will demonstrate a number of different design possibilities for your user interface.

- **iTunes.** This is Apple's most popular app — with good reason. iTunes has been available on the Mac since the first iPod was created in 2001. Ten years, millions of users, and billions of downloads later, iTunes is a fantastic app for delivering songs, videos, and apps, and it offers a great opportunity for you to see what Apple has done to provide iTunes users with what they really want.

Figure 1-1: Buttons, scrollbars, and entry fields in Safari.

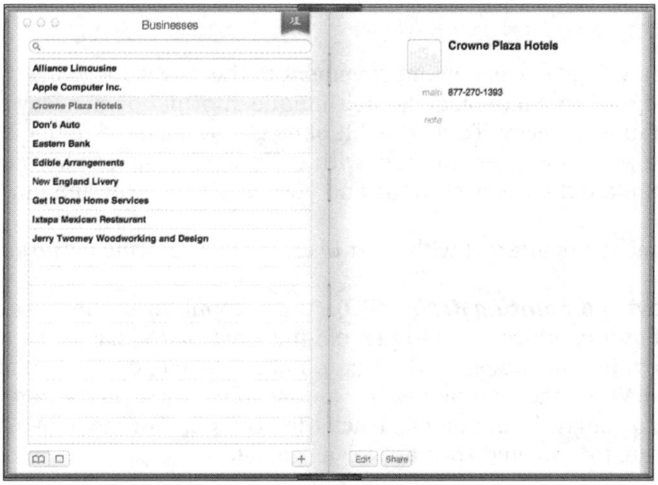

Figure 1-2: Users can quickly and easily navigate through their contacts in the Address Book.

- **App Store.** While the App Store is very similar to iTunes in many respects, it also provides another look at how to do things for your users. And it's great for getting an advance look at how to present your app when you're ready to deliver.

- **The Finder.** The Finder is the main interface between the user and the Macintosh. This is where users manage all of the items on their computer — hard drives, folders containing files, all the day-to-day bureaucratic tools that computers need. You should pay attention to the different ways the Finder allows users to do things, because these are the basic actions that users do all the time when they use their Macs.

Each of these apps, written and designed by Apple, demonstrates the basic user interface components and interactions that Mac users expect to see in your application. Mac users will be using the standard applications often, and so you should become familiar with how users get things done with them. The idea is to make sure your users feel at home with your app.

You can see in both Safari and Address Book some common user interface components:

- **Buttons** for ordering the app to perform an action
- **Icons** for representing information in a compact form
- **Text fields** for displaying unchanging text information
- **Text-entry fields**, such as the search field

Understanding how users interact with their Mac

Your app will give users an improvement in their lives by giving them the capability to store and manage their unique information in a way that is comfortable and easy. To do this bit of magic, you'll need to understand the different ways that users interact with their Macs — and how your app can accommodate their expectations and your app's features and functionality.

In general, users interact with their Macs in the following patterns:

- **Moving a *pointing device* (PD).** Apple popularized the use of a *graphical user interface* (GUI) to present information to Mac users, and also provided the mouse as the first pointing device for interacting with the GUI. When the user moves her mouse, the cursor on the screen moves accordingly. Your app can track the user's cursor movement, which is useful for drawing apps as well as games.

✓ **Clicking a button on a PD.** The most direct form of interaction between a user and her Mac is through the buttons on her PD. Clicking a button can select commands from a menu, or any items displayed on the Mac screen. Users click GUI buttons, click and drag files and windows, and will try to click everything your app displays.

✓ **Typing on the keyboard.** Every Mac except the Mac mini comes with a keyboard, and every app uses a keyboard to accept text information from users. Mac apps allow users to enact menu commands via their keyboards, as discussed in an upcoming subsection. Some games allow users to control aspects of playing the game through their keyboards (to take advantage of using ten fingers to deliver input to the game) in addition to the motion of the pointing device and the actions of its buttons.

✓ **Speaking into a microphone.** Mac OS X comes with the capability to hear and understand spoken commands. Users with accessibility challenges can take advantage of this feature to perform many tasks with their Macs that normally require a mouse or a keyboard. In addition, some apps capture and record input from the microphone to create podcasts or deliver network-based vocal communications.

Your apps can use any of these different forms for users to deliver information to and command your apps. The majority of users will use the keyboard and their favorite pointing device to interact with your app, and most apps conform to these two interactions.

Always think about ease of use when you're designing and implementing your apps. Mac users have been trained to expect the app they're using to be painless to interact with. Your users will be focused on entering and retrieving their information using your app; you should design your app to enable your users' actions to do so smoothly and efficiently. Your app should be easy to use with a pointing device in those areas where using a PD makes the most sense, such as selecting items on the screen or moving quickly through tables of data. Your app should likewise be easy to use when users are entering data from the keyboard through a source like a notepad app or a spreadsheet.

Pointing device (PD)

Your users' PDs (of whatever type) are the primary way they interact with the visual elements they see on the screen. Apple makes several different types of pointing devices, and other vendors make their own kinds:

✔ All PDs do the same basic thing: The user moves the device, and the pointer moves around the screen. To interact with objects on the screen: the user moves the mouse pointer over something and then clicks.

✔ Each PD may have additional features — the new Apple Magic Trackpad, for example, is a clickable pad that tracks finger movements and gestures, like the screen of an iPhone.

Users will choose the PDs that suit them best — I happen to like trackballs but I also like the Magic Trackpad. The end result is the same, no matter which PD is connected; you don't need to worry about how users are clicking around in your app when they're using the basic mouse-movement features of their PDs. However, Mac OS X Lion now incorporates *multi-touch gestures* similar to those available in iOS apps, so your app can take advantage of users using a multi-touch device such as the Magic Trackpad or the Magic Mouse.

Certain types of apps may be optimized to use particular types of pointing devices; be sure you understand the best ways to use the information that Mac OS X will provide your app for users and their interactions. Now that Mac OS X Lion can provide multi-touch and gesture information to your app, you can deliver an app that can use that information to deliver a better experience for your users.

Some types of apps that depend on a pointing device include these:

✔ Paint programs

✔ The Finder

✔ E-book readers

✔ Games

✔ DVD players

Keyboard

If your app will make use of text that the user types, then your users will be using their keyboards. Apple has tried to nudge Mac users to doing things with the PD more than with their keyboards, but so far users still love their keyboards. Many of the actions that users can perform with the mouse can also be performed with combinations of keys. An expert user will use the keyboard far more often than the PD — a keyboard offers much greater speed for getting things done; after all, you've got ten fingers that can do ten different things in a coordinated sequence — which is what they're doing when you type a sentence.

Types of apps that depend heavily on a keyboard include these:

- Spreadsheets
- Word processors
- Integrated development environments (IDEs)
- E-mail

To keep your users happy while using your app, provide *key-combinations* for the sets of actions they'll perform most frequently using your app. It's far easier to hit ⌘-S than it is to take my fingers off the keyboard while I'm typing this document, reach for my favorite trackball, drag the mouse pointer to select the Save menu item from the File menu, or click a Save toolbar button. If I use the keyboard, the interruption is a split second, and I can save in the middle of a sentence without losing track of what I want to write. The default application template I introduce in Chapter 3 includes the standard key-combinations for user actions such as creating, opening, closing, and saving files; printing data; and the usual edit functions of cut, copy, and paste. Your app should provide its own key-combinations for the actions that your app adds to its menus.

Seeing what your users see

Your users will have display devices attached to their Macs; your app can find that out and adjust accordingly. I'll show you in Chapter 5 how to use Interface Builder to make your screens' contents handle different display sizes automatically. What you need to know now is that your app will be running on screens of many different shapes and sizes.

Here are some of the different configurations possible:

- **Old-fashioned 4:3.** Not long ago, all screens had the same ratio of width to height: each screen was 33 percent wider than it was tall. Some of these are still out there. The first couple of generations of flat-panel LCD displays still copied this aspect ratio, and, yes, there are still some CRT screens around.

- **Widescreen.** This is the most common type of display; examples of it come in several different sizes. In addition, users may be able to rotate these displays to be taller than they are wide — your app should behave appropriately if or when the *aspect ratio* (the ratio of the screen's width to its height) changes.

- **Multiple.** Some users demand the most screen real estate they can get, and all Apple Macs come with multiple monitor ports to accommodate this need.

You can see examples of the different screen types in Figure 1-3.

Sometimes, working as a developer, you'll want an extra monitor so you can keep more of Xcode's windows around without cluttering up any one screen or jumping from one Desktop to another (Mission Control is Apple's app for creating virtual desktops).

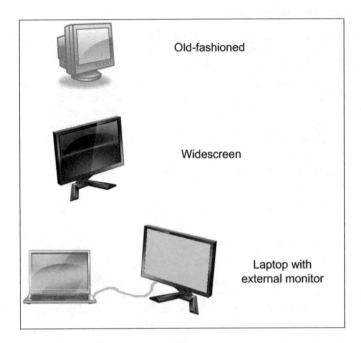

Old-fashioned

Widescreen

Laptop with external monitor

Figure 1-3: The different screen types and configurations your app may encounter on a Mac.

You may never need to think about how your users have configured their visual real estate, but your app should be responsive to screen changes whenever they occur. For instance, one app I use regularly on another OS runs into trouble whenever I bring my laptop home from work. At work I hook up an external monitor and this app's window may end up displayed on that screen. At home, however, I use only the laptop's screen, and launching this app causes its window to display *off-screen*. And there's nothing I can do about that. The app (obviously) remembers where I originally placed the window, but an improvement would be to make certain that this specific location is part of the area occupied by a physical screen. You'll need to be aware of the possibility for challenges such as this when creating your own apps.

Tooling Up

You are the most important tool in your software development toolkit. No matter what project you work on, alone or in a team, your expertise is more important than all the other tools you use to put together a Macintosh app. Your skill in using those tools is what makes the tools useful.

But you need a good set of software and hardware tools at hand before you start to do Mac development. The next sections cover the tools for making Macintosh apps.

Buying a great development Mac

There's no way around it: You'll need an Apple Macintosh as your development machine. The programming language you use (Objective-C) and the compiler (LLVM) are available to run on many platforms, but only Apple has the libraries and frameworks to run your apps on a Mac. And because you're creating a Mac app, you'll have to run it on a Mac anyway to see that it runs the way it should.

Your development machine will need to handle the following tasks when you're developing your Mac apps:

- **Editing code.** You'll be typing and editing lots of code, and every Mac available today — from a MacBook to an iMac to a Macintosh Pro — will support this. However, larger screens — such as an iMac (Model MC812LL/A) — are better than smaller — such as that on a 13-inch MacBook (MC516LL/A).

- **Editing the visual interface.** This task isn't much more draining than editing code, but it's always good to err on the side of higher speed and larger screen size.

- **Building the app.** You will perform this task many times during the development of each app, and this is one of the most power-hungry tasks for a computer to do. Building your code into an app and packaging it for delivery is very CPU- and memory-intensive, so you want a machine that has good processor speed, and as much memory as you can give it. Xcode 4 is optimized for running on the latest generation of Mac hardware, so you'll find newer Macs will build your apps faster than older Macs.

- **Executing and debugging the app.** Before you're ready to upload to the App Store, you will want to test your app to make sure it's got everything it needs — and to make sure it doesn't shatter into a thousand pieces. A debugging session also uses a lot of memory, and you want a speedy processor capable of running Xcode, its Debugger, *and* your app smoothly. Apple creates a wide range of different Macs for all users, but as a developer you'll benefit from a system that has these:

- Fast processor: 3 GHz or better

- Large amounts of memory: 8GB or higher

- Large widescreen display: 1920 pixels wide by 1200 pixels high

- Large hard drive: 1TB or more

- External hard drive: 2TB or more, for backups using Apple's TimeMachine

I prefer developing on Macintosh desktop machines rather than laptops — this may be due to the time period in which I started developing, back when a portable computer weighed 50 pounds and was carried in a suitcase. But don't let my bias prevent you from using a laptop. After all, a laptop allows you to develop *anywhere*, including at 30,000 feet. If you prefer a portable computer and can find a MacBook or MacBook Pro that's fast enough and has enough memory, don't hesitate to get it.

Table 1-1 outlines the specifications of the development Macintosh I used while writing the apps for this book.

Table 1-1	Requirements for a Development Macintosh
Equipment	*Optimum Requirements*
Processor	3.0 GHz quad-core Intel CPU
RAM	16GB
Operating system	OS X 10.7
Screen	27″ widescreen
Hard drive	1TB
Network connection	Broadband network access available today is all you need. If you can afford something faster — get it!

You *must* use a Mac that uses an Intel processor. Apple first introduced these in 2006 and now the Apple Store only sells Intel Macs. However, you may choose to purchase a used Mac instead; if you do, make sure the CPU inside is Intel, as shown in Figure 1-4.

Figure 1-4: Intel Inside.

Downloading the software you need

If you've just opened your new Mac, you will discover that Xcode hasn't been installed. But that's easy to rectify:

✔ Check for the latest and greatest version of Xcode available for download from Apple's App Store.

At the time of this writing, the latest version of Xcode is 4.1.1, and it's free to download if you're running OS X 10.7 Lion.

Figure 1-5 shows you the App Store page for Xcode.

Before you can download anything from http://developer.apple. com, Apple requires you to be a registered Mac developer, which I go over in Bonus Chapter 1 on the web site. Be sure you get that detail out of the way before you start trying to install Xcode.

Figure 1-5: Using the Mac OS X Install DVD to install Xcode on a new Mac.

Xcode tools

Your Mac app development efforts will require you to turn your ideas into the correct sequence of instructions for a Mac to execute. In addition, your app may need to use visual or audio resources and other data that will be embedded within it. To create this package of executable code and data, you'll use several tools that are automatically installed with Xcode. And to make sure your app works as perfectly as possible, Xcode also provides tools that will help you ensure that your app will be careful with memory and its performance.

The following are the major software tools you use to create Macintosh applications. All these tools are included with Xcode when you install it:

✔ **Xcode.** This is Apple's integrated development environment. Xcode includes the code editor, debugger, project manager, compiler, and package-maker. Xcode provides all this capability within itself, so you never need to leave Xcode to perform any of these functions.

✔ **Interface Builder.** You'll need Interface Builder to assist with the development of your app's graphical user interface. While you can do everything that IB does within code, you'll find that using IB to put together your screens graphically will save you a lot of time typing.

✔ **Instruments.** Apple has developed an app that can watch your app's use of memory — this is important while you're developing your app so you can avoid _memory leaks_. Apple will reject your app submission to the App Store if your app is leaking memory. (I go over memory leaks in Chapter 12; for now, just keep in mind that Instruments is instrumental to your app's successful appearance at the App Store.)

✔ **Shark.** You will use Shark to trace your app's performance hurdles — you will discover where your app is spending most of its time, and this can help you to improve the code in those areas so that your app doesn't keep your users waiting. Shark is an Apple app that installs with Xcode.

Other tools

Depending on what your app does, here are some other tools you should consider adding to your collection:

✔ **An image editor.** While your app may not depend on images for buttons or background screens, you will need to create an _application icon_ for Apple to display at the App Store.

I recommend GIMP, the GNU Image Manipulation Program. It's free, and you can find it at www.gimp.org. Alternatively, you can purchase Adobe's Photoshop Elements, which provides most of the same features at a price lower than the full version of Photoshop. You can find Photoshop Elements at www.adobe.com.

✔ **An audio editor.** If your app makes use of sounds, you will want something that can record audio and let you edit it.

If your audio needs are simple, such as providing audio help, I recommend Apple's GarageBand application. GarageBand is part of iLife, is bundled on new Macs, and is very easy to use.

✔ **A video editor.** With the advent of small, HD-quality video cameras, everyone today can be a video producer. If your app makes use of video — for instance, to provide your users with a tutorial — you will likely want a video editor app to assist with editing.

New Macs come with iMovie, a very useful — and free — video-editing app.

✔ **Backup software.** Every new Mac comes with Time Machine, Apple's backup software. You should definitely consider using this app to back up your work. Time Machine requires a separate hard disk, such as an external drive. Along with OS X 10.7 Lion, Apple has announced the creation of iCloud, an online storage service that comes with 5GB of free storage, which you can access from anywhere you have an Internet connection. You can purchase additional storage space as needed. Amazon (amazon.com) also has a cloud storage solution, and Mozy (mozy.com) provides online backup services.

Store your backups on a CD or DVD — *hard drives do fail*, and you will regret relying solely on their correct operation to maintain copies of the work you do.

If you assume that all your work can be lost with one power outage — it's as simple as tripping over your Mac's power cord — you will gain a healthy paranoia about ensuring that your work gets saved, somewhere. Back up your work — regularly. Your hours, days, or weeks of effort are worth the small amount of time it takes to move them off your computer and onto some other medium. Considering that you might be able to rewrite all your code in less time than it took to create it from scratch, you still have to spend that time rewriting it, instead of adding new features or fixing bugs. Do your backups.

Watching your language(s)

While the programming language of choice for Mac development is Objective-C, and while Objective-C is what I'll use to develop my Mac apps throughout this book, it isn't the only language available for use in developing Mac applications. Your app should use only the public APIs of Apple frameworks to avoid rejection during the App Store review process. In addition, your app cannot use optional technologies such as Java, as this will also cause a rejection of your app.

✔ The compiler used by Xcode — LLVM — supports the C and C++ programming languages as well. In addition, you aren't restricted to using the Objective-C Frameworks that Apple provides for you to develop Mac apps.

✔ Nokia supports a cross-platform development framework based on C++ called *Qt*; you can find more information about it at http://qt.nokia.com. If you are fairly adept with C++ application development, you may find Qt easier to handle, rather than jumping into a noticeably different programming language. And Qt was intended to assist in cross-platform development — a Qt app you write for the Mac is easy to move to Windows and Linux platforms, something not easily done for an Objective-C Mac app. Qt has its own limitations, but the appeal of easily moving your successful Mac app to another platform may be worth the effort.

Using Your Programming Skills

You will need some general skills to develop Mac applications:

✔ **Objective-C programming.** The Objective-C programming language is the primary development language used to develop Macintosh apps. It's based on the C programming language, so if you have a good background in C you'll recognize most of the syntax and program structures you encounter. In addition, you can create C-based source code modules, and Xcode will compile and integrate them into your app.

Objective-C is an *object-oriented language*, so you will need some understanding of object-oriented programming — if you're experienced with C++, your knowledge of that language can help (not to worry — the basics of Objective-C development show up later in this book). And you'll find that Objective-C can be used in conjunction with C++ source code modules as well, so if you have a library of platform-neutral C++ sources you can make use of them with only a few modifications.

In addition, Objective-C is a *dynamic* language, offering your app's code capabilities such as creating objects from just a class name, executing a method using just its name, and the ability to extend the classes provided in the Apple frameworks to suit your app's needs.

✔ **Debugging.** After you've implemented your app, there's a statistical likelihood that it won't be perfect. If you're lucky, those imperfections will make themselves apparent quickly and obviously. As you create more apps, you'll stop making the obvious and quickly fixed mistakes, which leaves the subtle and more challenging bugs. Your skills at debugging — looking at code as it runs, keeping track of what is going right and what is going wrong, and so on — will play an important part in completing your apps.

✔ **Software design patterns.** As with most modern computing platforms, your app will benefit from using software patterns where appropriate. You can create a functional and usable Mac application without relying on any of the canonical design patterns, but applications that are to have a long-duration existence will require a solid structure for operation *that the use of software patterns will support*. The most obvious of these is the Model-View-Controller (MVC) pattern, which enforces the separation of your app into pieces that are easy to manage. The basic Apple framework classes encourage using software design patterns — one of the fundamental classes for your app will be an NSViewController, which I describe along with MVC in Chapter 6.

Objective-C programming for Mac apps

The Objective-C programming language was created in the 1980s to add object-oriented features to the C language. Objective-C is the language I use in this book to demonstrate how to program Mac apps, because it's the language used by Apple for all of its applications. You should be familiar with C programming, and familiar with object-oriented programming in general. I'll go over some of the basic concepts here, but if you want a full experience, you should check out Neal Goldstein's *Objective-C For Dummies* (Wiley).

You may be familiar with *procedural programming*, where the computer moves from one program statement to the next in a straight line. If so, you're probably used to thinking of the operations of an application as being linear, one right after another. In *object-oriented programming*, your view of the application's operation will change: you will start to think of the app as a set of *objects*, with each object representing functionality coupled with the data that functionality will work with. The combination of this functionality and data is a mini-library of code called a *class*; the data is represented as *member variables*, and the code of a function in the class is called a *method*. The process of executing a particular method with a specific object is called *sending a message* to the object. Keep in mind that sending a message in Objective-C is different from calling a method in other OO languages such as C++. In Objective-C, the recipient of the message is determined when the code is executing — and that recipient is responsible for executing the code associated with the message or reporting an error to the OS. In C++, calling a method on an object means that the sequence of code to be executed is determined by the compiler, not the runtime environment. Because Objective-C puts the responsibility for handling a message onto the object receiving it, Objective-C classes can be more flexible in handling messages than C++ classes.

In addition to binding functionality and data together in one class, object-oriented programming provides the capability to *subclass* — that is, create a class that inherits data and functionality from a *parent* class. You create subclasses in order to

- Use the functionality and data of the parent class while adding your own new functionality and new data
- Replace the functionality of the parent class with your own improvements
- Execute the parent's functionality in addition to your own

Inheritance is a powerful programming concept, and you'll use it frequently during your development of Mac apps.

Each Objective-C class consists of two code files:

- **Header:** The header describes the structure of the class, including the member variables it contains, and the methods that can be called. In addition, the header provides information about the parent class. You will create a header file for every class you create, and you will use the header file to provide information to Xcode when it compiles the classes that want to know about a particular class. For instance, you create a class that represents a set of data values, such as the date, time, and text of a Notepad note. Then, when you want to display the contents of one set of those values in a View object, the view's class needs to know how to extract that information from a Note object — so you import the header file of the Note class into the source module for the View class.

  Listing 1-1 shows a simple header file for a Note object data class.

- **Source file:** The source file for a class provides implementations for the methods described by the header file. In addition, in order to override the implementation of a method in the parent class, you provide your new and improved method in the source file. Because of how Objective-C interprets inheritance, you only need to create declarations of new methods in the header file. The source file contains all the source code your class will execute.

  Listing 1-2 shows the Note object source code implementation.

Listing 1-1:   A very simple data class header file, Note.h

```
//
// Note.h
// NotePadApp
//

#import <Cocoa/Cocoa.h>

@interface Note : NSObject
{
    NSString* m_text;
    NSDate* m_timestamp;
}

- (void)setText:(NSString*)inText;
- (void)setTimestamp:(NSDate*)inTimestamp;
- (NSString*)getText;
- (NSDate*)getTimestamp;

@end
```

Listing 1-2: The very simple data class implementation, Note.m

```
//
// Note.m
// NotePadApp
//

#import "Note.h"

@implementation Note

- (id)init
{
    if (self = [super init])
    {
        // do some initialization
    }
    return (self);
}

- (void)setText:(NSString*)inText
{
    if (nil != m_text)
    {
        [m_text release];
    }
    m_text = inText;
    [m_text retain];
}

- (void)setTimestamp:(NSDate*)inTimestamp
{
    if (nil != m_ timestamp)
    {
        [m_text release];
    }
    m_ timestamp = inTimestamp;
    [m_ timestamp retain];
}

- (NSString*)getText
{
    return (m_text);
}

- (NSDate*)getTimestamp
{
    return (m_timestamp);
}

@end
```

The important things to take away from Listing 1-1 and Listing 1-2 are these:

✔ Comment lines start with "//". From that pair of characters onward on the same line, the Xcode compiler will ignore anything typed. This makes it really easy to remove a line of code that you might need to put back, which can happen a lot during debugging. You can also remove multiple lines of code by placing "/*" before the first line of code to be removed and "*/" after the last.

✔ You reference header files through #import statements. In C and C++, you would use #include; Objective-C understands that form as well, but #import improves upon this by ensuring that any one header file is included only once — eliminating the possibility of an infinite loop in which header file A includes header file B which includes header file C which includes header file A again.

✔ The declaration of the Note class starts with the @interface statement.

✔ The parent class of Note is the NSObject class, denoted to the right of the colon ":".

✔ In the header file, all member variables are enclosed by braces {}.

✔ In the header file, methods are declared and listed one line at a time, starting with a dash "–" and ending with a semicolon ";".

Methods can span multiple lines, but I prefer the one-line-per-method rule; it has the effect of keeping method names shorter, which means each one is simpler to understand. However, multiline method declarations and definitions can be easier to read, especially if you put each of the method's parameters on a separate line.

✔ The method declaration consists of a return value, such as (NSString*), surrounded by parentheses, and followed by the method name, which is a combination of its parameters and their types. Unlike C and C++, Objective-C methods take their parameters separated by text descriptions of what the parameter represents. The following code snippet shows the difference between Objective-C and C or C++ in declaring functions (in C) and methods (in C++ and Objective-C):

```
// C function or C++ method declaration
int addTwoValues( int value1, int value2 );
// Objective-C method declaration
- (int)addValue:(int)value1 toValue:(int)value2;
```

An example of a method that multiplies two Matrix objects by each other and returns a Matrix object representing their product might look like what you see in Listing 1-3. This is one of the major differences between Objective-C and C and C++, and you'll find yourself a little out of sorts when you switch between the two, especially if you've gotten used to the *other's* way of doing things.

✔ The declaration of the Note class ends with the @end statement.

✔ In the source file, the implementation for the Note class starts with the @ implementation statement.

✔ You can see all the four methods declared in the header file implemented in the source module.

✔ You can see one new method, - (id)init, also implemented. Because the exact same method is declared in the header file of the parent class or any ancestor class, you need not declare that method again in Note's header file, although doing so won't harm the app. The init method in Note.m will override the parent's method of the same name.

init is declared for the *root* class of all Objective-C classes, NSObject. You will never need to declare it in any Objective-C class you create as long as your class is a subclass of NSObject or any of its descendants.

✔ In the init method, the code executes [super init]. This is how you can execute a method declared in a parent class (also called the *superclass*) from within the overriding method of the child class. In addition, the brackets "[]" indicate that the code is sending the init message to the super object.

The return type for init is id. This is the type used to represent any object type that inherits from NSObject. It is used as a pointer to some object type, but without necessarily knowing what the actual type is. In C and C++, this is the equivalent of void*.

You'll get more of a handle on Objective-C and how to program Mac apps as I show you how to develop using Xcode.

Listing 1-3:   A Matrix-multiplication method in Objective-C

```
- (Matrix*)multiplyMatrix:(Matrix*)inMatrixA
          byMatrix:(Matrix*)inMatrixB;
```

In Objective-C, you only ever use *pointers* to objects. A pointer is just a fancy name for the address in computer memory where an object exists. But since you'll only ever be able to use pointers to objects instead of the objects themselves, you'll start thinking — and I will continue writing — of these as the objects. In Listing 1-3 you can see that Matrix* items are being passed into, manipulated, and returned by the method. These are *pointers* to Matrix objects, which is why the Matrix identifier is closely followed by an "*" character. Even though these are pointers to Matrix objects, it's easier to just call them Matrix objects. And my editors will have fewer words to make sure I spell correctly!

Your code can also include methods that take *scalar* values as parameters. A scalar is a simple variable type, such as the following C types:

```
int

short

long

float

double

char
```

Debugging

Xcode comes with a source-level debugger that makes tracking down and squashing bugs very easy. However, your own skills in debugging software apps are what matter most.

I assume that in your software application development experience your apps didn't always work perfectly. I'm guessing that you've presumably spent time analyzing code to find where the errors were hiding, and mercilessly corrected them. In general, debugging is still more art than science. Your tools can assist with shining light on the places where code goes wrong, but you still need creativity and imagination to know where to start shining that light. Small apps are usually easy to debug, but when your app has several dozen classes and layers, bugs find more places to hide.

You can find resources online and in print regarding debugging, as well as habits and approaches you can use to make your code easier to debug. I've worked on very few apps where no debugging was required before they ran flawlessly — that includes the sample apps I show you in the chapters that follow. All of them had quirks and gotchas that required analysis and imagination to overcome.

One lesson I've learned in my software development experience is that it's easier to find bugs if I test my software while I'm implementing it. For instance, usually after implementing a method for a class the first time, I build my app and include simple code to test it, just to make sure the initial implementation does exactly what I wanted it to do. Clearly, doing this for each line of code I implement would add many days to my development schedule, so normally I follow the implement-test-debug approach for methods that are more than a few lines of code. But you will find that testing your code at appropriate stopping points during implementation can greatly reduce the amount of time you spend debugging.

Using software patterns

Programmers have been developing software for a long enough time that a lot of the ways to solve problems have become standardized. *Software patterns* are a collection of these standard solutions to certain kinds of programming problems. You'll find not only that Apple has used them (and provided some of them as classes within the Mac app frameworks), but also that you can use them yourself to resolve the issues you encounter while writing your own apps.

You'll find that using software patterns can greatly simplify your code, and this leads you to developing code that's easier to maintain. Patterns tend to be simple and effective, focusing on delivering a limited set of functionality within your app. A class in your application that is the implementation of a particular software pattern for achieving a specific objective is straightforward and easy to test.

A simple example of a software pattern that you might use is one I use in many of the apps I develop: the Observer pattern. An Observer is an object that wants to know when another object has been modified — the Observer will adjust its behavior based on the new set of data in the other object. Apple provides classes within its core framework that support the Observer pattern, and Listing 1-4 shows a code snippet that makes use of these classes to support inter-object communication.

The `initialize` method of the class implementing the Observer behavior demonstrates how to use `NSNotificationCenter` to register the Observer to receive events named `notifyObserver`. In addition, the Observer provides the name of another method, `methodToCallOnNotify:`, when the named notification event occurs.

Any other object *posting* an event notification to the `NSNotificationCenter` will cause the Observer's registered method to be executed. You can use this type of software pattern to create apps that perform operations in the background and update the display while the user has control over the foreground.

The use of the `NSNotificationCenter` method `defaultCenter` is an example of another software pattern: the Singleton. Apple chose to use this pattern because there is generally no reason why you should create multiple notification managers in your app.

Listing 1-4:   Using the NSNotification and NSNotificationCenter to provide an Observer behavior

```
// in the Observer object class
- (void)initialize
{
    [[NSNotificationCenter defaultCenter] addObserver:self
        selector:@selector(methodToCallOnNotify:)
        name:@"notifyObserver" object:nil];
}

- (void)methodToCallOnNotify:(NSNotification*)inNotification
{
    // when a notification is broadcast by some other
    // object, this method gets executed
}

// in some other object class broadcasting a notification
- (void)updateObservers
{
    [[NSNotificationCenter defaultCenter] postNotificationNam
        e:@"notifyObserver" object:nil];
}
```

Understanding Macintosh Application Development Challenges

If writing solid Macintosh apps were easy, you wouldn't need this book. So you'll want to be prepared for the hurtling boulders of difficulty that will cross your path. Sometimes these challenges are caused by the limitations of the Macintosh or its operating system, OS X — you'll have to "code around" these types of problems. Other times, you'll find you've "coded yourself into a corner": for example, a decision of how to implement some part of your app at an earlier phase of development may force responsibilities on your code in later parts of your effort.

The following sections describe the challenges that you'll face in writing Macintosh applications.

Targeting an OS X version

Apple has a habit of releasing a major new version of OS X once every 12-24 months. In 2009 it was Snow Leopard, OS X 10.6. In 2011, the next version is Lion, OS X 10.7. Here are some of the improvements that Lion offers in OS X:

- **Full Screen Apps.** Lion provides users with the ability to launch an app that takes over the entire screen. Your app can take advantage of having every square pixel of screen real estate to itself.

- **Aqua.** Lion will improve the user interaction of Aqua, adding support for popovers (small, window-like displays), Overlay Scrollbars (scrollbars that appear when needed and disappear when not needed), and Multi-Touch Gestures and Animations (Apple's Magic Trackpad is available on its current laptops and as a Bluetooth add-on, and the Magic Mouse is also available). I imagine users will start expecting to take advantage of these features — which first arrived for the iPhone and iPad — in their Mac apps.

- **AV Foundation.** Apple is providing a new framework for Lion that includes Objective-C classes to play, examine, and compose audio-visual media from within your app. This will make it easier for you to capture audio and video from the user. For instance, you could create a game app that uses the user's voice to talk to other characters in the game, after reading through a script.

- **Auto Save and Versions.** In the old days — like, last week — users were cautioned to save early, and save often. Lion provides a built-in auto-save feature that will store changes to documents your app creates without requiring the user to take any action. And Lion's implementation of Versions will provide an automatically recorded history of changes made to documents, displaying a Time Machine–like interface that lets users browse through all the changes they've made.

- **Resume.** Before Lion, your app would have to keep track of the windows and their contents that users opened and left displayed onscreen when the user logged out or restarted the machine — assuming your app was considerate enough to do so. If it wasn't so considerate, it would require the users to re-open everything they could remember being open. Lion allows users to restore your app exactly where they left it. Apps left running when the logout or restart occurred will relaunch automatically. In addition, Lion will restore the state of an app that was terminated accidentally, such as from an application crash or a power outage.

- **File Coordination.** When your app has multiple threads of execution (I go over this in Chapter 9), accessing resources such as files from different threads could sometimes cause problems, such as one thread trying to read data from a file while another is trying to write data into it. Lion introduces File Coordination, which helps eliminate these kinds of difficulties.

✓ **Sandboxing and Privilege Separation.** On the iPhone and iPad, apps are *sandboxed* — your app can only access those parts of the file system assigned to your app and nothing else. This helps to ensure that well-behaved apps are not affected by apps misbehaving next door. Lion now brings this capability to the Mac desktop. Similarly, Privilege Separation helps system security by letting you factor your application into smaller pieces, each of which has its own privileges for operation on the machine. This enhances the overall security of the user's system and lets them feel comfortably in control over apps that are not running wild.

Mac OS X 10.7 Lion is now available and will be on the screens of your users, ready for your app to take advantage of its features.

Log in to the Apple developer website often — I recommend weekly — to keep on top of OS X releases. Doing so will save you from negative feedback and aggravation.

Apple also releases free updates to OS X between major releases — and because they're free, most users *will* install them. These updates range from simple bug-fixes for Apple apps up to major security fixes. Because your users are installing these updates, you should do likewise. You must ensure that your app runs on your users' machines.

Programming defensively

You want your app downloaded and used by tens of thousands of people worldwide. When that happens, each user becomes a quality assurance engineer for your app. These users will intentionally and accidentally discover new ways of breaking your application — causing unforeseen consequences to occur — that you never thought of. Your users will be your next major challenge.

Users follow a bell curve in terms of how they use your app. Most will behave exactly as you expect, following the anticipated modes of operation where they never encounter shortcomings in your app and never try to make the app do something incorrect. But a small group of users will push your app, by accident or on purpose, into a situation it can't handle. If you work for a large organization with a quality assurance department, a great many of these situations can be discovered and resolved before your code gets to the App Store. If you're a solo entrepreneur, this burden falls on your shoulders.

Most aberrant situations result from a user's input of invalid data into your app. This specific pathway to error can be prevented through the use of fixed-input entry fields: Your user interface can incorporate elements that restrict user input to particular data types or specific values. In addition, your app should "sanitize" the data that users provide as input, to make sure that nothing bad gets inside your app to wreak havoc.

As an example, your app might act as a gateway to blogs that the user visits often to contribute comments. You can hope that such websites do their own sanitizing, but your app can do that work ahead of time. The idea is to reduce the chance that the website will reject the data you transmit to it because of invalid characters that are, say, incorrect HTML tags.

Another invalid input entry will occur when your app displays text-entry fields for users to input data that your app will use. For instance, the following are examples of valid textual dates:

- 2/27/11
- February 27, 2011
- 2011-02-27

If your app lets users enter arbitrary text data into a plain text-entry field, you'll have to devise code within your app that can convert the data into a form more suitable for making comparisons and calculations. But a basic text-entry field also lets your users enter miscellaneous text such as `Karl's chapter due date`.

If your app tries to convert that value to an `NSDate` object (the standard Cocoa class for representing dates and times), the conversion will fail. A better way to ensure that only valid data values are entered is to use UI components that *limit* what a user is permitted to provide. In this case, using an `NSTextField` and adding an `NSDateFormatter` object will ensure that only dates can be entered into the field.

Another potential cause of problems is a user who tries to load your app with a set of data created by an older version of your app. The problems can range from simple (your app refuses to load the data) to complex (your app acts on data it doesn't fully understand — and uses it incorrectly). Neither of these outcomes will be pleasant for your users. I cover migration of older data to newer versions in Chapter 8, but you will inevitably run into this problem, and you'll need to code appropriately.

Stepping into a Brave, New World of Mac Apps

Apple has had tremendous success with its iPhone and iPad and the iOS App Store. With users now accustomed to using the App Store for downloading apps to their phones, Apple introduced the same capability for delivering desktop apps to their users — the Macintosh App Store. This online marketplace combines the familiar App Store ease-of-use with the delivery of high-quality, Apple-sanctioned desktop applications. The App Store provides many categories of apps for Mac users to download, such as Business, Education, Games, News, Social Networking, and Utilities.

For the complete list, please see Bonus Chapter 2 on the web site.

Some categories are further subdivided, to allow prospective buyers the ability to drill down through the store and find the app that's right for them. You, as a developer, should become familiar with the user's experience of searching and finding apps in the App Store, to place your app in the right category and to make sure your app shows off its best face.

Deciding what kind of app to create

If you already have an idea for an app, great! You're one giant step ahead on the road to App Store fortune and fame! This can be one of the most challenging parts of creating a Mac app — figuring out what to create.

Review the apps available at the App Store in a variety of different categories. Apple does suggest as part of their submission guidelines that there are some types of apps that are already overpopulated, and Apple will at its discretion reject apps that duplicate other apps, if there are many of them. So you'll want to get an idea of what's already available. Think of this exercise as window shopping. Your imagination will work in the background while you see what's already on the shelves, and all it takes is one example to trigger something wonderful. For instance, my app is intended to provide a logbook for diabetics to populate with the information useful for managing their diabetes on a daily basis. I found one app at the App Store, for about $40. Now that app provided a lot of different features, while I was thinking that a smaller app that did less would be useful, if I sold it for less. And that's how DiabeticPad was born.

After you're a registered Mac developer, you'll be able to access the Mac App Store review guidelines at

```
http://developer.apple.com/appstore/resources/approval/guidelines.html
```

I cover the process of becoming a registered Mac developer in Bonus Chapter 1 on the web site.

Brainstorming, alone or in groups

I am a co-founder of a small startup, BlazingApps. The other co-founders and I sit down irregularly for a brainstorming session: We go around the table and contribute an idea or many about different apps we've thought about since the previous meeting. I enjoy this kind of imaginative collaboration and highly recommend it.

For the solo entrepreneur, I highly recommend writing down any thoughts of ideas somewhere you can easily find them again — e-mailing yourself an idea is a great way to capture those ideas, especially if your e-mail is accessible from anywhere you have Internet access. You should write down everything, no matter how small or unimportant you might think it is. This way, you'll have a collection of thoughts and imaginings that you can use to spark more of the same — and this is what brainstorming is all about: the unrestricted generation of ideas. Some combination of these little pieces of your imagination, across a spectrum of your recorded notes, will gang up and prove to be an app worth creating. As a solo engineer, talking with other developers or even acquaintances can generate ideas. You can scan the many Macintosh online forums to pick up on what issues users are running into and develop ideas based on the problems they encounter and clearly want a solution for.

Becoming a Mac developer and App Store seller

Your first step toward Mac app development is to register with Apple as a Mac OS developer. You then gain access to a treasure chest of all things Macintosh, including

- Xcode downloads
- Sample code downloads
- All developer documentation
- Articles pertaining to Macintosh development
- The official Apple online development forums

The developer registration process is pretty straightforward. I go over the steps involved in Bonus Chapter 1 on the web site. Becoming an App Store seller is a little more complicated and has more steps to follow: that's because (you guessed it) money is involved. I go over the details of becoming an App Store seller of Macintosh apps as well in Bonus Chapter 1.

Read on!

Chapter 2

Mac OS X Coding with Xcode

· ·

In This Chapter

▶ Getting the hang of using Xcode

▶ Making Xcode work for you

▶ Getting familiar with the parts of a Macintosh project

· ·

*Y*our best friend, worst enemy, helpful assistant, cryptic co-conspirator, and all-around master toolbox of all Macintosh app development will be: Xcode. Apple created Xcode to do nearly everything you will need to do in order to create and support quality Macintosh applications. Those other things that Xcode doesn't handle for you, Xcode will ensure that you can get to the tools that keep all the other parts of your app and your development process in order.

In this chapter, I show you how to find and install the latest version of Xcode and the full set of Apple development tools, straight from Apple. I also demonstrate the construction of a more-than-simple application from start to finish, so that you can see the basic approach to follow when you create your own apps. I will also introduce Interface Builder, Xcode's integrated graphical tool that Apple designed to make your life easier when you create the visual interface of your application.

This book uses *Xcode*. On the web site, Bonus Chapter 1 shows how to become a Registered Apple Developer, sign on to the Mac Dev Center website, download the latest Xcode tools, and join the Mac Developer program.

Getting Familiar with Xcode

You will use Xcode for just about everything you need to create and build your application. Xcode is an integrated development environment (IDE) written and supported by Apple, which gives you the best possible tool to develop Macintosh applications. You will use the following components of Xcode for most of the work developing and testing your application:

- **Source Code Editor.** You use Xcode's text editor to create and edit the Objective-C, C, and C++ source files for your Macintosh application. You can use your own favorite editor (such as Emacs) if you prefer, but Xcode's editor incorporates context-sensitive help that can assist your development tasks — and a third-party editor might not provide such assistance. As you'll see later in this chapter, Xcode allows you to customize many of the visual aspects of your code as well.

- **Interface Builder.** Interface Builder is Apple's user-interface editor, and it gives you the capability to create and manipulate the visual portions of your app. In addition, you use Interface Builder to make connections between the code you write and the components of the visual interface. Interface Builder is bundled as an editor within Xcode.

- **Macintosh App Build Tool.** Xcode 4 uses the LLVM (Low Level Virtual Machine) compiler and linker to turn the human-readable source code you type into machine-readable instructions that a Mac computer's CPU will interpret and execute. The compiler and all the tools are installed when you install Xcode so it knows where to find them when you want to turn your code into a running app. The build tool is really a set of separate tools to turn all your hard work into a quality product. I go over the details of the build process later in this chapter.

- **Source-Level Debugger.** I make mistakes in my code, and the more apps you create, the greater the chances that one of your apps will do something you didn't expect or intend. Figure 2-1 shows you one of the results that a failure to do the right thing may lead to. You should make every effort to ensure your users never see this coming out of your apps. A debugger helps you track down and terminate with extreme prejudice the mistakes in your code that otherwise will send your users to your competition. Xcode's debugging tools provide you with a GUI-based approach to finding and fixing problems before your users see them. I will introduce you to Xcode's debugger later in this chapter and cover the debugger more extensively in Chapter 11.

- **CoreData Editor.** If your application is like most apps, your users will deliver their specific data into your app and your app will store it somewhere. CoreData is Apple's recommended approach to managing your users' data. Xcode comes with a visual tool that enables you to create structures for your data that CoreData can manage. You can even provide complex intra-structural relationships between different types of data, similar to creating tables that depend on each other within a relational database. You will find that CoreData offers many features for your app to exploit, and I cover CoreData and its editor in Chapter 8.

Figure 2-1: An application behaving badly. You don't want your users to see this.

You'll always want the latest and greatest versions of all the tools that Xcode comes with. I suggest that before you begin a new Xcode project you should check the Macintosh Developer downloads (`https://developer.apple.com/devcenter/mac/index.action`) to see whether there's anything new. In addition, you'll want to stay current with prerelease versions of Mac OS X — Apple may require that your app runs on upcoming versions of OS X as a condition for your app's presence in the App Store; this is certainly true for iPhone/iOS development and likely will also occur with OS X. I definitely recommend checking for new versions of Xcode and OS X just before your app is delivered to Apple, to cover the possibility that Apple has changed something that your app depends on.

Be careful! Your app should not *depend* on prereleases of OS X; if Apple hasn't officially released the new OS X version and you're building your app to use a prerelease, the app often won't run on users' Macs. You should develop your app for the version of OS X that will be available when your app is up at the App Store.

Xcode version 4.0 was released in March 2011, and that's what I use for the examples in this book.

Creating a Macintosh Application with Xcode

With Xcode by your side, you are at the start of your path to creating your first Macintosh app. The download and installation were both pretty straightforward, but now it's time to get interesting. The rest of this chapter describes the following tasks:

- ✔ Creating a new project
- ✔ Discovering what files are produced by Xcode for your app

✔ Creating and building a very basic display-type application using Xcode

✔ Creating and building a very basic document-type application using Xcode

✔ Using the Interface Builder to create the look of your app and connect it to your code

✔ Downloading and building a sample application

What type of app are you?

Your app will probably fall into one of the following two categories. There are other types of apps that Xcode can build, but these are the most common. I will go over the details of building each of these in this chapter.

Cocoa Application, window-based

This is a basic application that does not provide any document-related support. This means your app will have no default Save or New operations. You aren't prevented from adding these features and functionality, but Xcode does not add them automatically and you must manage them on your own.

Cocoa Application, document-based

This is a step up from the window-based application. Xcode will incorporate the features for creating new and saving old documents for your app — including managing multiple documents at the same time.

Cocoa is the name of the libraries of Objective-C code that you use to develop Macintosh apps. I cover Cocoa in more detail in Chapter 4.

Creating a new project

Your journey to creating a new Macintosh app begins with Xcode, and here's how you do it:

1. **Launch Xcode.**

   You can find Xcode in the Applications subfolder of the Developer folder at the top level of your Mac's hard drive.

   You see the Welcome to Xcode window, as shown in Figure 2-2.

2. **Click Create a new Xcode project.**

   Figure 2-3 is the dialog you should see next, which asks you to choose the type of project you want to create. Xcode provides several templates for projects — since I develop both iOS and Mac OS X apps, both types of templates are available for me.

Figure 2-2: The first step on your road to an app.

The dialog that Xcode displays at this point will remember what you selected the previous time you created a new project; if this is the first time you're running Xcode, you may see a dialog that doesn't show anything selected. Don't panic! You make those selections next.

Since this book is about Mac apps, you should review the items listed under the left (Mac OS X) pane.

Figure 2-3: Choosing the appropriate project template for your new app.

3. Click Application in the Mac OS X pane.

Doing so reveals the templates available for Mac apps.

4. Select "Cocoa Application" and then click "Next".

Xcode will display the dialog shown in Figure 2-4. This is the place for you to provide some high-level general information about the project you want Xcode to create.

Figure 2-4: Xcode gives you several options for your app (this simple app needs none of them).

5. Enter the Product Name and if needed, the Company Identifier, then click the Next button.

You provide the product name here — I've left the other options untouched, since I want to get you started building a simple app that's quick and easy to get up and running right away. The Company Identifier field may be pre-populated; Xcode remembers it for you from any previous project you created. You should provide your Company Identifier in this field in the form of a *reverse domain name*. For example, I use com. karlgkowalski because I have registered that as a domain name for myself. For a test app, you can just use the default Company Identifier provided by Xcode.

You must have a valid Company Identifier before you can submit an app to the App Store. This identifier should be a domain name you've registered for yourself, reversed as shown in the example. You can use any valid domain name for the Company Identifier, but you must register it to ensure you have the legal right to use it.

I've decided to call my simple Cocoa-window app `SimpleCocoa WindowApp`. I'm proficient at writing Mac apps, but need some help coming up with clever names (almost sounds like an app idea in itself).

You'll see the dialog shown in Figure 2-5. Xcode now asks you for a location to place all the files and folders it needs to create in order to get you started with a basic project.

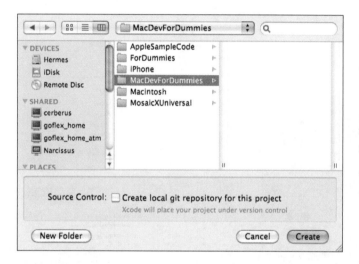

Figure 2-5: Xcode asks you for the location in which to place all the project files it will create.

6. **Select the location in which Xcode will create your project folder, then click the Create button.**

   Choose a good spot to store all your project information — Xcode will create a folder using your project name and create all the files it needs. Leave the checkbox next to Source Control unchecked.

   Xcode can create a version control system just for this project for you to record and track changes to your code. I discuss that in Bonus Chapter 3 on the website.

   Xcode will create a set of files and then open a window with the new project ready to go. Figure 2-6 shows you what you'll see when Xcode finishes getting everything ready. I will go over the details of the contents of this window later in the chapter.

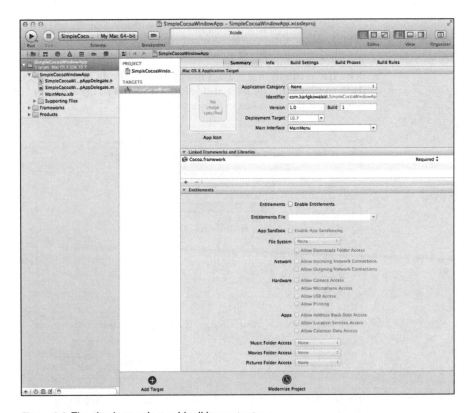

Figure 2-6: The simplest project, with all its contents.

7. **Click the Run button at the left side of the toolbar at the top of the window.**

The Run button looks like the "play" button on a DVD player. Get used to this button, because you'll be clicking it a lot. Xcode will perform several operations, and will write out a text message in the activity viewer in the center of the toolbar as each operation executes. For a simple app like this one, running on an average-powered machine, you might not see all of them flash by — larger apps with more source modules will take longer for Xcode to build.

I saw the following messages in my first build of SimpleCocoaWindowApp:

```
Building...

Precompiling 1 of 1 prefix headers.
```

A *prefix header* is a file that Xcode has created for your project, and it will be automatically included into every source code file you create for your app. Long ago someone came up with the idea that a speedier build would result from using a header file in nearly every compiled source file, compiling that file beforehand, and including it by default in every source file. Xcode created the file SimpleCocoaWindowApp_Prefix.pch and included it in the project. Figure 2-7 shows the contents of this file. Notice Line 6 in particular:

```
#import <Cocoa/Cocoa.h>
```

This line is an instruction to Xcode that it should find the Cocoa.h file in the Cocoa directory (the angle brackets <> are a hint to Xcode regarding where it should look to find this directory) and grab all its contents. This is the primary reason for the precompiling step: The contents of Cocoa.h are *very large*, and they include some *executable code*.

```
000                SimpleCocoaWindowApp - SimpleCocoaWindowApp-Prefix.pch
    ◀ ▶   SimpleCocoaWindowApp ⟩ SimpleCocoaWindowApp ⟩ Supporting Files ⟩ h SimpleCocoaWindowApp-Prefix.pch ⟩ No Selection
1  //
2  // Prefix header for all source files of the 'SimpleCocoaWindowApp' target in the 'SimpleCocoaWindowApp' project
3  //
4
5  #ifdef __OBJC__
6      #import <Cocoa/Cocoa.h>
7  #endif
8
```

Figure 2-7: The contents of the prefix header file Xcode created.

Your app's source and header files will access other header files, so that your code can use other classes that you create or classes provided by Cocoa. #import is a compiler directive telling the compiler to retrieve the contents of the file described in the remainder of the #import line. An #import line will have one of the following two forms:

```
#import "localHeaderFileName.h"
```

Xcode first searches the directory created for the project to find the file localHeaderFileName.h, and if it can't find the file there, Xcode searches the directories set in the Build Settings.

```
#import <systemHeaderFileName.h>
```

Xcode uses a list of predefined search directories to find the file `systemHeaderFileName.h`. The contents between the quotes and angle brackets can also include directory paths. Generally, the angle brackets are used for header files supplied by Xcode.

```
Compiling x of 2 source modules.
```

Xcode compiles each source file in your project and tells you which one it's currently compiling.

```
Build succeeded.
```

This is what you see when Xcode has done all the work it needs to do to create your app. You're also told if Xcode found anything questionable in your app that you might want to take a look at. I go over such warnings later in this chapter — right now, since Xcode was responsible for writing all the code currently in the app, you should see no warnings or errors. You should see two indications of success: a transient gray message with the text `Build Succeeded` and a line of text in the activity viewer that reads `No Issues`.

You can see in Figure 2-8 the window created when Xcode launches your app.

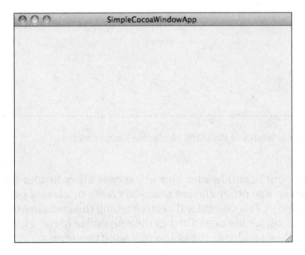

Figure 2-8: A plain-vanilla, incredibly boring app!

That's all you need to do to create a basic window-based `Cocoa` project. Your app will perform all the basic things that window apps perform, and it comes with all the default menus. But there's not much you can do with this app — it doesn't have anything interesting to tell or show you. I'll get you to add more features to this little app later on in this chapter, but next I go over the basic features and displays of the Xcode project window — because that's where you'll spend the majority of your time.

Xcode's visual details

Figure 2-6 is a display of the Xcode project window. You're interacting with the project window for the greater bulk of all the time you spend working on your Mac apps, and here's where I explain all the important parts of this window; it will be an indispensable part of your development experience. Figure 2-9 is a re-creation of this window, complete with the specific areas you need to know.

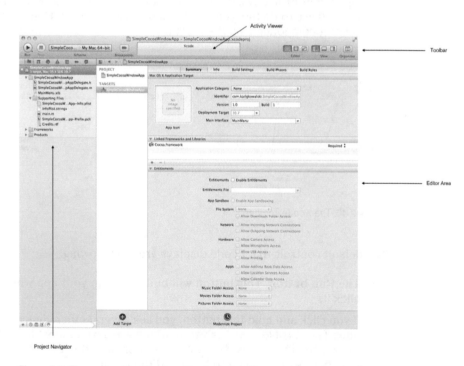

Figure 2-9: The parts of an Xcode project window. You can have many projects open at the same time, and each will have its own version of this window.

Those areas are

- ✔ **The Toolbar.** The buttons and other user interface (UI) controls you use to perform actions in and on your project are located here. (Farther along in this section, I explain each of the default controls and go over how to customize the toolbar.)

- ✔ **The Project navigator.** The panel on the left side of the window contains a set of items, some of which act like folders in a file system window. This panel provides access to all the files of your project.

- ✔ **The Editor area.** Here's where you'll spend a lot of your time tinkering with your app, editing source modules and other files (which include the user interface components and any data models — I go over UI editing in Chapter 5, and data model editing in Chapter 8).

The Toolbar

The top of your project window is a toolbar containing a set of UI controls that you will use to do things for, with, and to your project. Figure 2-10 shows the different components on the toolbar.

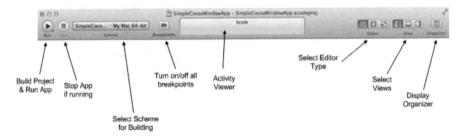

Figure 2-10: The Xcode Toolbar.

The default controls that Xcode displays are the following:

- ✔ **The Run button.** This button will build and run your app when you click it.

    If you click and hold this button, you see several other choices for running: Test, Profile, and Analyze — which are development tasks beyond the scope of this book. As a solo entrepreneur, I don't use any of these selections — I just want to build and run my app.

✓ **The Stop button.** After you click the Run button and Xcode launches your app, this button becomes enabled — you can stop your app without having to make it the foreground application. You might use this button if your app was caught in an infinite loop and you couldn't send any input into it.

✓ **The Scheme drop-down menu.** This menu contains the selection for some of the settings used in building your app. A *scheme* is simply a named set of build settings — you would use a release scheme to build a version of your app for distribution and a debug scheme while putting your app together. (I cover basic scheme settings later in this chapter.)

✓ **The Breakpoint State button.** This button gives you a quick way to enable and disable all breakpoints you set in your application. A *breakpoint* is an instruction to the Xcode Debugger that you want it to halt execution of your application when the CPU reaches the line of code where you set the breakpoint.

The Breakpoint State button is disabled when you create a new project and enabled automatically when you add your first breakpoint. You can then disable all breakpoints — which turns them off so the Debugger won't stop when it comes across them — by clicking the Breakpoint State button. Clicking the button a second time enables all the breakpoints.

✓ **The Activity Viewer.** Xcode provides a variety of different text and other visual messages in this pane in the center of the Toolbar. (I cover some of the important messages in this chapter.)

✓ **The Editor Selector.** Three buttons switch between different editing modes:

• You'll use the Standard editor (the left button) nearly all the time.

• The Assistant editor (middle button) displays a separate editor pane containing information that is logically related to the content of the Standard editor. For instance, if you've selected a header file from the Project navigator and you click the Assistant editor button, Xcode will show the corresponding source file in a separate pane. This can save you time when you're making changes in a header file such as adding a new method, because the source file is opened right next to the header file.

• The Version editor (right button) displays differences between the selected file in one pane and another version of that same file in a second pane.

This is useful if you've set up this project to use *source code control*, so you can track changes to your code. Briefly, source code control is a feature used to keep track of changes to your project files over time, so that you can track the evolution of your project from start to finish. For instance, you might use the Version editor's display of differences to discover where a change was made that introduced a bug.

✔ **The View selector.** This is a collection of toggle buttons for displaying or hiding selected views:

 • The left button is for displaying the Navigator area — that's the listing of files on the left side of the display. The Navigator area can show several other types of navigators, but you'll use the Project navigator the most.

 Keeping the Navigator area visible is very helpful — I jump from one module to the next fairly rapidly during my development.

 • The middle button displays the Debug area for your app when the Debugger is running at the bottom of the Editor area.

 • The right button displays the Utility area, which provides more information about the file shown as selected in the Navigator area.

 The Utility area also gives you some quick ways to add items to the file you're working on in the Standard editor — including code templates for Objective-C modules and UI components for Interface Builder modules.

I usually leave the Debug and Utility areas hidden unless I'm either running the Debugger or editing an Interface Builder file.

✔ **The Organizer button.** This button displays The Organizer Window, which gives you a display of several different sets of information related to general application development.

For Mac development, this is the window to use when you want to look up references in the documentation. I'll cover the Organizer Window in detail in this chapter.

Scheme settings

You can create different schemes for your app if you want to build different versions of the same app with different build settings. Figure 2-11 shows you the display of the build settings you see when you select Edit Scheme from the Scheme drop-down menu.

As a rule, I really only modify two of the settings in this scheme:

✔ **The Destination.** This build setting tells Xcode to build for either Mac 32-bit or Mac 64-bit, which means that Xcode is building your app to use (respectively) 32-bit addresses or 64-bit addresses.

I don't recommend changing this setting, unless you really need to run on a very old version of Mac OS X. All current Mac hardware is capable of running 64-bit apps.

✔ **The Build Configuration.** This build setting tells Xcode whether to build a Debug version of your app or a Release version.

I use Debug when I'm creating the app and then shift to Release after all the bugs have been caught and fixed and I'm about ready to upload my app to the App Store. The Debug build of your app will contain some extra information in the app itself for the Xcode Debugger to make use of, and you don't need that extra stuff in your released app.

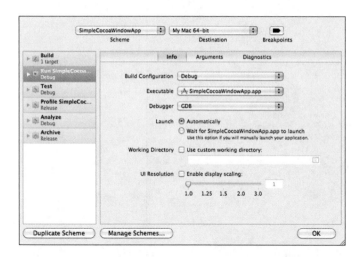

Figure 2-11: The default scheme for SimpleCocoaWindowApp.

The Navigator area

The left pane of the Project window is what you use to navigate through the files of your project and their contents in several different ways. Each navigation approach lets you view the components of your project in a manner that suits a different task, and each is represented by a button in the Navigator selector bar at the top of the pane, as shown in Figure 2-12.

Figure 2-12: The Navigator area.

> ## Address wars
>
> For a long time, every Mac OS was 32-bit: the OS used memory addresses that were 32 bits in length, allowing apps to access up to 4 billion bytes of memory, if that amount were available on the machine. This was a lot of memory space — more than necessary for apps other than some scientific, graphics, or simulator apps.
>
> Recent Macs have 64-bit hardware and versions of OS X that use 64-bit addresses to access memory. OS X still retains the capability to run 32-bit apps, but your app should be written to use 64-bit addresses because every Mac will support this size. Even if no one ever buys 16 quintillion bytes worth of memory, your app can get to all of it.
>
> Unless you know that your app's audience is using 32-bit Macs and you want to support them, keep Xcode set to build your app as a 64-bit executable.

From left to right, the selector buttons are

- ✔ **The Project navigator.** You use this list to display all the files and groups in your project. Selecting a file from this list displays the contents in the Editor area. For instance, selecting a `.m` file displays the contents of an Objective-C source file; selecting a `.xib` file displays the contents of an Interface Builder UI file.

- ✔ **The Symbol navigator.** You see a list of the Objective-C classes in your project when you click this button. Click the reveal-triangle to the left of each class name to see a list of methods and member variables for each class. Clicking a method or member variable takes you to its definition in the class file.

- ✔ **The Search navigator.** This display lets you find any text quickly within your project.

- ✔ **The Issue navigator.** Here's where Xcode displays any warnings or errors it finds when it opens, analyzes, or builds your project.

- ✔ **The Debug navigator.** While you're debugging your app, this navigator shows you information about the threads and the application stack.

- ✔ **Breakpoint navigator.** You can see all the breakpoints currently set in your code when you use the Breakpoint navigator. (I cover this feature in more detail in Chapter 11.)

- ✔ **Log navigator.** This display shows you the history of the tasks you've performed on this project — including building, running, and debugging. You can also review the details of the results. You might use this to see when your last successful build was run, or the log messages sent to the Debugger's Console.

I use the Project navigator display the most, because it lets me jump around my code. All the different files in the project — and there are a lot of them — will be displayed in the Project navigator. The major groups are the following:

✔ **The App's source files.** The item in the Project navigator area that is named with the App's name, represented by a folder icon, contains all the source files used to build the app. These include the following:

- Objective-C sources (.m) and headers (.h)

- Interface Builder (.xib) files

- CoreData model files, if any (.xcmodeldata)

- Precompiled header files (.pch)

- Strings (.strings)

- Property Lists (.plist)

- Credits (.rtf)

The folder icon in the Project navigator is a *group*. You create a group by clicking on an item in the Project navigator and selecting File➪New➪ New Group. This will create a new item in the navigator area that with a folder icon, and you can create new items and move other items inside this group. You might want to do this if a set of your Objective-C classes logically belong together.

✔ **Frameworks.** Your app will access a variety of Mac OS X code libraries called *Frameworks*. This folder contains the Frameworks that Xcode decided your project would need, and you can add more when you want to use Mac OS X code that isn't included by default. For instance, if your app will interact with the user's Address Book, you'll have to add the AddressBook framework to your application.

✔ **Products.** This folder contains the items that represent what your project is going to create.

For the SimpleCocoaWindowApp, there's only one product: SimpleCocoaWindowApp.

The Editor area

This is where you'll spend most of your time: typing and manipulating your app's code, its UI, and its data models. When you select a file from the Project navigator, the contents of that file will be displayed in the Editor area. Figure 2-13 shows the contents of the only class Xcode created for SimpleCocoaWindowApp, the file SimpleCocoaWindowAppAppDelegate.m.

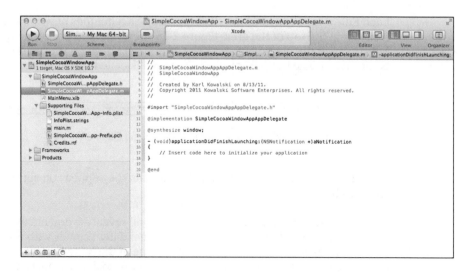

Figure 2-13: The Editor area, ready to edit the SimpleCocoaWindowAppAppDelegate.m module.

You can edit the contents of your files in a separate window. Instead of selecting a file from the Project navigator pane, double-click the file. An editor window will open up with that file's contents displayed, ready for you to work with. Figure 2-14 shows the `SimpleCocoaWindowAppAppDelega te.m` file in its own window, ready for edits. This window contains a subset of the components that the project window does, which means you're less likely to inadvertently click something you didn't want to click.

Figure 2-14: The SimpleCocoaWindowAppAppDelegate.m in its own editor window.

Each Editor area (or window) that appears has a number of very small controls lining the top of the area. Figure 2-15 shows the top part of a typical Editor area more clearly while `SimpleCocoaWindowAppAppDelegate.m` is being edited. The top part of the Editor area is called the *Jump bar*.

Figure 2-15: The controls in the Jump bar at the top of the Editor area.

You can see the different pieces, listed here as they appear on-screen from left to right:

- **The Related Items menu.** Clicking this will reveal several menu items, as you can see in Figure 2-16. Each active menu item comes with a submenu full of the names of files related to the one in the Editor area. For instance, the `SimpleCocoaWindowAppAppDelegate.m` file has one Counterpart (`SimpleCocoaWindowAppAppDelegate.h`), one Superclass (`NSObject`), and implements one Protocol (`NSApplicationDelegate`). Selecting any of these will open that particular file into the Editor area.

- **Back button.** If you've been editing multiple files, clicking this button will display the previous file you edited; it's similar to a web browser's Back button. This is a very quick way of moving from one file to another, which is helpful if you're adding methods and member variables in both the source and header files of a class.

- **Forward button.** You can move forward through the set of files you've been working with by clicking this button; it's similar to a web browser's Forward button.

- **The File's Project Location.** The location of the file within the project is laid out in a series of buttons. Each button allows you to access other files at that part of the project. In Figure 2-14, the project location of `Sim pleCocoaWindowAppAppDelegate.m` (the file in the Editor) starts at the Project, which leads to the `SimpleCocoaWindowApp` folder, which leads to the module itself. Clicking each of these buttons shows a menu displaying the other items in that level of the project.

- **Symbol drop-down menu.** Your source and header files contain a number of methods and member variables — these are called *symbols*. Figure 2-17 shows you what the symbols are for the `SimpleCocoa WindowAppAppDelegate.m` file.

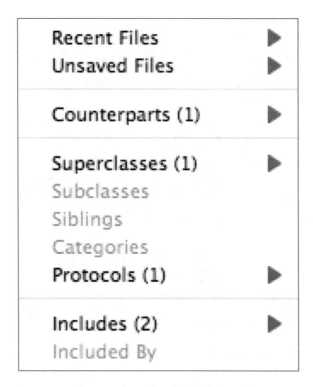

Figure 2-16: The menu items listed in the Related Files menu.

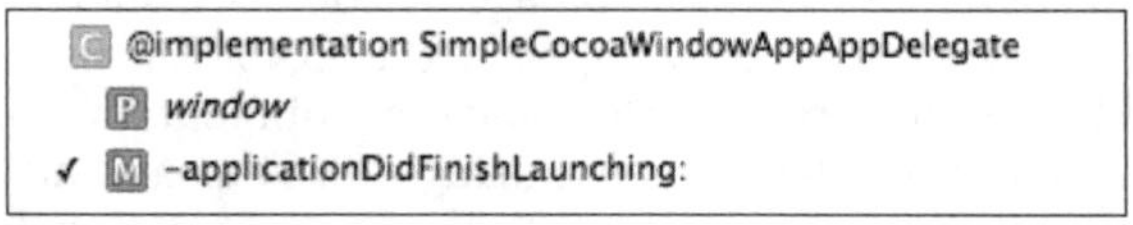

```
C  @implementation SimpleCocoaWindowAppAppDelegate
P  window
✓  M  -applicationDidFinishLaunching:
```

Figure 2-17: The list of symbols (methods and member variables) in the current file.

The Organizer window

You'll use the Xcode Organizer window to perform some tasks that aren't directly related to creating and editing your project. You can see the Organizer window displayed in Figure 2-18.

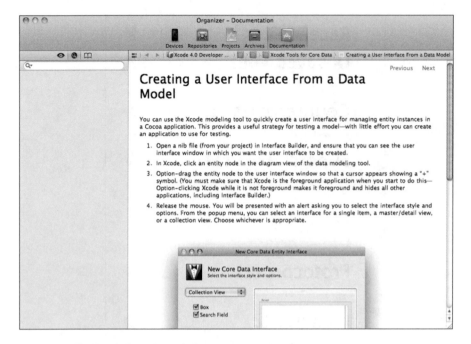

Figure 2-18: The Xcode Organizer window.

There are five different organizers:

✐ **Devices.** This organizer lets you manage iOS devices, such as the iPhone. This organizer will only appear if the iOS SDK is installed. You won't need to use this organizer for Mac development, but you should always consider future development using iOS. You can find more information on iOS development in *iPhone Application Development For Dummies, 3rd Edition*, by Neal Goldstein (John Wiley & Sons, Inc.).

✐ **Repositories.** You can create and manage your project's source code or version control system from here. Xcode supports Git and Subversion version control systems.

✐ **Projects.** This organizer lists all the projects you've created using Xcode and lets you open them.

✔ **Archives.** You will use this part of the Organizer to manage the product archives you create as a result of your Distribution Scheme. This becomes important when you want to submit your app to the App Store.

I cover the Archives in detail in Bonus Chapter 2 on the web site.

✔ **Documentation.** You'll use this organizer to view information from the Mac OS X reference library.

You're now loaded with data about the different parts of the Xcode environment. It's the perfect time to give you some improvements to make to `SimpleCocoaWindowApp` that will make use of all that info. Chapter 3 is the place to be!

Chapter 3

Giving Your App Something to Do

*H*ere I introduce to you one approach you can take for connecting your app's UI elements with the code that your app executes when it operates on the data that your users enter into the UI. This approach is explicit — you'll be adding all the code and making the connections yourself. Xcode 4 provides another approach as well, which I introduce after I walk you down the more explicit path.

Creating a Tip Calculator

Here's where I demonstrate the interaction between the UI and the code through a very simple example: I turn `SimpleCocoaWindowApp` (as demonstrated in Chapter 2) into a tip calculator with the following steps.

1. **Select** `SimpleCocoaWindowAppAppDelegate.h` **in the Project navigator.**

    This is the header file for our class, and it looks pretty bare-bones. The header file contains *declarations* of the parts of a class — this file can be `#imported` into other source modules as a "promise" of what the class provides. You're going to add some UI controls to the window, and this is the place to do it.

2. **Enter the purple-colored text shown in Listing 3-1.**

    I'm going to use purple to highlight the new code to add. You're adding four member variables and one new method. The member variables are added between the braces of the `@interface` declaration — this tells Xcode where to find the data portion of your class. The method is added after the braces surrounding the member variables — this tells Xcode where to find the functions that operate on the data of your class. I will explain in the next section what the different parts of the items you just added are.

3. Save the header file.

I have a habit of saving everything — very often — as this reduces the headaches and heartaches that come from power outages and the rare Xcode crash. Your own experience with computers and saving your data will determine how often you save your data. As computers have gotten faster, saving is usually just a combo-keypress away, so I recommend frequent saving.

You can enable Auto-Saving in Xcode's General preferences. Your changes will automatically be saved whenever you do a build or quit.

4. Select `SimpleCocoaWindowAppAppDelegate.m` **from the Project navigator.**

The editor pane will show the contents of the source file for this class. A source file contains the *implementation* of the promises made in the header file. You're going to add the method you declared in the header file.

5. Enter the purple-colored text shown in Listing 3-2 and save the source file.

Save the source file. Save early, save often!

6. Build the project but don't run it now.

You should see the `Build Succeeded` message in the Activity Viewer.

The code you've added performs the following operations:

1. It retrieves the data from the `NSTextField` called `m_amount`.

   The data is retrieved as an `NSString` object, because that's how `NSTextField` holds anything typed into the entry field on the screen.

2. It retrieves the data from the `NSTextField` called `m_tipPercentage`.

   The assumption is, of course, that this number is somewhere between 0 and 100. And once again, the data is retrieved as an `NSString` object.

3. It converts the two `NSString` objects into `double` values, so it's easier to multiply them together.

4. The two `double` values are multiplied to determine the tip amount.

5. The tip amount is converted into an `NSString` object.

6. The `NSString` object containing the tip amount is used to set the value of the tip amount for the `NSTextField` `m_tipAmount`.

The code you've just added to the `SimpleCocoaWindowAppAppDelegate` source and header files is to prepare for adding the user interface components in the next set of steps. Your app is a combination of UI components connected to your code; so far you've just added the code to the app.

Listing 3-1: Modifications for SimpleCocoaWindowAppAppDelegate.h

```
//
// SimpleCocoaWindowAppAppDelegate.h
// SimpleCocoaWindowApp
//
// Created by Karl Kowalski on 2/12/11
// Copyright 2011 Kowalski Software Enterprises.
// All rights reserved.
//

#import <Cocoa/Cocoa.h>

@interface SimpleCocoaWindowAppAppDelegate: NSObject
          <NSApplicationDelegate>
{
@private
    NSWindow *window;
    IBOutlet NSTextField* m_amount;
    IBOutlet NSTextField* m_tipPercent;
    IBOutlet NSButton* m_calculate;
    IBOutlet NSTextField* m_tipAmount;
}

@property (assign) IBOutlet NSWindow *window;

- (IBAction)calculateTip:(id)inSender;

@end
```

Listing 3-2:   Modifications for SimpleCocoaWindowAppAppDelegate.m

```
//
// SimpleCocoaWindowAppAppDelegate.m
// SimpleCocoaWindowApp
//
// Created by Karl Kowalski on 2/12/11
// Copyright 2011 Kowalski Software Enterprises.
// All rights reserved.
//

#import "SimpleCocoaWindowAppAppDelegate.h"

@implementation SimpleCocoaWindowAppAppDelegate

@synthesize window;

- (void)applicationDidFinishLaunching:(NSNotification*)
          aNotification
{
    // Insert code here to initialize your application
}

- (IBAction)calculateTip:(id)inSender
{
    NSString* amountValue = [m_amount stringValue];
    NSString* tipPercentage = [m_tipPercent stringValue];
    double amountValueD = [amountValue doubleValue];
    double tipPercentageD = [tipPercentage doubleValue];
    double tipAmount = amountValueD * tipPercentageD / 100.0;
    NSString* tipAmountString = [NSString
          stringWithFormat:@"%.2f", tipAmount];
    [m_tipAmount setStringValue:tipAmountString];
}

@end
```

Now you're going to jump feet-first into building a user interface. Here's how you do that:

1. **In the Project navigator, select the MainMenu.xib item.**

   This will display the Interface Builder file containing your user interface. Figure 3-1 shows what Interface Builder's Editor area looks like. The Editor area contains the following items:

   - **The Dock.** The Dock contains the items you can edit using Interface Builder. It's divided into two sections: the top contains *proxy objects*, which will reference real objects that will exist when the application is running; and *instance objects*, which are instances of objects that will be created when this XIB file is loaded by the application — each window object would come with its own font manager object and `SimpleCocoaWindowAppAppDelegate` object. A XIB file contains the information Cocoa needs to recreate the visual components of your app that you put together using Interface Builder.

- **The Application menubar.** This menubar is what users will use when the application is running; this is not the Xcode menubar. You can add menu items to any of the menus in the application menubar to give more functionality to your app.

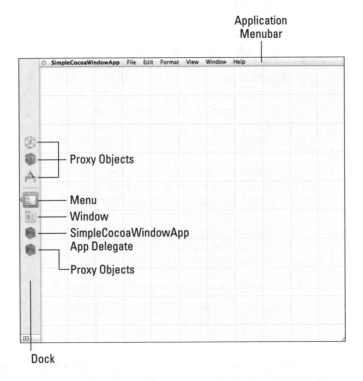

Figure 3-1: The MainMenu.xib file opened in the Editor area.

2. Click the Window icon in the left sidebar of the IB Editor.

This should be the fifth icon from the top — hold your mouse over the icon to make Xcode display a hint, which should say `Window — SimpleCocoaWindowApp`. It's also the icon that looks like a tiny Mac window.

After you click it, the window should appear over the graph paper–like background.

3. **Click the Show Utility view button on the toolbar.**

This view gives you access to the library of UI components you can drag and drop onto the window in your user interface.

Since the Utility view occupies part of your Project window, you will want to maximize this window to use all the available screen space.

4. **Click the Show the Object library button in the Utility view selector bar.**

Figure 3-2 shows the display of the Object library. You may want to increase the vertical height of this display, to save on scrolling. You will be doing a lot of drag-and-drop actions from this view into your window.

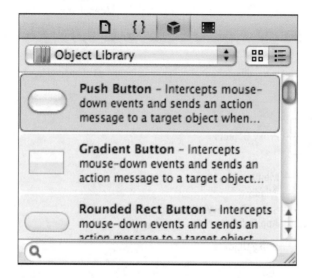

Figure 3-2: The Library window, displaying the UI components for data input and data display.

5. **In the Utility view, select Object Library⇨Cocoa⇨Controls from the drop-down menu.**

6. **Drag a Label from the Object Library and drop it anywhere onto the window.**

You can use the search field at the bottom of the Object Library area to filter the set of UI components displayed. If you enter the word **Label** in the field, the set of displayed components is reduced to two, making it easier to grab.

7. **Click the Attributes Inspector button at the top of the Utility view.**

8. **Change the Title attribute to** Amount.

   You can also double-click the Label and type the text directly into it.

9. **Resize the label on the screen.**

   Xcode doesn't auto-resize it for you when you change the text using the Attributes Inspector, so here's the drill: Click and drag one of the blue dots on the side of the label in the window to resize the label horizontally. Instead of using the Attributes Inspector, you can also change the title attribute by double-clicking the label and editing the text right on the window; this has the added bonus of forcing Xcode to auto-resize the label to the new width.

10. **Drag a Text Field from the Object Library and drop it to the right of the Amount label.**

    The Interface Builder Editor will provide you some blue dashed lines, called *guides*, as you move the text field control around the window near the Amount label. This is Xcode offering you "help" by giving you indications of where you might consider dropping the control, as governed by Apple's knowledge about how human users like to see things. These are hints, not requirements.

11. **Repeat Step 9 and Step 10 for a Tip Percentage label and its corresponding text field. Place the pair just below the Amount label and its corresponding text field.**

12. **Drag a Push Button from the Object Library window and drop it onto the SimpleCocoaWindowApp window, right below the Tip Percentage text field.**

13. **Modify the button's text label to read** Calculate.

14. **Drag two Labels from the Library window and drop both below the Calculate button such that one is aligned with the Amount and Tip Percentage labels and the other is aligned with the Amount and Tip Percentage text fields.**

15. **Change the Title of the left label to** Tip Amount:.

    The label on the left is where the tip amount will be displayed; I've changed its Title to <tipAmount> as a reminder of what the data will be.

16. **Save everything.**

    The SimpleCocoaWindowApp window should look like the display in Figure 3-3.

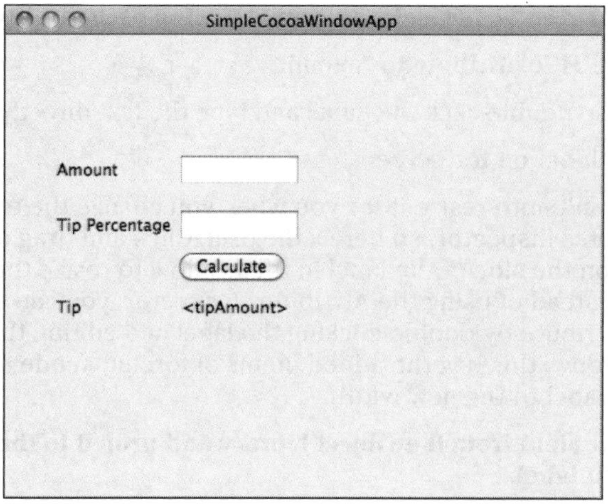

Figure 3-3: The final look of the SimpleCocoaWindowApp.

You've now modified the UI display of `SimpleCocoaWindowApp`, but there's still one step missing: You need to connect the UI components — the labels, button, and the text fields — to the code. In the next steps, you'll be dragging from components in the window to the `SimpleCocoaWindowAppDelegate` *instance*, which represents the actual `SimpleCocoaWindowAppDelegate` object created when the application is launched. This is the object whose code, in source module `SimpleCocoaWindowAppDelegate.m`, you edited in the procedure right before this one. You use this instance within the visual editor as if it were the actual `SimpleCocoaWindowAppDelegate` object containing the window that gets displayed on the screen. You can reference the contents of that instance — the class members and methods — with the instance in the editor. And that's how you connect the visual elements of the `SimpleCocoaWindowApp` window with the code you've implemented. So let's get to it.

1. **Control-Drag from the** `SimpleCocoaWindowApp` **instance to the text field next to the Amount label and release.**

   You should see a small window pop up, as shown in Figure 3-4. This window contains the possible items within the `SimpleCocoaWindow AppAppDelegate` member variables that you can connect to.

2. **Select** m_amount **from the choices in the small pop-up window.**

   Congratulations! You've now connected the member variable m_amount to its text field. This is how you connect member variables in the class to items on the window: by dragging *from* the class instance *to* the item on the screen, and selecting the member variable from the pop-up window.

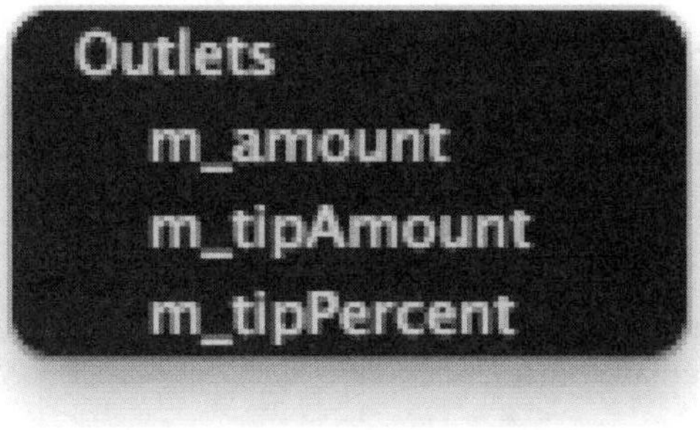

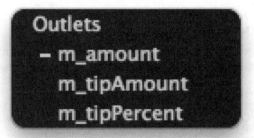

Figure 3-4: The Connection Options window for the connection to the amount. Choose any member variables from the SimpleCocoaWindowApp class.

3. **Control-Drag from the instance to the text field next to the Tip Percentage label and release.**

You'll see another pop-up window, shown in Figure 3-5. Notice that the m_amount item has a "-" next to it — this indicates that this member variable is already connected to something.

Figure 3-5: The connection options window for the connection to the tip percentage. You can see that m_amount is already connected, so you will probably want to connect to a different item.

4. **Select** m_tipPercent.

   Another member variable connected!

5. **Control-Drag from the instance to the label next to the Tip Amount label and release.**

6. **Select the final remaining member variable,** m_tipAmount, **from the list.**

7. **Control-Drag from the instance to the button and release.**

8. **Select the only option, the** m_calculate **member variable.**

   Notice that the editor only lets you make connections between consistent types of items: you cannot connect the m_amount member variable to the Calculate button.

You have now connected the member variables of your class with the components they represent in your interface. When Xcode compiles your app, the information provided in the MainMenu.xib file will be available for your app to use when your application is running. While you made these connections *visually* using the visual editor, when your application is running and the window is created and displayed, these connections are automatically made *programmatically* by the code provided as part of the Cocoa Framework of classes, from which SimpleCocoaWindowAppAppDelegate is created. (Chapter 4 goes over the details of how applications create their visual interfaces when executing.)

The final steps to creating the functional tip calculator are these:

1. **Control-Drag from the button on the** SimpleCocoaWindowApp **window to the instance, and then release.**

   This operation is called *setting the button's action*. When it's done, you see another little pop-up window revealed, as shown in Figure 3-6.

Figure 3-6: The pop-up shown when you connect a button to a method inside the class.

2. **Select** `calculateTip:`.

   You've now told Xcode that when the button is pressed, the `calculateTip:` method should be executed.

3. **Save the** `MainMenu.xib` **file to ensure that all your changes are remembered.**

   That's it. Your app's code and its data members are now connected to the user interface.

Now it's time to return to the Xcode project and get everything put together.

 If you want to see all the connections for the instance in MainMenu.xib, to make sure that you didn't leave anything disconnected accidentally, Control-click the instance object. You see the complete set of member variables and methods and what they're connected to. Figure 3-7 shows you what the finished connections of `SimpleCocoaWindowApp` look like. You can see all the different elements of the class — the Outlets — listed, as well as the method that should be called when the button is clicked — the Received Action; a little dot to the right of each element is filled in with solid white, indicating that each one is connected.

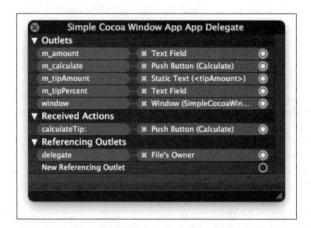

Figure 3-7: The completely connected SimpleCocoaWindowApp AppDelegate instance.

Now your only remaining task is to get back into Xcode and rebuild the project. Just click the Run button. Your app launches, and you can calculate tips from an amount and a percentage. Figure 3-8 shows what this looks like. Just think: Now you can pull out your MacBook at every fine-dining establishment you visit and be sure to calculate the proper amount for the tip.

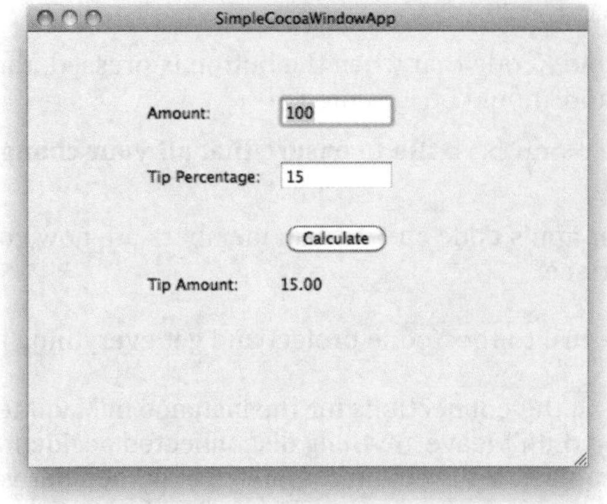

SimpleCocoaWindowApp

Amount: 100

Tip Percentage: 15

(Calculate)

Tip Amount: 15.00

Figure 3-8: The SimpleCocoaWindowApp, improved to function
as a tip calculator.

Take a deep breath and relax. You've created a functional Macintosh application, from (nearly) scratch. You've added UI components and connected
them to your code. Your code calculates tip values based on the data entered
in two text fields.

Sometimes I need to follow my own advice. When I first built and ran the app,
the tip calculation didn't happen! My instinct was to see whether I'd somehow gotten the calculation part wrong, so I set a breakpoint at the beginning
of the calculateTip: method and launched the app with the Debugger.
The Debugger should have halted at the line of code where I'd put the breakpoint — but it didn't. It was almost like the button wasn't connected to this
method. I knew I'd made the connection in Interface Builder from the button
to the SimpleCocoaWindowAppAppDelegate instance object, which should
have triggered the method to be called — except *I forgot to save MainMenu.
xib*. The Interface Builder Editor hadn't recorded that particular information
for Xcode to know what it was supposed to do. It's true, even experts make
simple mistakes. When I saved the MainMenu.xib file and rebuilt, the code
worked exactly as written. Save early, save often! Or else make sure you turn
on the Autosaving preference in Xcode so that your changes are saved when
you Build and Run.

The process you've just walked through here is a very explicit approach to creating a user interface backed by code. Xcode 4 offers an improved way for you to achieve the same result: Create the user interface with Interface Builder *first*, and then Control-drag components from the user interface to the source and header files of the application. Here's what you can do:

1. **Create a new Project in Xcode, and call it** SimpleCocoaWindowApp2.

   Use the exact same settings as before.

2. **Select** `MainMenu.xib` **from the Project navigator.**

3. **Click the button to Show the Assistant editor.**

   You'll see Xcode open the header file, `SimpleCocoaWindowApp2AppDe legate.h` in the Assistant's side window as shown in Figure 3-9.

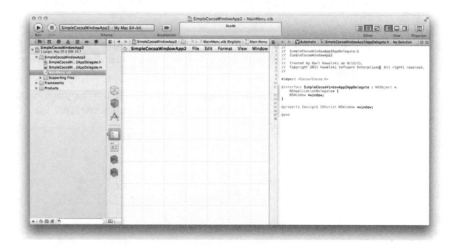

Figure 3-9: Interface Builder open to edit MainMenu.xib, with the Assistant view shown.

4. **Select the Window object in the Interface Builder Dock.**

5. **Add a Label, a Button, and a Text Entry field to the window, as shown in Figure 3-10.**

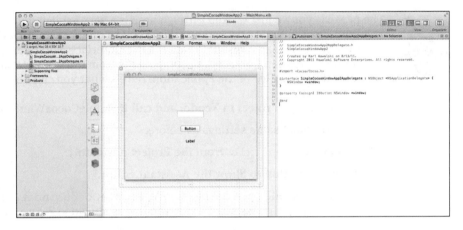

Figure 3-10: Three UI components added to the window in MainMenu.xib.

6. **Control-drag from the Label component into the header file, to the end of the line containing the @interface directive, after the curly brace.**

When you release the mouse button, you'll see the small window in Figure 3-11 appear. You're creating a member variable for the Label within the header file.

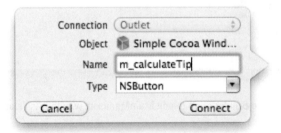

Figure 3-11: The Connection creator. Xcode will create an IBOutlet in your header file and connect it to the UI component.

7. **Name the member variable m_label and click the Connect button.**

The header file will now have the following line added automatically:

```
IBOutlet NSTextField *m_label;
```

8. **Control-drag from the Text Entry field into the header file, below the** `@property` **directive.**

   You'll see another small window displayed.

9. **Name the member variable m_textField and click the Connect button.**

   Xcode adds several lines of code to the header file:

   • A member variable declaration after the `@private` directive:

     `NSTextField *m_textField;`

   • An `@property` declaration for the new member variable:

     `@property (assign) IBOutlet NSTextField *m_textField;`

   • A line into the source file `SimpleCocoaWindowApp2App Delegate.m`:

     `@synthesize m_textField;`

10. **Control-drag from the Button into the header file below the** `@property` **directive.**

    Once again, the little window is displayed.

11. **Change the Connection drop-down menu to Action instead of Outlet. Name the action** clickButton **and click the Connect button.**

    Xcode adds the `clickButton` method declaration to the header file, and adds the method definition to the source file. This method is empty, which means you'll still have to fill it with the code

Analysis of the changes to SimpleCocoaWindowApp

The modifications you made to `SimpleCocoaWindowApp` involved both the header file and the source file. Your changes were the following:

✔ You added four new member variables, each with the qualifier `IBOutlet`, to the header file. This qualifier is a hint to Xcode that these variables are used in the Interface Builder Editor; when the Interface Builder Editor reads the header file, it will pick up these variables and allow you to reference them when making connections.

✔ You added a new method to the header file and also to the source file. This method had a return type of `IBAction`, although no data is actually returned from the method. `IBAction` is a hint to Xcode that this method is going to be referenced by the Interface Builder Editor. Like the `IBOutlet` qualifier for the member variables, the Interface Builder Editor allows you to reference the method when making connections. Every method that you create to be called from a UI action will have the pattern shown in Listing 3-3. This pattern is called a *method signature*.

If you opted to use the alternate approach for creating the UI components first, here's what happened:

- You added UI components to the app's window.

- Xcode created the member variables for the Label and the Text Field and set up the connection between the UI components and the member variables for you. The member variable representing the Text Field was added as a property, and both member variables were given the IBOutlet qualifier.

- Xcode created the calculateTip: method declaration in the header file with the qualifier IBAction. Xcode also implemented an empty calculateTip; method in your source file and set up the connection between the button and the method so that clicking the button would send the calculateTip; message to the SimpleCocoaWindowApp2AppDelegate object.

Listing 3-3:   A code snippet showing an IBAction method signature

```
- (IBAction)name_of_method:(id)inSender;
```

When a UI component in your application triggers a connected method, the code in the application framework will call the method on the object to which the method is connected. In the case of SimpleCocoaWindowApp, that object is the SimpleCocoaWindowAppAppDelegate. In addition to calling the method, the code in the application framework will pass a parameter to the method, of type id. This parameter is always an object — it is the object that triggered the method being called. When the calculateTip: method is executed, the object passed in is the NSButton object m_calculate. Why does the application framework provide the object when it calls the connected method? Because it's possible to assign multiple UI components to trigger the same method, and while SimpleCocoaWindowApp doesn't do this, one of your future apps may take advantage of this capability. For instance, you could remove the Tip Percentage text field, and replace the Calculate button with three separate buttons, each with its own tip percentage value. You then connect each button with the calculateTip: method, and you can then calculate a different tip by determining which button was passed into the method. Your user would then only have to enter the amount used to calculate the tip and pick the percentage using the button that matches what their chosen tip should be.

Analysis of the calculateTip: method

You've absorbed a lot of information already in this chapter, but I would like to go over the operations that take place when the user clicks the Calculate button.

You (or Xcode) connected the button in the `SimpleCocoaWindowApp` window to the method in the `SimpleCocoaWindowAppAppDelegate` instance, so that when the button is pressed the application's `calculate Tip:` method will be called. Here are the details of what happens during the execution of `calculateTip:`.

1. The first operation is to get the value stored in the `m_amount` text field. The `NSTextField` object has a `stringValue` method which returns an `NSString` object.

2. The code retrieves the value stored in the `m_tipPercent` text field as an `NSString`.

3. These two values are each converted to the primitive data type `double`. An `NSString` object comes with a `doubleValue` method that performs this conversion.

4. The code calculates the tip amount by multiplying the two `double` values and dividing by 100.

5. An `NSString` object is created using the creation method `string WithFormat:`. This method takes an `NSString` as a parameter hard-coded to be `@"%.2f"`, which is the C-language formatter that creates a numeric text string showing two decimal places in the resulting text.

6. The tip amount `NSString` is set to be the value of the `m_tipAmount` label.

Most of the work is done behind the scenes by the `Cocoa` application framework. The framework manages the objects that make up your application, including all the UI components and the other class objects that are available for use such as `NSString`.

Your code can use data in several different forms, but the two most used will be *objects* and *primitive data*. A primitive data type is simply a basic unit of data, such as the integer value 1, the letter *K*, or the floating-point value 3.14159. An object is more complex, as it contains both data types and code — methods — for working with that data. I will cover objects in more detail in Chapter 4.

Dude, where's my app?

The Xcode project builds your app according to the code you write and the UI components (and their connection information) you include using Interface Builder. Now, where did that all go?

When you create a new project with Xcode, Xcode creates a folder named with your project name and places all the files and folders it needs inside this folder. In this folder are the following items:

✔ The `SimpleCocoaWindowApp` folder, which contains the source files (as listed in Figure 3-12)

✔ The *folder* named `SimpleCocoaWindowApp.xcodeproj`

> Yes, you heard correctly: This item is a folder, even though it looks like a file. This is an Apple construction called a *Package* — it's actually a folder, but if you double-click it, you launch Xcode and open the `SimpleCocoaWindowApp` project. You can display the contents by right-clicking the file in the Finder and selecting Show Package Contents. Doing so displays a standard Finder window with the files contained in the folder.

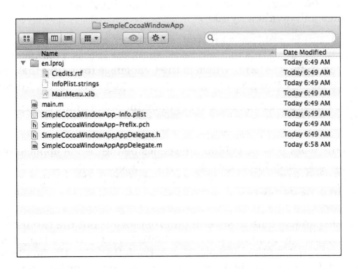

Figure 3-12: Xcode puts all the source files and folders for your app into one folder, so you always know where to find them.

When you perform a build or a run of your application with Xcode, the application will be created in a location separate from the project. You can find the app in the following location in the Finder:

```
YourHomeFolder/Library/Developer/Xcode/DerivedData/
          appName-uniqueID
```

This folder contains the following subfolder path to your application:

```
Build/Products/Debug/appName
```

If you double-click this app, you will launch it.

Normally you will launch your app from within Xcode while you're working on it. However, in order to deliver your app to another Macintosh for testing — or (more important) to the App Store for money-making — you must *Archive* your app.

Archiving your app

An *application archive* is a copy of your application as it exists at a particular time, placed in a file that you can share with others or — when your app is ready to submit to the App Store — upload to Apple. You create an application archive using Xcode. Here's how you do it:

1. **In the Xcode project window, select Product⇨Archive.**

   Doing so creates an Archive version of your app, which you can see in the Organizer window, as shown in Figure 3-13.

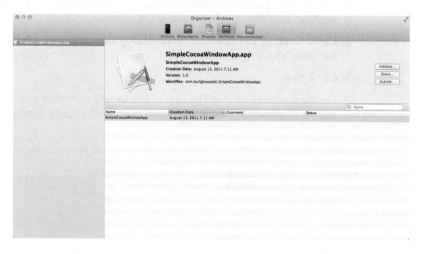

Figure 3-13: The Xcode Organizer window, showing the archive of SimpleCocoaWindowApp.

2. **Select the archive you just created in the Organizer window, and click Share.**

   You see the dialog shown in Figure 3-14.

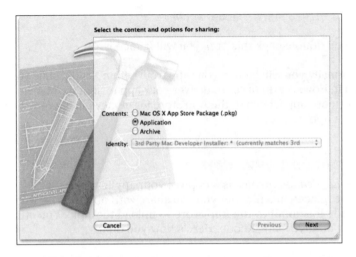

Figure 3-14: You can share your app with others, such as beta-testers, using an archive of your app.

3. **Select the Application radio button to make sure you create the archive as a Mac app on your hard drive.**

4. **Click Next; in the familiar Save dialog that appears, pick a good place for your app to get delivered.**

5. **Click Save.**

   On my machine, I saved the app in the same folder that contains the project folder, as shown in Figure 3-15. Your app is now ready to use on any Mac.

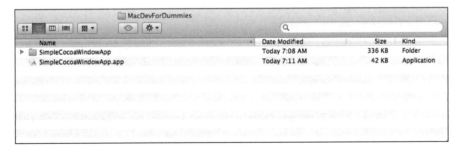

Figure 3-15: SimpleCocoaWindowApp saved as an application from an archive on my Mac.

Setting Xcode to Your Preferred Preferences

Software development with an integrated development environment (IDE) such as Xcode has evolved over the 20-plus years that IDEs have been around. Apple provides Xcode with a variety of options, or *preferences*, that you can modify to suit your preferred ways of doing things and your preferred ways of showing things. I won't cover all the preferences available, but will point you to some that I find useful; you can explore the rest on your own.

1. **Select Xcode⇨Preferences.**

   This will display the Preferences window shown in Figure 3-16. It's set to display the General preferences, which is selected for you in the toolbar at the top of the window. Xcode will remember where you left off the next time you open this window.

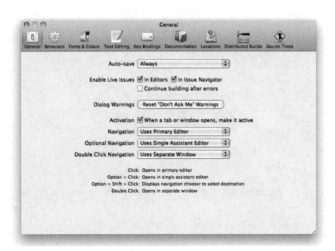

Figure 3-16: The Xcode preferences window in its initial state the first time you open it.

2. **Select Text Editing in the toolbar.**

   You see the display shown in Figure 3-17.

3. **Select Fonts & Colors in the toolbar.**

   This will show you the display in Figure 3-18. You can change the colors and even the fonts of your text editor to correspond to the different kinds of text you type. I fell in love with this feature the first time I experienced it in the early 1990s. While I prefer all my code to be in the standard Courier font (a legacy of my growing up with dot-matrix printers), using color to highlight different syntactical elements was wonderful. I would know instantly when the name of the member variable I typed was correct because the text would change color from black to whatever color I chose for member variables. If the color hadn't changed by the time I'd finished typing, I knew I had typed something wrong. And Xcode lets you create and store your own color theme (essentially a color scheme) — you first duplicate the Basic theme and give the duplicate a new name. Then you can modify the duplicate to suit your color preferences.

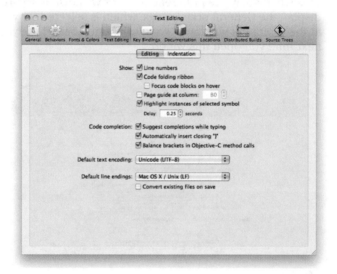

Figure 3-17: The Text Editing preferences.

4. **Select the Documentation item.**

You'll see the display as shown in Figure 3-19. As you'll find in the course of your Mac app development experience, the Apple reference documentation is an absolute necessity. You can always get to it through the Apple Developer website, but you can download it as well — which speeds up searches. In Figure 3-19 you can see I've got the Mac OS X 10.6 Core Library and Xcode 4.0 Developer Library already installed, and two others are available for me to download. Now you can download all the information you may need about programming a Mac without harming a tree.

Figure 3-18: The Fonts & Colors preferences. You too can turn your source code into a psychedelic delight.

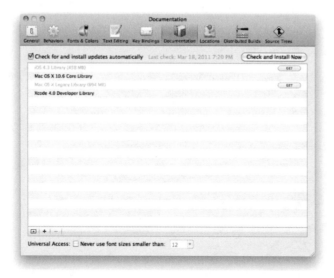

Figure 3-19: The environmentally friendly documentation manager.

Such are the most interesting and useful sets of preferences that you can adjust to meet your perfect Xcode display. Your preferences are stored for you automatically when you close this window.

Chapter 4

Objective-C and Cocoa Applications

*F*rom the very beginning, Apple has always recommended Mac developers to create OS X Mac apps using the Objective-C programming language. Although Apple provided an SDK called Carbon to assist developers from older Mac operating systems to transition their apps over to OS X, Objective-C is the primary programming language used on the Mac for the majority of its apps. You'll need a good foundation in Objective-C to get access to the greatest features and functionality that OS X has to offer you. And Apple also provides several libraries of Objective-C classes known collectively as *Cocoa*, which your apps will use to exploit all the capabilities of the Mac platform. Objective-C and Cocoa together are the tools you use to get your ideas running as apps on users' Macs.

I'm going to cover the basics of Objective-C programming in this chapter, so you'll be ready to start coding in later chapters — and so you can tell the difference between an `alloc` and an `initWithFrame:`. Here you get a look at Cocoa and the different frameworks that your apps can use — as well as those that Xcode adds to your project automatically. And finally, you'll get an anatomy of a running Mac app, from start to finish, so you'll know why your app is doing what it's doing.

You can also create Mac apps using the C and C++ programming languages. However, you'll find the standard Cocoa frameworks are easier to use when you're programming in Objective-C — and that's what I use in this book for all examples. You can create source and header files for C functions — and the classes you create using Objective-C can use these without any modification. Using C++ code is a little more challenging, but Objective-C provides a means for your apps to use C++ modules as well, using Objective-C++. The use of Objective-C++ is beyond the scope of this book.

Objective-C

You're going to spend a lot of time using Objective-C, so I'll cover this first. Objective-C is an object-oriented programming language based on the C programming language. Because it's object-oriented, you'll create your apps as collections of Objective-C classes. A *class* is a description of a set of data and the functions that act on that data. As with the C++ programming language, Objective-C classes usually consist of two files that contain the code for the class:

- ✔ **Source files:** A *source file* contains the *definition* of the class. You'll put all the code that a class will execute within the source module for the class. Source files use .m as their file extension, and Xcode knows that the contents of an .m file are to be compiled using the LLVM compiler.

- ✔ **Header files:** A *header file* contains the *declaration* of the class. You use this when you want other classes to know how to use the data and functions of a particular class. Header files use .h as their file extension.

When you instruct Xcode to create a new Objective-C class, it creates both the header file and the source file for you automatically. Depending on the parent class, Xcode also provides a bare-bones minimum amount of code for the class, to get you started.

In Objective-C, every Cocoa class is a subclass or *child* class of another Cocoa class named NSObject. There may be a line of *ancestor* classes between NSObject and your subclass, making your subclass a grandchild or great-great-great grandchild, but every Cocoa class can trace its ancestry to NSObject. Subclasses *inherit* their functionality and data from their ancestors, and this is part of what makes object-oriented programming so useful. Each class you create as a subclass of a Cocoa class will come with data and functions that are already built-in. And you can add your own data and functionality to your class so your app can use these features. The data elements of a class are called *member variables*. The functions in a class are called *methods*. Your classes will declare their member variables and methods within the header file, as you can see in Listing 4-1.

Note the intentional colorization in the book's code listings. I added it only in this book — it's not something Xcode did. Xcode does, however, provide the capability to color different aspects of the textual display of your code in its Preferences panel (which I go over in Chapter 3).

Because Objective-C is based on C, you can program using all the standard C programming concepts and constructs you've encountered if you've ever programmed C. You can even use C code libraries in your projects, if you've already got some. Because Mac OS X is Unix-based, it comes with all the standard Unix C libraries for your apps to use.

Listing 4-1: A simple Objective-C class header file

```
//
//  VerySimpleClass.h
//  CocoaWindows
//
//  Created by Karl Kowalski on 4/28/11.
//  Copyright 2011 Kowalski Software Enterprises.
//  All rights reserved.
//

#import <Foundation/Foundation.h>


@interface VerySimpleClass : NSObject {
    NSInteger m_anInt;
    NSString* m_aString;

@private
    NSString* m_propertyString;
}

- (NSString*)getString;
- (NSInteger)getInteger;
- (void)setString:(NSString*)inNewString;
- (void)setInteger:(NSInteger)inNewInt;

@property (assign) NSString* m_propertyString;


@end
```

This is similar to what you'll see when you make Xcode create a subclass of `NSObject`. The header file consists of the following pieces:

- **The introductory comments (**blue**).** These include the name of the header file, the app it was created for, and the copyright notice.

- **The** `#import` **statement (**green**).** For this class, the `Foundation.h` header file is imported. An `#import` statement is similar to the `#include` statement in C and C++, but it improves upon that older form by checking for whether the header file being `#import`ed has already been `#import`ed by some other header file. This removes a problem that C and C++ code modules would sometimes encounter: the recursive inclusion of a header file.

- **The class declaration (**orange**).** The declaration of every class starts with the `@interface` directive and concludes with the `@end` directive. Xcode does not create any member variables or methods for a class that is directly descended from `NSObject`, but there are some classes you'll create where Xcode does add member variables and methods for you.

The `@` at the beginning of a statement is a *compiler directive*. You'll use compiler directives in your code to indicate to the compiler something it's supposed to do that doesn't get translated into executable code. Objective-C uses the `@` character preceding a keyword — for example, `@private`, `@interface`, `@end`, `@property`, `@synthesize`, and `@implementation` — as commands to the compiler. Objective-C also includes standard C programming-language directives, such as `#include` and `#define`.

- **The member variables and methods (**purple**).** You enter member variables between the braces and method declarations after the closing brace but before the `@end`. Included in this group is the declaration beginning with the compiler directive `@property`. This is a command to the compiler to do some extra work for this member variable; I'll cover this command in more detail in the description of the source file.

The `@private` is another compiler directive that you can use in Objective-C to tell the compiler to restrict access to this member variable from other parts of your code. I generally don't use this feature — my apps and their classes don't have anything to hide — but there are times when you may want to impose this restriction — as when you're creating a library for other developers to use in their apps, and you don't want their code to be able to use yours directly. You can find information about `@private` and other Objective-C directives for member variable protection in Table 4-1.

The header file contains the information Xcode's compiler needs to know in order to reference the member variables and the methods in classes that will make use of objects made from this class.

You can see the contents of the source module for this class in Listing 4-2. Again, the colorization is from me, not Xcode.

Listing 4-2: The implementation of the VerySimpleClass

```
//
//  VerySimpleClass.m
//  CocoaWindows
//
//  Created by Karl Kowalski on 4/28/11.
//  Copyright 2011 Kowalski Software Enterprises.
//  All rights reserved.
//

#import "VerySimpleClass.h"


@implementation VerySimpleClass

@synthesize m_propertyString;

- (id)init
{
    self = [super init];
    if (self)
    {
        // Initialization code here.
    }

    return self;
}

- (void)dealloc
{
    [m_aString release];
    [super dealloc];
}

- (NSString*)getString
{
    return (m_aString);
}
```

(continued)

Listing 4-2 *(continued)*

```
- (NSInteger)getInteger
{
    return (m_anInt);
}

- (void)setString:(NSString*)inNewString
{
    [m_aString release];
    m_aString = inNewString;
    [m_aString retain];
}

- (void)setInteger:(NSInteger)inNewInt
{
    m_anInt = inNewInt;
}


@end
```

I've divided up the source module into more colors than the header file, because there's a little more going on:

✔ The top of the module (blue) is once again the comments describing the file and the copyright.

✔ The #import line (green) is for the class's header file, so that when Xcode compiles this module it gets a preview of what to expect. Xcode will provide a warning if something you've declared in the header file is not implemented in the source module. Xcode will flag an error if you've implemented something in the source module that's not declared in the header file.

✔ The @synthesize directive (purple). This compiler directive is required as a result of using the @property directive in the header file for this member variable. By turning m_propertyString into a *property* and adding this directive, you are giving a command to the compiler to create *getter* and *setter* methods (described below) for this member variable.

If you declare a member variable in the header file with the compiler directive @property, you *must* also declare it within the source file with the compiler directive @synthesize.

✓ The first two methods (orange), `init` and `dealloc`, are implemented for you by Xcode when the module is created. In addition, the `@implementation` and `@end` directive bound the methods that are implemented for this class — all the methods you declare for your own classes must be implemented within the `@implementation` and `@end` statements. I'll go over the contents of these methods in the next section.

✓ The next four methods (purple) are the implementations of the methods I added to the header file for this class. These methods consist of two *getters* (methods that return values) and two *setters* (methods that set values) for the member variables. Since almost every class you'll create will have member variables holding information, you'll want to provide a way for other classes to modify and retrieve that information.

Objects

The source module and header file provide the declaration and definition of the classes you'll create. An *object* is what your app will create and use to store the information that your classes are describing. An object is a runtime *instance* of a class, a concrete version of the data and the code that can manipulate that data. For example, you might make an app that stores different audio recordings for users to store verbal notes, as a kind of audio notepad. You could create a class to represent each recording, and make it contain the following information:

✓ Date and time of the recording

✓ The length of the recording in seconds

✓ The recorded audio signal

✓ A list of text keywords describing the recording

Every time the user creates a recording and saves it, your app will create a new object from your class definition and add the appropriate information for that instance of the class. Each of the pieces of information listed above would be stored as a member variable within the object. In this way, your classes describe how each object behaves, while the member variables contain the data that makes each object unique. As another example, you could create a class to represent automobiles driving on a race track. Each car would have its own number and color, and while the app was running a race, each would have its own speed.

Every Macintosh app built using Cocoa has many objects that are managed by the app while it executes. There's an NSApplication object which you can consider to be the primary object, since its methods create and manage all the other objects that the app uses.

Every Cocoa app project that Xcode creates includes a main.m source module. In this module is one function, main. This is the function that will execute first when the app is launched. In this function Xcode will create one line shown in this code snippet.

```
return NSApplicationMain( argc, (const char**)argv );
```

This code is the application's starting point. NSApplicationMain is a function call that performs a variety of operations before handing over execution to your code.

Do not modify this code — your application depends on the operations it performs to ensure that your app is set up properly.

In the init method of the class shown in Listing 4-2, you can see two items in the code, self and super. self is code within a class for an object to reference itself. If you're familiar with Java or C++, self is the Objective-C equivalent of the this pointer in those two languages. You use self when you want to execute a method defined for your class from within another method of your class. While in Java and C++ your code is not required to use the this pointer to execute a class's own methods, in Objective-C you must do it this way. Your code will tell the object to execute one of its methods on itself.

You will use the super object whenever you want to execute a method as it was written for your class's parent class. One of the features of an object-oriented language is that you have the ability to *override* a method implemented for a parent class of your subclass. In this way, you can provide behavior for your objects that differs from the parent class's behavior. For instance, you might subclass the Cocoa class NSView, which is used to represent items drawn on the screen, in order to draw the cars driving on the racetrack. NSView comes with a method called drawRect: that's executed by the app's code when it's time to draw things on the screen. The app only knows it has a bunch of NSView objects that need to be drawn; the app does not know that some of those objects are of the CarView class, which your app created to show its cars on the screen. Your CarView class, which subclasses NSView, implements its own version of drawRect: so that when your app tells all the displayed objects to draw themselves, the drawRect: of the CarView is executed, instead of the drawRect: of the NSView.

But there may still be a need to execute the parent class's method at some point. So Objective-C uses the keyword `super` to provide a way for your code to execute the method you've rewritten. In the `dealloc` method in Listing 4-2, the parent's `dealloc` method is called, in order to ensure that the parent class cleans itself up after the subclass has performed its own cleaning.

Member variables

Member variables are the data that an instance of a class contains. Each instance has its own member variables that your app can modify as it chooses. In the above example of the audio app, the date and time when the recording was created would be stored in a member variable, of the class `NSDate`. You can name your member variables as you prefer, with one restriction:

A member variable's name cannot start with a number, a math symbol, or a punctuation character, with the single exception of the underscore (_).

I use the following naming convention when creating member variables: I add `m_` to the beginning of each name. You will find a variety of other suggestions to follow for naming member variables, methods, classes, and all the other items you will name within your applications. You will eventually follow your own conventions, but you should strive to be consistent. I've found that this makes my code easier for me to read days, months, and years after I've first written it. Your naming conventions can change over time, but you'll find that eventually they will stabilize.

The following are all valid names for member variables in Objective-C:

```
t
T
timeStamp
time_stamp
_timeStamP
Time_3_Stamp
```

The following are invalid names for member variables, which Xcode will note as errors:

```
3Stamp (starts with a number)
&time (starts with punctuation)
=timestamp (starts with math symbol)
```

You can actually start a member variable's name with an asterisk (*) and Xcode will not inform you of an error, but the result will not be what you might expect. Xcode treats an * in front of a member variable as an indication that the variable is an address of a block of memory, also known as a *pointer*, described below.

Pointers

In Listing 4-1 (given earlier), the NSString member variable named m_aString is declared as follows:

```
NSString* m_aString;
```

This declaration tells Xcode that my VerySimpleClass has a member variable that is a pointer to an object of type NSString. A pointer is literally an address in memory, and starting at that memory location is the contents of the object or data type that the pointer is pointing to. In Objective-C and Cocoa, every instance of a class in your app will be a pointer to an object. Xcode will note an error if you ever write a line of code like this:

```
NSString m_aString; // error
```

The other member variable in Listing 4-1 is of type NSInteger. Xcode knows that this type is not a class and so it doesn't require an * in front of the name. Cocoa provides renamings of the integer numeric types you would normally find in C and C++:

✔ NSInteger for int

✔ NSUInteger for unsigned int

You can still use int and unsigned int in your code and Cocoa will know that they're equivalent to NSInteger and NSUInteger, respectively.

The * character is used to declare a variable to be a pointer. You can use either of the following forms to declare pointer variables — they are equivalent. I prefer the first one, because I find it easier to read:

```
NSString* aString;
NSString *aString;
```

Protection of member variables

Your class member variables come with a level of protection that reduces access to the member variables by code in other classes. Table 4-1 lists the levels of member variable protection that exist in Objective-C:

Table 4-1		Levels of Member Variable Protection
Level	*Code Statement*	*Description*
Public	@public	The member variable is accessible to any code that uses an instance of the class.
Protected	@protected	The member variable is accessible only within methods of this class and any subclass. This is the default protection level.
Private	@private	The member variable is accessible only from within the class that declares it.

You usually want your member variables to come with the default level of protection, @protected. In order to gain access to protected member variables, you will also want to create methods that can retrieve the information in the member variables (*getters*) as well as methods that can set the information for member variables (*setters*).

Creating objects

Your app's code will sometimes need to create instances of your classes or Cocoa classes while your app runs. There are two ways to create objects in Objective-C:

↳ By using the alloc method

↳ By using a class *convenience* method

alloc

You'll use the alloc method most frequently. alloc is short for *allocate*, which means to reserve space. Your code will create a new instance of a class by allocating space out of the computer's memory to hold the member variables and the locations of the methods implemented for the class. An example of creating an instance of the VerySimpleClass looks like this:

```
VerySimpleClass* anInstance = [VerySimpleClass alloc];
```

That's all the code you need to write in order to create an instance of any class in your app or in the Cocoa framework. The alloc method is a part of the NSObject class implementation, so your code never needs to create its own as long as your classes are descendants of NSObject. Since Xcode takes care of this when you tell it to create a new class, you don't have to do anything extra.

Convenience methods

Some classes come with methods built-in that take care of creating and initializing instances of themselves. You'll find these methods to be convenient, hence their designation as *convenience methods*. You'll probably find yourself using some of the following convenience methods in NSString very often:

- stringWithFormat: allows you to create an NSString instance with data formatted using the same formatting characters as C.

- stringWithContentsOfFile: allows you to create an NSString instance initialized with the text found in a file located in the file system.

- stringWithContentsOfURL: allows you to create an NSString instance initialized with the stream of HTML coming from a URL.

Here's a code example of creating an NSString instance by formatting some data:

```
int temperatureInt = 75; // nice warm day
NSString* aString = [NSString stringWithFormat:@"Today's temp
        is: %d", temperatureInt];
```

When the code just given here is executed in the app, the variable aString will contain the text Today's temp is: 75.

If convenience methods look kind of like class methods, you're right: They are.

Methods

Whenever you want an object to do something, your application code calls one of its methods. You'll be doing this a lot, so I'm going to go over the details here.

Your app sends *messages* to Objective-C *objects*; this is similar to *calling methods* on objects in other object-oriented languages such as C++. The difference between the two is subtle: In Objective-C, the object receiving the message determines at runtime whether it can execute a particular method — and if it cannot, an exception is raised. In C++ and similar languages, the compiler determines whether the object can perform the execution. For most of your Objective-C development efforts, this difference is minimal and these two phrases — *sending a message* and *calling a method* — can be used interchangeably.

You'll create methods for your classes every time you want your class to perform an operation, such as modifying the information contained in its member variables. You'll also execute methods on instances of classes that Cocoa provides. In Objective-C, your code will execute a method on an instance of a class as shown in this code snippet:

```
[instanceOfSomeClass methodName];
```

You will see the above syntax in almost every code example in this book, and every sample code you download from Apple. The above code snippet executes a method named `methodName` on the variable named `instanceOfSomeClass`. This method takes no parameters and does not return any values back to the code that called it. The declaration of this method in the class header file would look like this:

```
- (void)methodName;
```

And in the source file, the implementation of this method would look like this:

```
- (void)methodName
{
    // do something
}
```

You might implement a method like this for the audio recording example to play the recording. Since the recorded audio signal is a member variable in the class, you wouldn't need to pass a parameter into the method in order to play the sound. And since the method is only going to play a prerecorded sound, there's no need to return a value back to the code that called this method.

You can see in the following code snippet a method that takes in two parameters and returns an integer value that indicates success or failure:

```
- (NSUInteger)writeData:(NSData*)inData toFile:(NSString*)
            inFilePath
{
    //
    NSUInteger resultValue = 0; // assume successful
    // do something with the data
    // if it doesn't work, resultValue will be > 0
    return (resultValue);
}
```

You can see that parameter values are passed into the method by using the method's name split up by colon (`:`) characters. The value returned by the method is declared at the beginning of the method name.

When turning Objective-C code into machine-level executable instructions, the compiler converts messages into a form called a *selector*. A selector is simply a string that represents the concatenation of the method's name, without the arguments. So the selector for the method just given would be

```
writeData:toFile:
```

When your code sends a message to an Objective-C object, the compiler turns the executable statement into a function call, and passes the selector for the message plus the values of the parameters into that function.

You can call the methods I've introduced so far on an instance created from a class. There's also a second type of method that you can implement, called a `class method`. Class methods are different because you cannot call them on instances of a class; you must call them independently of all instances. The convenience methods mentioned here are class methods, and your code executes them like this:

```
NSString* aStringObj = [NSString stringWithString:@"this is
        an NSString"];
```

In addition, `alloc` is a class method of `NSObject` and therefore also of each class you create in your app, so your code will execute a class method every time you create an instance of a class. You declare a class method in your own classes as shown in the following snippet from a header file:

```
+ (NSString*)getSomeValue;
```

This method declaration and its implementation start with +, which differentiates them from instance methods that start with –.

You execute this class method as follows:

```
NSString* valueString = [YourClass getSomeValue];
```

Protocols

You create some of your classes as simple descendants of classes that Apple has created within Cocoa. However, sometimes you'll want your classes to provide specific behaviors that another class can make use of, without the other class knowing the basic implementation of your class. A *protocol* is how you declare one of your classes to provide specific methods for any other class able to exercise the protocol. You might use a protocol to add methods that update a modification date & time for several different data storage classes so that your app can support a manager class that keeps track of objects of different types — and update each object's modification state — without having to know the specific details of each object's class.

The Objective-C protocol is equivalent to the Java language interface.

A protocol gives you the capability to declare methods that any of your classes can implement. You can define a protocol in a header file as simply as this:

```
//
// NotificationBroadcaster.h
//
//
@protocol NotificationBroadcaster
 (void)sendNotification:(NSString*)inName
          withObject:(NSObject*)inObj;
@end
```

The protocol in the snippet just given declares a method that classes adopting the protocol must implement. A class adopting this protocol is making a promise that it has a method that will be executed when the sendNotification:withObject: message is received by an instance of the class.

You can create a class to adopt a protocol by declaring it within its header file:

```
//
// AdoptiveClass.h
//

#import "NotificationBroadcaster.h"

@interface AdoptiveClass : NSObject <NotificationBroadcaster>
{
    // add member variables here
}
// add properties and methods here
@end
```

AdoptiveClass does not need to declare the methods of the protocol, so you're saved some typing. You will need to implement the methods of the protocol in the source file:

```
//
// AdoptiveClass.m
//

#import "AdoptiveClass.h"

@implementation AdoptiveClass

- (void)sendNotification:(NSString*)inName
         withObject:(NSObject*)inObj
{
    [[NSNotificationCenter defaultCenter]
         postNotificationName:inName object:inObj];
}

@end
```

Your app can create multiple classes with this same protocol, and all instances of those classes in your app will have a method that can be called to broadcast notifications to objects listening for them. Your app can maintain a collection of objects of different classes, each of which adopts this protocol, and can then iterate over the entire collection and have each object in the collection broadcast a notification. For instance, an app that manages library resources such as books, CDs, and DVDs could keep objects of each of those different types in one huge collection, and then send a message to each of them to broadcast to a display object the due-date status for each checked-out item.

Protocol methods can be of two types:

 ✔ **Required:** The class must implement the method. This is the default type.

 ✔ **Optional:** The class does not have to implement the method. You can declare methods to be optional by placing the compiler directive @optional before the list of methods that don't have to be implemented.

You've already encountered a class that adopts a protocol in Chapter 3: the SimpleCocoaWindowAppAppDelegate class. *Delegates* are another powerful feature in Cocoa, so I discuss them next.

Delegates

A *delegate* is an object that can be used by another object to perform certain actions when necessary. You can create delegate classes for your apps to implement functionality for Cocoa classes used in your app, so that your classes provide unique responses in certain situations. To do this, Cocoa provides you with a large number of delegate protocols that you can have your classes adopt. Here are just a few of the delegates you can use:

- ✔ NSApplicationDelegate. This delegate is used in the NSApplication class to give your app an opportunity to perform your own response to certain messages sent to the application object.

  This is the protocol adopted by SimpleCocoaWindowAppAppDelegate to give the Chapter 3 app a chance to do its unique operations. All of NSApplicationDelegate's methods are optional, so SimpleCocoa WindowAppAppDelegate only implements applicationDidFinish Launching:, which is called when the NSApplication has reached the moment during its startup at which everything has been initialized and the app is just about ready to display itself for the user.

- ✔ NSAnimationDelegate. Cocoa provides a delegate protocol your app can use to perform operations at certain moments during the execution of an animation.

  When Cocoa is executing an animation for your app, the animation code will call methods of an NSAnimationDelegate object at moments such as right before the animation is about to be started, right after it ended, as well as at various points during the animation's progression from start to finish.

- ✔ NSImageDelegate. Because image files can be large, and because images may be loaded from network-based locations, Cocoa provides the NSImageDelegate class which gives you an approach for listening in on the loading process for an NSImage.

- ✔ NSWindowDelegate. You can create a class to be a delegate of an NSWindow so that your app can respond when certain actions take place on an NSWindow. For instance, your app can keep track of a window that a user moves, resizes, miniaturizes, closes, or has been placed on a different screen.

- ✔ NSTableViewDelegate. The NSTableView object is the visual representation of a two-dimensional table displayed in an app's window.

  When the user clicks in the table on the screen, the NSTableView Delegate object assigned to the NSTableView will be sent messages indicating what the user is doing. In addition, the NSTableView Delegate object is also used by its NSTableView to provide the NSTableView with information regarding visual and functional aspects of the displayed table, such as whether a specific cell in the table can be edited or whether a selection in a table cell will cause the entire row to be selected.

To create a delegate object to act as an `NSWindowDelegate`, you perform the following steps:

1. **Create a class based on** `NSObject`.

   In the code examples that follow, I've called the class `MyWindowDelegate`.

2. **Adopt the** `NSWindowDelegate` **protocol in the header file of the class, as shown in the following code snippet:**

   ```
   @interface MyWindowDelegate : NSObject <NSWindowDelegate>
   ```

3. **In the source file, implement the methods you want your delegate to support.**

   For instance, in `MyWindowDelegate.m` I've implemented two methods I want my delegate to respond to:

   ```
   - (void)windowDidChangeScreen:(NSNotification*)
           inNotification
   {
       // this will be called when the delegate's window has
       // been moved to a different screen, so you can do
       // something important
   }

   - (void)windowDidDeminiaturize:(NSNotification*)
           inNotification
   {
       // the window has now been returned from its
       // miniaturized status, so maybe your app will
       // check the web feed for updated information
       // from the user's favorite social networking
       // site
   }
   ```

4. **Create an instance of your delegate class, and then assign it to an object you want to receive delegate messages for.**

   I want the `NSWindow` that comes with `SimpleCocoaWindowAppApp Delegate` to use `MyWindowDelegate` when it changes screens or deminiaturizes, so I add the following code to its `applicationDid FinishLaunching:` method:

   ```
   - (void)applicationDidFinishLaunching:(NSNotification*)
           inNotification
   {
       MyWindowDelegate* myDelegate = [[MyWindowDelegate
           alloc] init];
       [window setDelegate:myDelegate];
       // now when the window changes screens or
       // deminiaturizes, the delegate's methods
       // will be called
   }
   ```

You use delegates to extend the behavior of Cocoa's classes that accept delegates. You could accomplish this by using class inheritance, but delegates are simpler and easier. Not every Cocoa class uses delegates, so you're limited in where you can make use of this feature. But Apple has added delegate capability to the Cocoa classes that can make good use of it.

Before you choose to create a subclass of some Cocoa class whose behaviors you want to change, check to see whether the class offers to accept a delegate object you can make for its delegate protocol methods. You'll create a leaner app by using delegates than creating subclasses.

Managing memory

Every time your app creates an instance of a class, your app is requesting and receiving a block of memory from the computer's RAM. In the Objective-C programming language, your app is responsible for keeping track of each block of memory it requests and receives. Even though the amount of memory available to apps on current Macintosh computers is pretty large, your app should really be careful and very frugal when it comes to requesting memory. And your app should also be very diligent about freeing up that memory when it's no longer needed. Your app is responsible for cleaning up the objects it creates when those objects are no longer in use.

I first learned to do Macintosh development with Objective-C in the old days, when memory management was the responsibility of the code that was requesting the memory. Today you can set your Xcode project to do *garbage collection* automatically while your app is running, as long as your app is executing on Mac OS X version 10.5 or later. I still do Mac programming the old-fashioned way, because I understand it better and because I know what's going on. The rest of this section will describe the details of the memory management operations your code will need to implement if garbage collection isn't turned on; this is the old-fashioned way. The technical note at the end of the section describes how to turn on garbage collection in an Xcode project.

The Cocoa framework does provide some assistance for you through the use of a mechanism called the *retain count* — literally a count of how many different places your app is maintaining a pointer to a specific instance of a class. Unfortunately, Cocoa does not keep track of this count completely automatically. Your app is partially responsible for making sure the retain count of its objects is kept up to date. Your code can call the following methods to manage the retain count of an object:

✔ retain. This method increments the object's retain count by one. Calling a class's `alloc` method automatically also calls `retain` on the object that is returned by `alloc`.

✔ release. This method decrements the object's retain count by one. If the retain count is reduced to zero, Cocoa assumes that no piece of your code is still keeping a pointer to this object — and the object's memory is returned to the pool of available memory to be used for satisfying memory requests such as creating new objects.

✔ autorelease. This method *temporarily* gives the object an increment in its retain count, but at *some point in the future* the object's memory will be returned to the pool of available memory, just as if its retain count had gone to zero. The NSString object's convenience method stringWithString: (for example) calls autorelease on the object that's returned, as will other convenience methods.

The best way to demonstrate how to use these methods is with an example. Listing 4-3 shows several methods in a class that create new objects and use retain, release, and autorelease on the objects.

Listing 4-3:   Code snippet of methods exercising retain, release, and autorelease

```
- (void)setStringValue:(NSString*)inNewValue
{
    if (nil != m_memberString)
    {
        [m_memberString release];
    }
    m_memberString = inNewValue;
    [m_memberString retain];
}

- (NSString*)getStringValue
{
    return (m_memberString);
}

- (void)temporaryDataUsage
{
    NSString* filePathObj = [NSString
        stringWithString:@"full_path_to_file"];
    NSData* dataFromFile = [NSData dataWithContentsOfFile:fil
        ePathObj];
    // use the NSData object to do important stuff
    // the dataFromFile object is autoreleased
}

- (void)dealloc
{
    [m_memberString release];
    [super dealloc];
}
```

In the first method, `setStringValue:`, the code first checks to see whether the member variable `m_memberString` has already been set to a value. If it has a non-`nil` value, then the code presumes that the object that `m_member String` points to was `retained` by this same code when *it* was the input parameter to this method. Therefore the code executes `release` on this object, so that its memory will be reclaimed by the OS the next time the application checks for objects that need to have their memory freed up. Next, the member variable is set to point to the incoming `NSString` object. Finally, the retain method of `m_memberString` is called, indicating that the incoming `NSString` object is being referenced by the object whose `set StringValue:` method was executed.

I've shown the second method, `getStringValue`, as a means of counter-example. When this class is asked to return the `NSString` object that its member variable is pointing to, the code does not call `retain` or `release`. It is the responsibility of the app code that is executing the `getStringValue` method to `retain` the object that has been returned from this method.

If you always implement your getter and setter methods as shown in Listing 4-3 — and if you always assume that the calling code is responsible for retaining the pointers that it receives from other getter methods — then you will reduce the chances that your app is calling `retain` or `release` incorrectly. The usual problem you'll run into is when you call `release` on an object that another part of your code is still expecting to use. This can lead to your app crashing in unexpected ways.

Implementing a getter method as shown above does not prevent the calling code from executing the `release` method on the returned object. To reduce the chances of calling release too early, you should only call release in the `dealloc` method of your class, or within the setter methods you implement.

The third method of the code snippet, `temporaryDataUsage`, demonstrates two class methods, one each for `NSString` and `NSData`. The `NSString` convenience method `stringWithString:` will return a pointer to an `NSString` object that holds the text `full_path_to_file`. In real code, this text would be the full directory path to a file that the code is going to load into an `NSData` object. The `NSData` convenience method `dataWith ContentsOfFile:` will find the file at the path specified in the `NSString` object, open it, and read its complete contents, returning a pointer to an `NSData` object that your app can use to interpret the data. Both of these convenience methods return objects that have had the `autorelease` method called upon them. This means that your code does not have to release them, and they will both have their memory freed automatically at some point in time after the method has finished executing. Your code can call the `retain` method on either of these objects, but then your code would have to accept responsibility for calling the `release` method at some future moment.

Your code is responsible for matching every `retain` method call your code makes on an object with a call to that object's `release` method. If you call `retain` more than you call `release`, your app will reduce the amount of memory it has available to store information. If you call `release` more than you call `retain`, at some moment your app will try to use an object that has had its memory taken away — and the usual result is a crash. To avoid these problems, you must write your apps consistently, remembering the following:

✓ Convenience methods always call `autorelease` for you, meaning the objects you receive are temporary unless you `retain` them yourself.

✓ `alloc` methods always call `retain` for you — meaning the objects you receive are permanent and you have to `release` them explicitly.

✓ Every `retain` method you call must be matched by an explicit call to `release`.

The final method in Listing 4-3 is the `dealloc` method, which will be called automatically by a part of your Cocoa application when an object's retain count reaches zero. You can see that the member variable `m_memberString` has its `release` method called within this method. The `m_memberString` variable was retained when the assignment was made in a prior call to `set StringValue:`.

In the `dealloc` method, my code does not check for whether `m_member String` contains a pointer to a valid `NSString` object. You can call any method on an object even if the object is `nil`. All member variables of an instance of a class are automatically assigned `nil` when the instance is created. Cocoa ignores any method called on a `nil` object, without reporting any error.

Objective-C 2.0 and Mac OS X version 10.5 introduced automatic garbage collection for Cocoa applications. This removes the strict requirement that your app keep a solid track of all the memory it has requested from the OS. This is a build setting you must select for the project after Xcode has created it — the default is Unsupported, which means your code is responsible for managing its own memory. You can modify this setting by following these steps:

1. **Launch Xcode and open the project for which you want to turn on automatic garbage collection.**

2. **Select the Project in the Project navigator and the Build Settings tab in the editor.**

3. **Scroll down to the LLVM compiler 2.0 – Code Generation section.**

4. Change the setting for Objective-C Garbage Collection to Required (as shown in Figure 4-1).

Your project will now ignore all `retain`, `release`, and `autorelease` messages sent to your app's objects, and Cocoa will handle all of the memory management for your app.

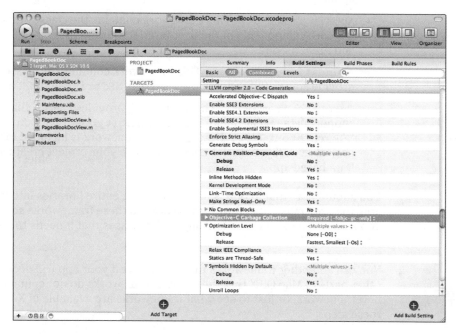

Figure 4-1: The build settings for an Objective-C app that performs its own memory management.

You've now completed the basics of the Objective-C programming language — including classes, objects and instances, member variables, methods, and memory management. You'll make use of this knowledge in all your Mac apps, with every class you create and with the Cocoa classes that your app creates and uses.

Using Cocoa Frameworks

A *Cocoa framework* is a library of code and data that Apple has created and which ships with Mac OS X. The latest version of Xcode will build using the Cocoa frameworks that work with the latest version of OS X, although you can choose to build apps to run on an earlier version. For instance, Xcode 4.1 comes with the Cocoa frameworks for both OS X 10.7 Lion and OS X 10.6 Snow Leopard. When you create a minimalist Xcode project, Xcode creates the project with the following frameworks already attached:

- ✔ Cocoa.framework. This contains the basic functions for Cocoa applications.

- ✔ AppKit.framework. This framework contains the classes that make up the core components of the user interface classes, such as NSControl and NSDocument.

- ✔ Foundation.framework. This framework contains the classes that provide some utility capabilities, such as NSString and NSData.

- ✔ CoreData.framework. This framework provides classes that support data management, such as NSEntityDescription and NSPersistentStore. Note that this framework is included in your project even if you do not choose to make your project create a Core Data-based app.

You should note that Xcode is not copying the entire libraries into your app; the project is created with references to these frameworks so that your app's code knows where to find any of the classes that it needs to perform its operations.

You can add other frameworks to your project if your app will need to access other parts of Mac OS X that these basic frameworks do not contain. To add a new framework, or just to see what frameworks are available in Xcode, follow these steps:

1. **Launch Xcode and then open an existing project or create a new one.**

2. **In the Project navigator, right-click the Frameworks folder and select Add Files to** YourProjectName.

   The Open File panel slides out over the window.

3. **Select the Developer folder at the top level of your hard disk.**

   This is where Xcode keeps all of its files.

4. **Navigate through the following folder selections:** SDKs⇨MacOSX10.7. sdk⇨System⇨Library ⇨Frameworks.

   You should see a list of folders named FrameworkName.framework, as shown in Figure 4-2.

   Each folder shown in the figure is a framework that you can add to your project. For instance, if your app will access the user's Address Book, you would add the AddressBook.framework to your project.

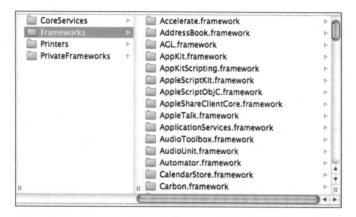

Figure 4-2: The top of the list of frameworks you can add to your Xcode projects.

The following list is a subset of some of the frameworks I've found useful in some of my own Mac apps:

- ✓ AddressBook. Provides classes and functions for reading and writing information into the user's AddressBook collection of contacts. Your app could use this to send group e-mails to everyone in the user's set of contacts who has a .mac account — with the user's permission, of course.

- ✓ CalendarStore. This framework gives you classes and functions to read and write calendar information for the user's iCal data. Your app can create items in their calendars that remind them to take out the trash or return a library book.

- ✓ CoreAudio. You can use the functions in this framework to record audio from your user's Mac microphone. You could create an app that acts as an audio notepad.

- ✓ DVDPlayback. The functions in this framework provide your app with access to the DVD player on the user's Mac.

- ✓ IOKit. The functions in IOKit provide your app with access to all the devices such as hard drives connected to the user's Mac. Although there are other classes you can use to retrieve similar information, the IOKit gives you every bit of detail you will ever want regarding the inner workings of the components of a user's machine. For instance, a hard-drive maintenance app would use the functions in IOKit to find out the manufacturer of a hard drive, the drive's serial number, or the number of sectors on a formatted disk.

✔ OpenGL. This standard graphics library provides a consistent and highly optimized approach for drawing and animating three-dimensional images. Your app could use this to demonstrate solutions to 3-D puzzles.

✔ WebKit. Your app can use this set of classes to read and manipulate HTML and other web-based forms of documents such as XML. You could create your own browser app using WebKit.

Your projects can take advantage of any of these and many other frameworks to add features that will set your apps apart from all the others available at the App Store. Combinations of these features will give your apps unique capabilities to generate a greater following of loyal users. Instead of just directing your users to your app's website for help, your app could provide users with assistance in using your app by downloading HTML from your app's website and displaying it in an app window with the help of WebKit. Even better, for help with specific menu items or components on your app's windows you could display the specific information from your website as the user moves their mouse over different zones of your display. Your app could provide audio feedback for users with vision challenges by announcing the name of components when the user's mouse hesitates over them. The possibilities are endless.

Understanding the Application Life Cycle

The general behavior of a Mac application follows this approach:

1. The user double-clicks the app's icon on their Desktop.

2. The application is launched showing its main screen.

3. The user manipulates the controls and menus and adds some information.

4. The user selects the Quit menu item.

5. The application exits.

Figure 4-3 shows a more detailed display of what happens when an application is launched.

As you saw earlier, the first code statement to be executed is in the main function, in the module main.m. Here's what that statement looks like, again:

```
return (NSApplicationMain( argc, (const char**)argv );
```

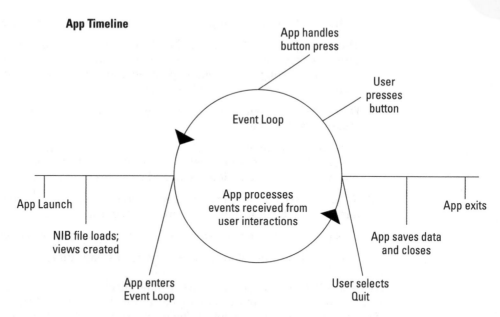

Figure 4-3: The life of an application from launch to Quit.

Your application then follows this process:

1. The NSApplicationMain function — provided for you in the Cocoa frameworks — performs some basic initialization.

2. NSApplicationMain creates an object that represents your application, as a member of the class NSApplication.

   There can be only one NSApplication object in an executing app.

3. The NSApplication object loads your app's main XIB file, which is usually MainMenu.xib.

4. After loading the XIB file, the NSApplication object will display the main window.

5. The app creates and launches the main event loop.

   This is a method that loops within itself, until circumstances cause it to stop.

6. In the event loop, your app retrieves events from an event queue.

   The queue holds all the events that the OS supplies it, such as the user pressing a mouse key or a keyboard key. In addition, at the beginning of each cycle through the event loop, objects that have a retain count of zero have their `dealloc` method called.

7. For each event, your app determines what happened and what the app's response should be.

   For instance, if the user selects an item from one of your app's menus, the app determines which method of which object has been targeted to receive the menu-selection event, and executes it.

8. If the user selects Quit from the application menu, the event loop is terminated and the app begins the process of cleaning itself up.

   This process may include saving any data the user has provided.

9. The app closes the windows presently on display and exits.

Your app will follow this process every time a user launches it. Usually you won't need to worry about what happens during the setup and shutdown of your app, and you'll concentrate on what happens when your users click your app's controls or make changes to the contents of your app's windows. But hopefully you'll remember the process outlined above so you will understand what your app does from start to finish, and you'll know where every operation your app performs occurs during its lifetime.

Part II
A View to an App

The 5th Wave — By Rich Tennant

"Yes, I have experience with nonprofit organizations. I created a game called 'Cap the Oil Well.'"

In this part . . .

After you have the tools you need to develop Mac apps, it's time to explore more thoroughly the pieces of a Macintosh application. The beginning of this part expands your understanding of Interface Builder and the user interface components of a Macintosh app: buttons, menus, checkboxes, etc. Moving forward, you'll discover how to enhance that knowledge with a greater understanding of Macintosh app views and the controllers that manage them. In the last chapter of this part you'll see how you can create your own custom views, so you can display your app's information in your own fashion. You can then give your Mac app a definitive user experience that no other app has.

Chapter 5

Using Interface Builder to Lay Out Your Views

. . . .

In This Chapter

▶ Learning Xcode's UI Tool

▶ Starting from the defaults

▶ Adding views

▶ Adding UI elements

▶ Testing your UI

▶ Connecting to your app

. . . .

A pple has completely integrated Interface Builder, their graphical user interface editing tool, into Xcode 4.0. This improvement means you only need one tool, Xcode, to do all your creation and editing of your app.

Interface Builder is a visual tool that you use to create the graphical user interfaces for your Mac apps. You'll put your app's appearance together visually, by simply dragging and dropping objects from the UI component Object Library onto the windows and views of your app. The Object Library contains all the different visual interface elements that Apple packs into OS X. You can put together really clever and visually appealing displays for the information you present to your app's users. And best of all, you'll be following the guidance of Apple's Human Interface Guidelines while using Interface Builder — this will assist you in making sure that your Mac apps are likelier to survive the scrutiny of the App Store submission review process. Most important, you'll be living up to the expectations of Mac users who've come to take cleanly designed Macintosh apps for granted.

In this chapter, I take you on a tour of the IB Editor and show you how to use its features and functionality by producing a new app. You'll be exploring how to use the IB Editor to create and lay out the visual interface of your app and connect the components you'll add to the code they work with. By the end of the chapter, you'll master the techniques of providing a visual and interactive experience for your users and connecting that experience to your app's code that's running behind the scenes.

Going with the Flow

Xcode gives you the opportunity to choose one of two general categories of apps you can create with a UI:

- **Single Window:** Your app consists of a single window in which your users perform all their interactions. This kind of app is easy to manage: All your information is in one place, and selections from the menu are all directed toward this window. One example of this type of app would be a calculator: Your users only need one and want that one-and-only every time they launch your app. Most games are examples of Single Window apps. In Mac OS X 10.7 Lion, you'll be able to create full-screen apps: Your app will take advantage every pixel available on its screen.

- **Document-Based:** You can think of this type of app as multiple Single Window apps. Each window displays information independently of other sibling windows that might be visible. A web browser is a good example of this type of app: Each window might display the contents downloaded from a different web page. Each web window behaves the same way, rendering the HTML data that came from the page's URL, but each window is showing different data.

If your app is going to save information that the users provide in files on their Macs' hard drives, a Document-Based app is a better choice — for the most part, this type of app takes care of managing the saving of information for you. And I'm definitely in favor of letting Xcode put together all the details of managing files and saving and reading them.

Choosing a template for your project will lock you into a particular structure for your app. This doesn't mean you cannot change your mind later when you run into challenges for implementing features in your app. But you should spend some time scoping out the different things your app will do, and use that information to choose wisely.

One more handy consideration: Whichever template you choose, you're not limited to putting your data onscreen in only one type of display. Interface Builder and the Cocoa UI classes let you create a variety of different views, each of which can be tailored to show the information your users need to see — in the best way possible. Each display of information can be presented in a separate window, and both the Single Window and Document-Based app templates can support this behavior.

You'll have to decide which type of app is right for your goal before you create the project. Figure 5-1 shows the Project Options screen where you make this decision. The checkbox Create Document-Based Application should be checked if your app falls into that category.

Figure 5-1: Set the option to Document-Based at this point.

From code to screen and back again

You'll create, edit, and lay out the visual components of your windows using Interface Builder. You'll write code to support all your visual components, so that when the user clicks a button, your app will do the right thing. This means your visual components must be *connected* to your app's code. And the connection requires that your code be properly set up to

 ✔ Accept connections from the visual components created in Interface Builder

 ✔ Deliver the results of code calculations back to the visual components

These connections have two types of end points:

✔ An `IBOutlet` is associated with member variables in your Objective-C classes. This is a signal to the compiler that a specific member variable should be made *visible* to Interface Builder for use as a connection end point.

An `IBOutlet` member variable represents the visual component when the application is running. For instance, you could place a Text Field on your app's main window for use as a label to display text messages to the user in an instant-messaging app. When a new text message comes in, the code in your app selects the `Text Field` member variable and sets its text to the new information. The communication happens from the member variable to the component on display, and this is how the connection will be made in Interface Builder: from the object that contains the code to the visual component on the window. Each `IBOutlet` member variable can point to only one visual component, but multiple `IBOutlet` member variables can point to the same visual component.

An `IBAction` is associated with methods in your Objective-C class. This tells the compiler that a specific method should be made available for components in Interface Builder to execute when the user causes the component to perform an action.

You would use an `IBAction` to assign a specific method to execute when the user selects a button on your app's window. Returning to our instant-messaging app, after the user has read the new message, she types in a response and clicks the Send button. Because you made a connection from the button to your app's `sendMessage:` method in your window's Objective-C class, that method will be executed whenever the Send button is clicked. Each `IBAction` method can be executed by any number of visual components.

Interface Builder in Xcode 4 gives you the capability to automatically create `IBActions` and `IBOutlets` by control-dragging from your UI directly into the class header file. This will save you time when creating your UI components and connecting them to your code files.

In Chapter 3 you developed a small application with a simple user interface to familiarize yourself with Xcode. You'll go a little deeper in implementing a user interface in this chapter so that you become familiar with Interface Builder and how it interacts with your source code modules. I cover different aspects of creating and modifying user interfaces through the process of creating some simple applications.

Touring Interface Builder

Your first encounter with Interface Builder was with Chapter 3's tip calculator app. Your first project in this chapter will introduce you to the details of Interface Builder and its tools.

1. **Launch Xcode.**

2. **Create a new Project using the Cocoa Application template. Leave the Create Document-Based Application checkbox unchecked.**

   I've named my app `UISimple` as shown in Figure 5-2.

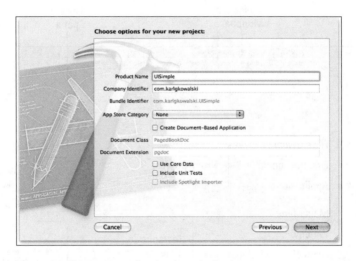

Figure 5-2: Name your project but keep it simple.

3. **Click Next.**

4. **Choose a location for your project and click Create.**

5. **Select the `MainMenu.xib` file from the Project Navigator.**

   Xcode displays Interface Builder with `MainMenu.xib` on display.

   Show the Utilities view; you'll need to access it many times during this session.

The `MainMenu.xib` file will contain all of the visual components you add to create your user interface.

The XIB file is a text file which lists all of your user interface in an XML-based format. Although I think you should take a look at the contents of this file, I believe you should obey the following rule: *Look but Don't Touch.* The data within the XIB file is loaded by your Cocoa app and is used to create objects to represent in code the displayed components on the user's screens. Modifying the contents of this file can break your app in subtle ways that can be difficult to track down. It's okay to look, but one false deletion or addition can confuse the Cocoa objects that are trying to build your app's screens.

Figure 5-3 shows Interface Builder's display of `MainMenu.xib`, with the smaller panes separated to explain each one's purpose.

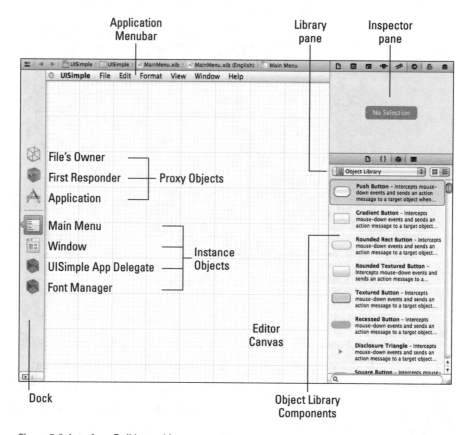

Figure 5-3: Interface Builder and its contents.

The four main panes are

✔ **The Dock.** This pane contains objects that will be automatically created when the XIB file is loaded into your application to create the user interface. You can see the seven objects that are created by default for a Single-Window type application:

- File's Owner
- First Responder
- Application
- Main Menu (where you edit the menus for your app)
- Window (where you place your UI components)
- UISimple App Delegate
- Font Manager

✔ **The Editor Canvas**

✔ **The Inspector pane**

✔ **The Library pane**

Your next task is to add some UI components to the window so that they'll be on display when the user launches your app. Before you do this, I show you the different pieces of Interface Builder you'll be using to work with the UI components.

1. **Select the Window icon in the Dock.**

   You'll see a small window displayed in the editor area, with the name UISimple at the top. Figure 5-4 shows the Editor's canvas area with the UISimple window highlighted in blue.

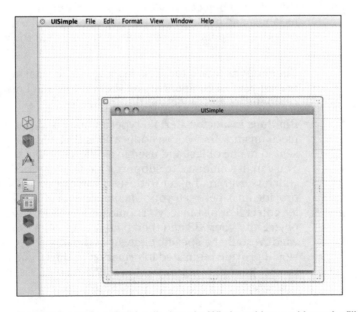

Figure 5-4: Interface Builder displays the Window object, waiting to be filled.

With the window highlighted, the buttons in the Inspector selector bar (at the top of the Inspector pane) now show you a variety of information about the window. The Inspector provides these different types of data for the components you select from either the Dock or the Editor Canvas. The Inspector selector bar contains the following items:

- **File inspector.** You can find information about the file selected in the Project navigator, which in this case is the MainMenu.xib.

- **Quick Help.** You use Quick Help to get a capsule summary of the object selected on the canvas, which includes links to documentation and programming guides where available.

- **Identity inspector.** This inspector provides more information regarding the class of the object selected in the Editor Canvas. You won't usually modify anything in this panel, but you will when you want to force Interface Builder to use your preferred class for a particular object, instead of its own default choice. Your object must be a subclass of the object selected. For example, if you create a custom view subclass of Cocoa's NSView class, you would add an NSView object to your app's window and then change its class to your custom class using the Identity inspector.

- **Attributes inspector.** You can set options for the specific class selected in the Editor Canvas. Figure 5-5 shows the attributes you can set for the NSWindow class.

- **Size inspector.** You can set various size and position attributes of the selected object using this inspector. For UI components such as labels and buttons, this panel includes settings that determine how the components move and/or resize when the window's size changes.

- **Connections inspector.** This inspector is for making connections among your UI components on the window and between those components and objects sitting in the Dock.

- **Bindings inspector.** Certain types of objects support *binding* — a mechanism within Cocoa applications that allows data to be represented in one object and used in a different object within the app. You can use bindings to support a *Model-View-Controller* (MVC, which I cover in Chapter 6) design: you can set up bindings to provide links between your UI components (views) to your controller object. For instance, you could add an NSArrayController object into your XIB and then bind it to UI components in your window so that a specific element of the NSArrayController would provide requested information to the UI components. You can set your UI components to reflect the data inside an item that the NSArrayController selects.

- **View Effects inspector.** You use this inspector to adjust some of the visual characteristics of the selected UI component, such as the component's transparency or animation.

You'll use the different Inspector options while you create your app's visual interface. Each one gives you different information about the UI component selected in Interface Builder.

Figure 5-5: The `UISimple` window's attributes.

Looking through the Library

The Object Library contains all the UI components you can drag and drop onto your windows and views. You'll also find some nonvisual components in the Library, such as the `NSArrayController` I mentioned in the previous section. To see all the items contained in the entire Library, do the following:

1. **Select the Object Library item in the drop-down menu at the top of the Library panel.**

2. **Select the Icon View button.**

   What you get is a matrix of all the objects contained in the entire library.

   You can also choose the List View button to get a linear listing of the same objects along with a short text description for each.

3. **Select any one of the items in either listing, and leave your mouse hovering over the selection.**

   Interface Builds displays a pop-up window containing more detailed information about the item you've selected. Figure 5-6 shows the pop-up window for the selection of the PDFThumbnailView.

   Click the Done button to close the pop-up window.

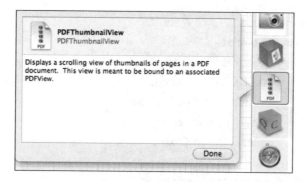

Figure 5-6: Descriptive text appears when you select and hover.

You can reduce the number of components by selecting submenus from the Object Library drop-down menu. I find this makes it easier and quicker to find the particular component I'm looking for. (Of course, being adventurous, I did enjoy scrolling through all the icons while writing this section. But that's just me.) You can also enter text into the search field at the bottom of the pane to filter the contents, which can get you to a desired component faster.

When you're building your app's user interfaces for all your app's windows, you'll make extensive use of the library and its components. So let's add something to the window.

1. **Drag a Label from the Library and hold it anywhere over the window.**

   You see the window highlighted by a gradient blue color, and the Label will display a green circle containing a plus sign to indicate that you're *copying* the Label to the window. In addition, a small label "View" appears in the lower-right corner of the window. You use these visual cues to confirm that you're about to add the object to the window.

2. **While holding the Label, drag it to the center of the window.**

   Figure 5-7 shows the Label held at the center of the window, just before you drop it.

   You'll know you're at the center because you'll see blue dashed guides beneath the Label as you move it over the window — in particular, when you cross the horizontal and vertical centers. When both lines are displayed, you're at dead center. I recommend finding one of the guides and then moving along it until you find the second.

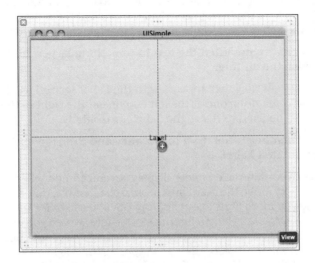

Figure 5-7: A Label in the center of the window.

3. **Drop the Label at the center of the window.**

4. **Click and drag the Label you just dropped to the top of the window.**

   About one Label's height away from the top, you'll see another dashed blue guide, indicating that Interface Builder believes that's about as high as you should go. You can go higher, and if you do, you see another guideline appear when Interface Builder *really* thinks you should stop. You can go even higher, until the lowest part of the Label's text is just below the title bar of the window. But that's it. You'll experience the same guide behavior on all four sides of the window. Interface Builder will guide you visually along what Apple's Human Interface guidelines suggest for placing UI components within views and windows. Place the Label anywhere you like within the window.

   You should follow Interface Builder's suggestions where they make sense. By doing so, you're adhering to Apple's beliefs about what will bring increased User Happiness (it helps to think of that concept in caps). Since your goal is to get your app through Apple's App Store submission review, you don't want your app rejected because of any User Experience violations. However, you can push the User Experience envelope — Apple will judge expensive apps more strictly than free ones, for instance. And full-screen animated games clearly are going to be judged differently from spreadsheet and word-processing apps.

5. **Double-click the Label.**

This action highlights the text *Label* so you can modify it.

You can change this to any text you choose, but I recommend at this point making the text longer than the original "Label" so you can see how the Label resizes automatically to accommodate your new text.

6. **When you've modified the text to something larger, hit the Return key to finish the editing.**

Your Label's new text appears with the Label resized to fit. You should see two blue dots, one at the left and one at the right of the Label. These can also be used to resize the Label horizontally.

7. **Select another Label from the Library and drag it over the window near the first Label.**

You can see Interface Builder display several additional guide lines as you slowly move the new Label around the first one. Interface Builder is giving you more hints about appropriate placement for this new Label, based on Apple's Human Interface guidelines, which you can find at `http://developer.apple.com/library/mac/#documentation/UserExperience/Conceptual/AppleHIGuidelines/Intro/intro.html`. The rationale for each one should be fairly obvious, and if you move the new Label slowly enough, you pick up some *stickiness* when the moving Label is near a place that Interface Builder thinks is an appropriate position. For instance, if you move the center of the new Label an inch or so below the first and then slowly slide it to the right, you'll see the blue guide line appear when the right side of the new Label is in line with the right side of the first one, and the new Label will seem to stick in place while the mouse cursor moves along past it. Interface Builder is giving you an opportunity to leave the new Label aligned with the first one on their right sides. You'll see similar behavior regarding other possible alignments.

I noticed that there seemed to be one alignment that was unique: when I moved a component to be just below and to the right of a Label component. It only happens for this *specific* combination. A dashed blue guide line will appear to let you align one component to be *indented* below a Label component. Apple is happy to let you know when you're about to do something they believe is a good User Experience.

8. **Drop the Label wherever you think is appropriate.**

You're just testing out Interface Builder, so it won't really matter — you won't be submitting this to Apple, so your window can look as beautiful as you want.

9. **Drag and drop different UI components to different places on your window.**

   You'll get a better feel for the dashed-blue guides and how they can assist your placement of the different components. I recommend choosing a wide variety of the different components. You've already got a couple of Labels, so add some Buttons and Checkboxes.

10. **Single-click a component to select it. Press and hold the Option key and move your cursor around the window.**

    As your cursor passes over other components, the Interface Builder displays guides and numbers to tell you about the distances between the selected component and the one the cursor is over. If you move the cursor over an area of the window where no other component lies, the display shows the distance between each edge of the selected component and the sides of the window.

TIP

You can use the mouse to move items, but for really precise pixel-by-pixel positioning you should use the arrow keys. Interface Builder will still display guides to help you.

As mentioned before, the Library comes chock-full of UI components you can add to windows and views. As you've seen, the Library groups these components by their Frameworks, as shown in Table 5-1.

Table 5-1	UI Components in the Library
Framework	Contains These Types of Components
Cocoa	Windows, views, labels, menus, buttons, radio groups, sliders, progress indicators, and others.
Address Book	Address Book People Picker View
DiscRecorder	MSF Formatter, an object for use with disc recording
Image Kit	Views for use with peripheral devices such as scanners and cameras
OSAKit	Objects used to help make your application scriptable
PDFKit	Views you use for displaying PDF documents
QTKit	Views you can use to work with QuickTime movies.
Quartz Composer	Objects for displaying Quartz Composer compositions
WebKit	Views for displaying web content
Custom Objects	Third-party controls or your own custom controls and objects

To further assist in tracking down some of the components you use most often, the Library subdivides the Cocoa Framework into these groups:

- **Controls.** You'll find Buttons and Labels here, as well as Checkboxes, Radio Groups, and Sliders.

- **Data Views.** Here you'll find some more complex views, including my favorite, the Table View. You'll also find controls that can be used within these complex views, so that you can create a Table View that contains checkboxes.

- **Layout Views.** The objects in this group will help you provide some layout management for complicated views. In addition, the Custom View object lives here, providing you with a way to save space for view objects that you create classes for within your app.

- **Objects & Controllers.** The items in this group provide you with a way to add objects to your XIB file that aren't UI components themselves but are used by UI components. For instance, you could use an Array Controller to provide access to a collection of movie information, and your UI would be populated with the name, release date, and runtime of each movie when selected by the controller.

- **Windows & Menus.** You'll find windows, menus, and toolbars in this collection.

Because the User Experience is so important, you'll find yourself editing and refining the windows and views you create using the IB Editor very frequently, to get the right look and feel for your app. As a result, expect to spend some time dragging components out of the Library and manipulating them on your windows. As I mention earlier, you'll spend most of your time in the Cocoa Framework with its collection of UI components.

The inspectors

In addition to the Library, you'll also be manipulating the settings in the various *inspectors* that live in the Inspector pane. Each time you select an object in the Interface Builder, you can use the inspectors to find and modify the various settings of that object. To see how the inspectors work, perform these steps:

1. **Select the window object.**

   You'll see a blue highlight around the window when it's the object that's selected. The best way to make sure you select the window and not anything else is to click its title bar.

2. **Show the Attributes inspector by clicking its button in the Inspector pane.**

   Figure 5-8 shows the attributes for the selected window object. Different objects will show different sets of attributes in the different inspectors. For instance, the attributes of a Button are different from the attributes of a window.

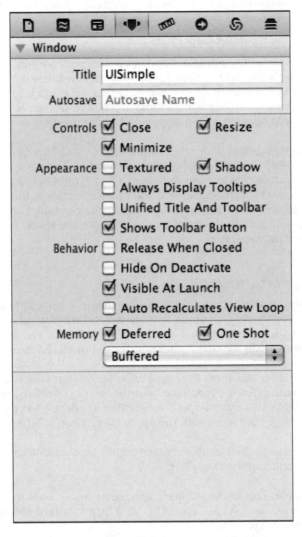

Figure 5-8: The Attribute inspector displaying the window's attributes.

3. **Show the Size inspector.**

   The Size inspector provides details about the component's size and, for controls, lets you set options for determining how the control reacts when the window containing it resizes. (I'll go over this in detail in a later section.)

4. **Show the Connections inspector.**

   You use this inspector to list all connections made to or from the selected object.

5. **Show the Bindings inspector.**

   You use bindings to make Xcode populate your user interface automatically with data from a specific source, such as the selected element of an Array Controller. As mentioned earlier, bindings implement links between a controller and its views in an MVC design. In Chapter 8, I show you how to use bindings with UI components.

The inspectors deliver more details about the components in your user interface than the visual display can provide you. The visual interaction — dragging components around the display and dropping them in the right spots — is great for the initial creation of your windows, but you'll eventually have to use the inspectors to get all the finer details correct. You'll end up spending a lot of time working with both the visual part of Interface Builder and its inspectors.

Modifying your menus

Nearly every Macintosh app comes with a menu — games are the major exception, but I've played some that use a standard Mac menu bar just like the one on a spreadsheet app. The Cocoa app projects you create with Xcode will give you an XIB file that comes with a pre-populated menu bar.

Interface Builder will show the *application's* menu bar within the Xcode project window; *Xcode's* menu bar is at the top of your Mac screen. You use Xcode's menus to perform operations within Xcode, while you add menu functionality to your apps with the application menu in Interface Builder.

The `UISimple` project you've created comes with a menu that includes the following menus in the menu bar:

- ✔ **UISimple.** This is the standard app menu you've seen in nearly every Macintosh app. If your app is going to be a standard Mac app, this menu is a necessity.

- ✔ **File.** Your users will expect the standard menu items in this menu, such as New, Open, and Save.

✔ **Edit.** If your app provides text entry or other forms of editing, you'll need an Edit menu because your users will expect it.

✔ **Format.** Users expect to find text-formatting submenus here, so if your app allows users to change fonts and perform basic formatting, you'll need this menu's help.

✔ **View.** The default items in this menu relate to the use of a toolbar. Your app can add commands to this menu that manipulate your app's views. For instance, Xcode's View menu provides menu items to display any of its views such as Project navigator.

✔ **Window.** Users can use items in this menu to support some window operations. In Xcode, for example, this menu contains items that let you access the Welcome to Xcode display you see when you launch Xcode, or the windows of the various open projects. This menu is pre-populated with the Minimize, Zoom, and Bring All to Front menu items; in a Document-Based Cocoa app, each open document window appears as a menu item that users can select to make it the active window.

✔ **Help.** You can provide menu items in this menu to support your users when they're looking for information about your app and how to do things with it.

You're free to add more top-level menus, and even remove those that don't apply. As I mentioned, there are some apps that don't provide menus in a menu bar at all. But if you're going to provide menus for your users, here are some rules to keep in mind:

✔ **The app menu is not optional; you must provide one.** This menu contains items such as the About App item and the Quit item. Users expect this menu and its items, and I believe that the Apple App Store submission reviewers will not be happy if this menu is missing, if your app is providing any menus in the menu bar.

✔ **The File menu is recommended.** Most apps use files for some purpose during their operation, so letting the user browse for, select, and save files using the File menu is something just about every app will have to do. In addition, the Print functionality is part of the File menu. An example of an app that does not provide a File menu is Apple's System Preferences app.

✔ **The Edit menu is strongly recommended.** Even game apps can make use of text editing — if your role-playing app lets your users name the characters they create, your users might decide to search the web for the coolest character name, then copy and paste that text into your app's name-entry field. The essential elements of the Edit menu are the Cut, Copy, and Paste menu items — if you provide an Edit menu, your users will expect these items and their associated behaviors.

To edit your app's menus, here's what you do:

1. **Click the Main Menu icon in Interface Builder's Dock.**

   The Menu editor can be dismissed by clicking the X in the gray circle on the left side of the application menu display; clicking the Main Menu icon brings it right back.

2. **Click the View menu.**

   Doing so highlights the menu name in the menu bar, and the menu's contents appear as they would in the app.

3. **Delete the menu.**

   This app will not require a View menu, and Apple won't reject your app if it has no View menu. You could Cut the menu, but that leaves a place-holder for it in the menu bar, which puts a noticeable space between the Format and Window menus. Use the Delete key on your keyboard to completely remove both the menu and its contents.

4. **Drag a Submenu Menu Item object from the Library's Windows & Menus palette and drop it in the menu bar between the Format and Window menus. In the Attributes inspector, set the Title to Colors.**

5. **Click the Colors menu in the menu bar.**

   The first item has already been added for you.

6. **Select the Item and change its text to Red.**

7. **Drag a Menu Item from the Library and drop it just at the bottom of the Red menu item.**

   You see a blue line below the text *Red*, indicating where the new menu item will be dropped. Change the text of this item to **Green**.

8. **Drag one more Menu Item from the Library and drop it below the Green Menu Item. Change this item's text to Blue.**

9. **Choose File:Save to save your changes.**

10. **Choose Editor:Simulate Document to launch the Cocoa Simulator and display your interface.**

    The Cocoa Simulator displays your window and menus as a test bed — you have some limited default functionality, but nothing of what your app does in its own code. The Colors menu is shown but its items are grayed out. Your buttons also won't execute any actions in your app. You aren't using the actual application; this is just a test display of the user interface you've put together. In earlier days, this was useful because it was faster to display the components of the interface than it was to do a complete build-and-run. With today's faster and more powerful machines, however, you may find it just as quick to do a full build of your app and run it as you do to simulate your interface. The benefit of doing a full build is that you get all the functionality you added in your code and made available through the connections.

11. **Quit the Cocoa Simulator and return to Xcode.**

12. **Click the Run button to run your app.**

You'll probably notice right away that something's wrong: The menu items in the Colors menu are *disabled*. When your app is executing and you click the Colors menu, the Cocoa framework displays the menu items you added, but those menu items that are not connected to IBAction methods in your app will be disabled — there's no reason for a menu to be enabled if there's nothing that will execute when it's selected. Part of the idea here is to reduce confusion for the user — when a user selects a menu item, she is telling your app to do something. If your app hasn't connected that menu item to a specific method — giving it something to do — then the user won't know what just happened. By intentionally disabling those methods that are not set to do anything, the Cocoa framework prevents this confusion. So let's fix that:

1. **Click the Show the Assistant editor button.**

   Xcode displays the header file UISimpleAppDelegate.h.

2. **Click the Colors menu to display its three menu items.**

3. **Hold down the Control key and click the Red menu item. While holding the Control key down, drag a line from the menu item into the UISimpleAppDelegate.h editor, right above the @end directive.**

4. **In the Connection pop-up window, set the Connection type to Action, and set the name to** handleColorRed, **and then click Connect.**

5. **Control-drag from the Green menu item into the** UISimpleApp Delegate, h **editor, set the Connection type to** Action **and the name to** handleColorGreen, **and then click Connect.**

6. **Control-drag from the Blue menu item into the** UISimpleApp Delegate, h **editor, set the Connection type to** Action **and the name to** handleColorBlue, **and click Connect.**

   The contents of the UISimpleAppDelegate.h file should look similar to that shown in Listing 5-1. And the contents of UISimpleAppDelegate.m should look similar to that shown in Listing 5-2. Xcode has automatically added IBAction methods to your app's delegate class and connected them to the menu items.

7. **Click the Run button.**

   Xcode saves, builds, and runs your application.

Figure 5-9 shows the Colors menu selected with all three menu items enabled.

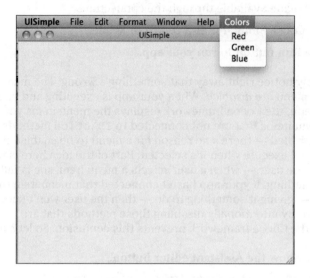

Figure 5-9: UISimple's Colors menu, fully enabled.

Listing 5-1:   The three methods to be called by the three menu items

```
//
//  UISimpleAppDelegate.h
//  UISimple
//

#import <Cocoa/Cocoa.h>

@interface UISimpleAppDelegate : NSObject
            <NSApplicationDelegate>
{
@private
  NSWindow* window;
}

@property (assign) IBOutlet NSWindow* window;

- (IBAction)handleColorRed:(id)inSender;
- (IBAction)handleColorGreen:(id)inSender;
- (IBAction)handleColorBlue:(id)inSender;

@end
```

Listing 5-2: **The functional menu methods**

```
//
// UISimpleAppDelegate.m
// UISimple
//

#import "UISimpleAppDelegate.h"

@implementation UISimpleAppDelegate
@synthesize window;
- (void)applicationDidFinishLaunching: (NSNotification*)
          aNotification
{
    // Insert code to initialize your application
}

- (IBAction)handleColorRed:(id)inSender
{
}

- (IBAction)handleColorGreen:(id)inSender
{
}

- (IBAction)handleColorBlue:(id)inSender
{
}

@end
```

Your menu methods don't have to do anything — the Cocoa framework only
checks to see that clicking a menu will cause the execution of some method
but doesn't look into whether any code gets executed in the method. One
benefit of this arrangement is that you can create *stub* methods: Your code
will implement empty methods to support the menus to start with, and you
can add functionality piece by piece later on — which is what you're going to
do next.

1. **If** UISimple **is running, quit it.**

2. **In Xcode, select** MainMenu.xib **from the Project Navigator.**

3. **Click the Colors menu to display the menu items.**

4. **Click the Red menu item to select it. In the Attributes inspector, click**
   in the field next to Key Equivalent.

You're going to create a key combination to perform the menu action when the user presses the correct keys.

5. **Press ⌘-R.**

You should see the result as shown in Figure 5-10. You'll also see the key combination appear in the menu.

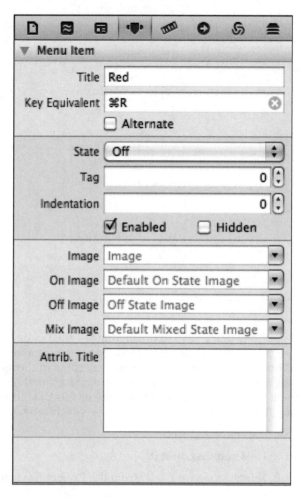

Figure 5-10: You've just assigned ⌘-R to the Red menu item in the Colors menu.

6. **Assign key combinations to the Green and Blue menus as well.**

   And don't forget to save your changes.

   Be careful: ⌘-B and ⌘-G are already in use by other menu items. You can either find those menu items and remove their assigned key combinations, remove the menu items themselves, or else choose something other than ⌘-B and ⌘-G. Neither the IB Editor nor Xcode will complain if two menu items have the same key combinations, but your app won't behave as you expect: When running, one of the menu items will respond to the key combination and the other one will not. (Hint: That won't make the user happy.)

7. **Click the Run button.**

   Xcode will launch `UISimple` and you can use the key combinations you assigned to trigger the menus.

   You should see the Colors menu flash when you press the ⌘-R key combination to trigger the Red menu item.

The next step is to add some real functionality to those menu actions. Here goes:

1. **If `UISimple` is still running, quit it.**

2. **Select `MainMenu.xib` from the Project Navigator. If the Assistant editor is not visible, click the Show the Assistant editor button.**

3. **Add a Label to the window. Set the Label's text to** `"Now is the time for all good Colors to come to the aid of Interface Builder"`.

4. **Control-drag from the Label to the right of the "{" following the @** `interface` **directive in** `UISimpleAppDelegate.h`. **In the pop-up window, set the name to** `m_label` **and click Connect.**

   Xcode creates a member variable in the `UISimpleAppDelegate` class for the Label you just added to the window and makes the connection. The header file UISimpleAppDelegate.h should look similar to the code shown in Listing 5-3.

5. **Add the green code from Listing 5-4 into** `UISimpleAppDelegate.m`.

6. **Click the Run button and test your color-changing app.**

   The text will change to the colors you chose for each of the three methods, and you can use key combinations instead of a mouse to select the particular menu item.

Listing 5-3:   A member variable to reference the Label

```
//
// UISimpleAppDelegate.h
// UISimple
//

#import <Cocoa/Cocoa.h>

@interface UISimpleAppDelegate : NSObject
            <NSApplicationDelegate>
{
    IBOutlet NSTextField* m_label;
@private
  NSWindow* window;
}

@property (assign) IBOutlet NSWindow* window;

- (IBAction)handleColorRed:(id)inSender;
- (IBAction)handleColorGreen:(id)inSender;
- (IBAction)handleColorBlue:(id)inSender;

@end
```

Listing 5-4:   Responding to the menu items by changing the text color as appropriate

```
//
// UISimpleAppDelegate.m
// UISimple
//

#import "UISimpleAppDelegate.h"

@implementation UISimpleAppDelegate
@synthesize window;
- (void)applicationDidFinishLaunching: (NSNotification*)
          aNotification
{
    // Insert code to initialize your application
}

- (IBAction)handleColorRed:(id)inSender
{
    [m_label setTextColor:[NSColor redColor]];
}
```

```
- (IBAction)handleColorGreen:(id)inSender
{
    [m_label setTextColor:[NSColor greenColor]];
}

- (IBAction)handleColorBlue:(id)inSender
{
    [m_label setTextColor:[NSColor blueColor]];
}

@end
```

Your app uses menus to change the color of a field of text in its window. You implemented this behavior with hardly any code — most of the work was dragging and dropping items into the menus and the window, and making connections between items in Interface Builder. Next we're going to make the code more interactive.

1. **Quit** `UISimple` **if it's still running.**

2. **Select** `MainMenu.xib` **from the Project Navigator. Click the Show the Assistant editor button if the Assistant editor is not displayed.**

3. **Drag and drop a Horizontal Slider onto the window.**

4. **Control-drag from the Horizontal Slider into** `UISimple AppDelegate.h` **editor, below the** **m_label** **member variable.**

5. **In the pop-up Connection window, set the name to** **m_opacity,** **and click Connect.**

6. **Control-drag from the Horizontal Slider into** `UISimpleApp Delegate.h` **editor, just before the** `@end` **directive.**

7. **In the pop-up Connection window, select Action from the Connection drop-down menu, and set the name to** **handleOpacitySlider.** **Click Connect.**

   You should now see the code in `UISimpleAppDelegate.h` as shown in Listing 5-5.

8. **Add the green code lines as shown in Listing 5-6.**

9. **Build and run** `UISimple.`

   You can now change the transparency (or opacity) of the text in addition to its color. The Horizontal Slider's values run from 0.0 through

100.0 for default; the opacity value is retrieved from the slider and divided by 100.0 to set it to run from 0.0 to 1.00. This is used as the *alpha* value for the NSColor object, which is what determines how transparent the text will be.

Listing 5-5: Adding a slider to change the text transparency

```
//
// UISimpleAppDelegate.h
// UISimple
//

#import <Cocoa/Cocoa.h>

@interface UISimpleAppDelegate : NSObject
          <NSApplicationDelegate>
{
    IBOutlet NSTextField* m_label;
    IBOutlet NSSlider* m_opacity;
@private
  NSWindow* window;
}

@property (assign) IBOutlet NSWindow* window;

- (IBAction)handleColorRed:(id)inSender;
- (IBAction)handleColorGreen:(id)inSender;
- (IBAction)handleColorBlue:(id)inSender;
- (IBAction)handleOpacitySlider:(id)inSender;

@end
```

Listing 5-6: Implementing the code to modify text transparency

```
//
// UISimpleAppDelegate.m
// UISimple
//

#import "UISimpleAppDelegate.h"

@implementation UISimpleAppDelegate
@synthesize window;
- (void)applicationDidFinishLaunching:(NSNotification*)
          aNotification
{
    // Insert code to initialize your application
```

```
        [self handleColorRed:nil]; // set red as the initial
            color
    }

- (IBAction)handleColorRed:(id)inSender
{
    CGFloat opacity = [m_opacity doubleValue]/100.0;
    [m_label setTextColor:[NSColor colorWithDeviceRed:1.00
            green:0.00 blue:0.00 alpha:opacity]];
}

- (IBAction)handleColorGreen:(id)inSender
{
    CGFloat opacity = [m_opacity doubleValue]/100.0;
    [m_label setTextColor:[NSColor colorWithDeviceRed:0.00
            green:1.00 blue:0.00 alpha:opacity]];
}

- (IBAction)handleColorBlue:(id)inSender
{
    CGFloat opacity = [m_opacity doubleValue]/100.0;
    [m_label setTextColor:[NSColor colorWithDeviceRed:0.00
            green:0.00 blue:1.00 alpha:opacity]];
}

- (IBAction)handleOpacitySlider:(id)inSender
{
    NSColor* textColor = [m_label textColor];
    CGFloat redValue = 0.00;
    CGFloat greenValue = 0.00;
    CGFloat blueValue = 0.00;
    CGFloat alphaValue = 0.00;
    [textColor getRed:&redValue green:&greenValue
            blue:&blueValue alpha:&alphaValue];
    [m_label setTextColor:[NSColor
            colorWithDeviceRed:redValue green:greenValue
            blue:blueValue alpha:[m_opacity
            doubleValue]/100.0]];
}

@end
```

Sizing up your windows

One of the benefits of using a large monitor for my Mac is that I can place many windows in it and fill up the screen so that I can jump from one app to the next just by clicking that app's windows. Of course, the more apps I have running, the more space gets used up by each one's windows. I will end up resizing my apps' windows so that the most-used app gets the most space and is thus more easily reached when I need to return to it. Your users can also use multiple monitors, or make use of OS X Lion's Mission Control and multiple virtual Desktops to give all of their apps more space to grow into.

The default app window created for your project by Xcode is resizable, so you don't have to implement any code to give your users the ability to change the size of the windows you display for them. However, you do have to decide how you want the components within your windows to behave when their containing window gets resized. A long time ago, you would have to implement many lines of code for your app to execute every time a window was resized, to calculate each component's new size based on the new size of the window. Interface Builder makes this aspect of app development easy, and you can achieve a great deal of what you want without writing a single line of code. And in OS X Lion, your app can become a full-screen app, which will allow your app to be resized to the edges of the user's monitor, adjusting its contents according to the Size settings you select within Interface Builder.

You do this bit of magic by using the Size inspector — for all the components of your window, as well as the window itself.

1. **Quit the** `UISimple` **app if it's still running.**

2. **Select** `MainMenu.xib` **from the Project Navigator.**

3. **Single-click the text label, and click the Show Size inspector button in the Inspector panel.**

   You should see something like what's in Figure 5-11.

4. **In the Autosizing tool, click the I-shaped red bars to the right and below the box in the middle.**

   The display should look like each side of the smaller box is connected to each side of the larger box by a red bar.

5. **Single-click the Horizontal Slider.**

6. **In the Autosizing tool, click all four of the I-shaped red bars so that only the bars to the right and below the box in the middle are solid red. Save your changes.**

7. **Single-click the window's title bar to select it.**

8. **Click the Minimum Size checkbox in the Constraints section.**

Doing so fixes the minimum size of the window to its current size; when the window is resized, it will never be smaller than what you see at this point in Interface Builder.

9. **Click the Run button.**

Alternatively, since you didn't make any code changes, you could select Editor: Simulate Document. Resize the window, and notice the effect of the changes you've made.

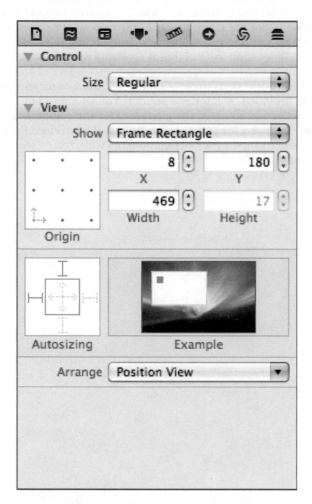

Figure 5-11: The Size inspector, showing size information about the label.

Congratulations — you've made a resizable window whose contents adjust their positions and sizes depending on the settings you selected with the Autosizing tool of the Size inspector. Your selections for the Autosizing tool can create some interesting sizing relationships and help you lay out the components within your windows and views. For instance, the Autosizing settings are managed relative to the view that contains the component you're adjusting the settings for. In this example, the components were both within a single window, but you could place a view within the window and put some components within that view. Then you would assign Autosizing behaviors for the view with respect to the window that contains it, and assign Autosizing behaviors for the components of the view with respect to that view. (Got that?) By layering your views and architecting the resizing of those views you can concoct some very elaborate resizing of views within views.

You've now got the basic skills to create the user interface of your app using the components provided by Interface Builder. You've linked your code to your UI components and adjusted the attributes for the components for display to the user. There's a lot you can do with just the Interface Builder skills in this chapter, and the code your UI components will execute when your users interact with your UI.

Chapter 6

Controlling Your Windows and Views

*I*n 1984, Apple revealed the Macintosh, the first mass-market computer that introduced a new way for ordinary humans to interact with their computers. The highlight of this new approach was the use of windows (framed screen areas) to display the information that users would work with. Today, you'll find the use of computer windows everywhere, including an operating system of that name. Apple lit the torch, and the world has followed.

Nearly all Macintosh apps provide windows, and chances are your apps will also do so. In this chapter, I show you the basics of using windows in your Mac apps. I'll also cover *views*, which are objects that can be displayed within a window. Every user interface component is a subclass of the Cocoa class NSView. All the windows your app will create will contain views to display your app's information, or provide your users with controls and components to interact with your app. You'll also find information on a useful *architectural pattern*, called Model-View-Controller (MVC), which your apps can use to organize your windows and views and coordinate your users' actions with changes to the data stored within your apps. Your next steps will guide you to a much more structured approach to writing Mac apps — which will help you keep your code easy to understand and easy to reuse.

You can write Macintosh apps that don't display windows to perform their operations. For instance, a web server app does not require any user interaction; it just sits and runs in the background. But in this chapter, I'm going to limit my explanations and examples to the use of windows and views.

Opening Windows

Mac windows are distinctively familiar, and Cocoa apps you build with Xcode will come with a standard Mac window ready for your app to use. Every NSWindow object your app displays appears as a standard Mac window, like that shown in Figure 6-1. Because your users expect to see windows like this, and because your app must adhere to your users' expectations, your apps display windows just like this one, displaying your app's own content. Of course, there are exceptions to this principle, such as a full-screen game or an app that shows movies using every available pixel. The standard Mac app comes with a standard window, so I'll give you the information you need to create and manage windows in your apps.

Figure 6-1: The normal Mac window, recognized and loved by millions of users worldwide.

There are several types of windows that Cocoa offers for your apps to use:

- **Window:** You'll use this type of window most often. This is the basic form of NSWindow.

- **Panel:** You can use panels for supporting your app's main windows. For instance, if your app has preferences for its behaviors that users may want to personalize, such as the font size for the text in your app's displays, you would use a preferences panel to give your users a separate window in which to change those settings. NSPanel is the Cocoa class that provides panel functionality. Panels are meant to assist your users during their interaction with the main window of your app. As such, panels are removed from the screen when your app is not *active*, that is, when the user has selected another app to work with while yours is still running.

- **Textured Window:** An NSWindow that comes with a textured background.

- **HUD Window:** This is an NSWindow that is semi-transparent, which lets you create a window that acts like a Heads-Up-Display. You might use this instead of an ordinary NSPanel for making changes to a main window, in order to let your users see the changes as they make them. For example, Interface Builder displays HUD Windows to show the connections that are available or already connected for a UI component. And Apple apps such as iDVD and iMovie use HUD windows as well.

- **Window and Drawer:** Your windows can come with drawers. Cocoa provides a class, NSDrawer, that acts as a slide-out component your apps can connect with your windows. Each window has its own accompanying drawer which can be used to contain components and information your app provides for the specific window the drawer is attached to. Each NSDrawer object has a custom NSView that contains all the UI components the NSDrawer displays when open.

You can see examples of all of these windows in Figure 6-2.

State of your window

Apple has defined three different states that your app's windows can be in while your app is executing:

- **Inactive:** An *inactive* window is one that isn't accepting input from the user until the user clicks it. For example, your app may have multiple windows displaying images downloaded from different web sites. Only one window is active, while the rest are all inactive. An *active* window can receive input from the keyboard; an inactive window won't respond to the user's key presses.

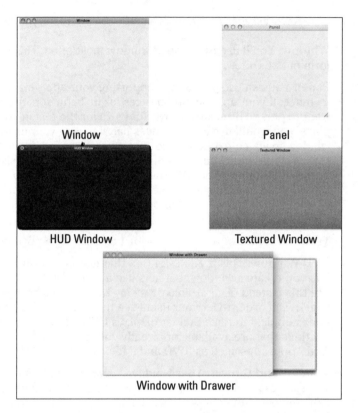

Figure 6-2: You can create a variety of different windows for your app to display.

✔ **Key:** A *key* window is the window that receives keyboard input from the user. Your app's key window, if displayed, is the primary receiver for all messages from menus and panels. Your app can have only one key window at a time, and a window is made the key window when a user clicks it. An example of a key window would be the panel that is displayed in Apple's TextEdit app when a user selects Edit ➪ Find ➪ Find. When the user presses a key on the keyboard, this panel will receive it. If the user clicks back in the main window, the panel becomes inactive but is still visible; if the user switches to a different app, the main window for TextEdit will be visible but the Find window will disappear.

✔ **Main:** A *main* window is the window where your user is currently working. A main window may also be the key window, but at other times it may not. An example of this is the font window used in Apple's TextEdit app, as shown in Figure 6-3. The font window is the key window, while the TextEdit document "Untitled" is the main window.

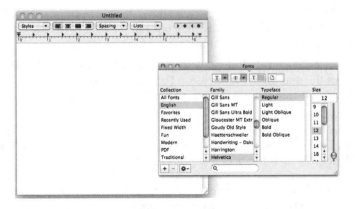

Figure 6-3: The TextEdit Font key window and the main window.

Generally, you won't need to think too much about what state your windows are in while your app is running, because the OS and the Cocoa framework take care of that for you. This information will become useful for understanding the behavior of your app when multiple windows and panels are displayed and menus are selected and keys are being pressed — you'll need to keep track of which window is the main and which is the key in order to ensure that you know where the result of a menu selection or a key press will appear. The following two pieces of information are important to remember:

✔ A user action such as a key press or a menu selection is first associated with the *key* window.

✔ If the key window is a panel and it cannot handle the action, the action is next associated with the *main* window.

If you keep that order straight, you can keep on top of what's happening in your views.

Introducing MVC

A *software design pattern* is a fancy term used to describe a consistent architecture of code created to solve a particular type of problem that has happened fairly often in software development. The Model-View-Controller (MVC) concept, for example, is a design pattern that is useful for managing the relationship between your app's data, your app's display of that data, and your user's interactions with that data on display. An app that implements MVC incorporates three different types of objects:

✔ **Model:** An object that represents the data that your app will display and allow the user to interact with. If your app uses Core Data, you'll rely on its data model to be the Model for your app.

✔ **View:** An object that displays data to your app's users. DiabeticPad displays the data of a specific Core Data entity object using the UI components of its main window, and this will be the View.

✔ **Controller:** An object that responds to the user's interactions with your app. The NSDocument subclass in DiabeticPad, CoreDataDiabeticPadDoc acts as the Controller, because it's the object to which the user's actions are directed.

Here's a simple example of a real-world system that will help you understand the components of MVC and how they work together. You've either driven or been a passenger in an automobile, so this analogy should be very familiar:

✔ The car's dashboard is the *View*, displaying the various pieces of information to the driver.

✔ The systems and sensors tracking such data as the amount of gasoline in the tank, the number of miles driven, and the temperature of the water in the radiator represent the *Model*.

✔ The computer monitoring the data and responding to the driver's inputs is the *Controller*.

When the driver fills up her tank with gas, she resets the trip odometer to zero. This causes the Controller to set a value in the Model. Sometime later, when the driver wants to know how many miles she's gone since the last fill-up, she presses a button to show the trip odometer: the Controller instructs the Model to retrieve a count of the mileage and display it in the View. In addition, as she drives her car, the Model reports to the Controller the amount of gasoline remaining in the tank and tells the View to display that value; when she has topped the tank off, the View shows the gas tank to be full, again as reported by the Model.

The MVC pattern separates the components of the app into three separate parts, each of which has responsibility for and control over its own supporting elements. By using the MVC pattern and by strictly keeping the three parts separate, you can easily adjust and modify each component independently from the other two, without completely rewriting the other components. Each part minimizes the interactions that the others can initiate upon it, limiting the chances for errors to occur. In addition, should the need arise, you can easily replace one part with a new and improved version — again without disturbing the operation of the other parts. So when the driver decides to take a break, she lets her friend drive her car, thus replacing the original Controller with another, while the View and the Model both stay the same. Some time later, the driver might decide to upgrade the dashboard with a heads-up display like those used in aircraft; she thus would be changing the View without affecting the Model or the Controller.

Figure 6-4 shows you a picture of the MVC design pattern. The Controller communicates *directly* with both the View and the Model, as indicated by the solid lines connecting the Controller to the other two objects. This means your classes that operate as Controllers maintain an Objective-C object that is a member of a View class and a Model class. The Model and View both connect back to the Controller *indirectly*, usually through an intermediate class or operation. This is shown as a dashed line in Figure 6-4. Your View and Model classes can communicate using NSNotifications in Cocoa, as described in the last section in this chapter, "Using notifications." Lastly, note the solid line connecting the View and the Model: the View classes will communicate with the Model directly, in order to speed the process of updating the View based on information stored in the Model.

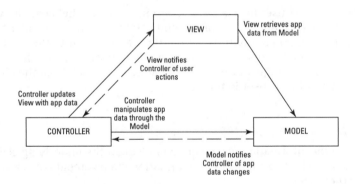

Figure 6-4: The MVC design pattern, showing the interactions between the three components.

Your apps will become more modular as you use the MVC design pattern. Your apps will be composed of separate, indivisible parts, which you can reuse in other places within an app or across several apps. For instance, a calendar app might have a Model class that represents a user's identity. This same class could be used in an e-mail or voicemail app, to identify incoming mail or calls, so that my wife's phone calls get forwarded to my cell phone, while her parents' calls go to the "In-laws" voicemail repository.

Using MVC in Your App

MVC theory is great, but now it's time to use that theory while you develop your own app. In the rest of this chapter, I walk you through the creation of an app that uses MVC to manage its displays, handle its users' interactions, and manipulate its stored data. Since it's helpful to keep track of your stocks in the stock market, you're going to step through the creation of a simple stock-trading app that you can use to track shares and the value you've invested in one stock. You design the app to work like this:

- Your Model class will keep track of all the transactions in one stock. The View class will act as the front end of the app (the part that's facing the user); as such, it displays the information stored in the Model and accepts input from the user. The Controller will act as the middleman between the Model and the View.

- Whenever the app needs to display the total number of shares owned and the current share price, the Controller will retrieve that information from the Model and deliver it to the View to show to the user.

- Any time the user makes a stock purchase or sale, he'll use the View to enter the data about the transaction and trigger the Controller to take the information out of the user interface and hand it to the Model, allowing the Model to update the information in its data store. The Controller will then also request the updated information back from the Model, to present it to the user in the View.

Starting with the Model

You'll use the information just given to implement the underlying classes used by the Model to support the information management tasks it performs. Follow these steps:

1. **Launch Xcode and select File⇨New⇨New Project... from the menu.**

   You'll see the usual new Project window.

2. **Choose Mac OS X Application from the left column, choose Cocoa Application from the list of templates, and click the Next button.**

3. **Give the project a name and click the Next button.**

   I called mine `StockMarketer`, as shown in Figure 6-5. There's no need to make this project use Core Data or be Document-based.

4. **Save the project in an appropriate location and click Create.**

   You now have a basic project to which you'll add components to support an MVC design.

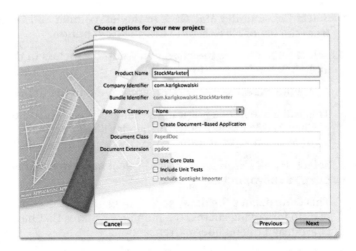

Figure 6-5: Creating the StockMarketer project in Xcode.

5. **Select the StockMarketer group in the Project navigator and select File⇨New ⇨New File.**

   You'll see the New File sheet slide out, shown in Figure 6-6.

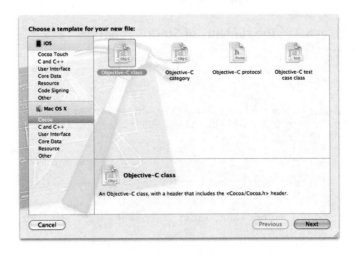

Figure 6-6: Creating the StockAccount class in Xcode.

6. **Select Cocoa under Mac OS X in the left column and Objective-C class from the list of classes and click the Next button.**

7. **Select** NSObject **as the class you want to subclass in the next panel, and click the Next button.**

8. **Name the class** StockAccount **and save it in the default location.**

   This will make Xcode put it in the same place as the other classes in the project. Xcode creates both the header file (StockAccount.h) and the source file (StockAccount.m) for this class, automatically.

9. **Select** StockAccount.h **in the Project navigator and add the code in** purple **shown in Listing 6-1.**

   This code defines the data representing a stock account — the amount of cash for buying shares, the number of shares that have been purchased, and the number of transactions.

10. **Select** StockAccount.m **in the Project navigator and add the code in** purple **shown in Listing 6-2.**

    This code is the implementation of the StockAccount class. This will be the Model used by StockMarketer. In this sample app, the account will be created with 1,000 shares and $10,000.00 cash to start with. The Model will also keep track of the number of transactions. In a real stock market application, you would provide an initializer method to set the initial values of this data.

Listing 6-1:   The contents of StockAccount.h

```
//
//   StockAccount.h
//   StockMarketer
//
//   Created by Karl Kowalski on 4/24/11.
//   Copyright 2011 Kowalski Software Enterprises.
//   All rights reserved.
//

#import <Foundation/Foundation.h>


@interface StockAccount : NSObject
{
@private
    NSUInteger   m_shares;
    double       m_cash;
    NSUInteger   m_numberTransactions;
}
```

```
- (double)getCash;
- (NSUInteger)getShares;
- (BOOL)purchaseShares:(NSUInteger)inShares atPrice:(double)
        inPrice;
- (BOOL)sellShares:(NSUInteger)inShares atPrice:(double)
        inPrice;
- (NSUInteger)getNumberTransactions;

@end
```

Listing 6-2:   The implementation code for StockAccount.m

```
//
//  StockAccount.m
//  StockMarketer
//
//  Created by Karl Kowalski on 4/24/11.
//  Copyright 2011 Kowalski Software Enterprises.
//  All rights reserved.
//

#import "StockAccount.h"


@implementation StockAccount

- (id)init
{
    self = [super init];
    if (self)
    {
        // initialize cash and shares
        m_cash = 10000.0;
        m_shares = 1000;
        m_numberTransactions = 0;
    }
    return (self);
}

- (void)dealloc
{    [super dealloc];
}

- (double)getCash
{
    return (m_cash);
}
```

(continued)

Listing 6-2 *(continued)*

```objc
- (NSUInteger)getShares
{
    return (m_shares);
}

- (BOOL)purchaseShares:(NSUInteger)inShares atPrice:(double)
            inPrice
{
    double cost = (double)inShares * inPrice;
    BOOL success = (cost < m_cash);
    if (YES == success)
    {
        // can only buy with available cash
        m_cash = m_cash - cost;
        m_shares += inShares;
        m_ numberTransactions++;
    }
    return (success);
}

- (BOOL)sellShares:(NSUInteger)inShares atPrice:(double)
            inPrice
{
    // can only sell if we have the shares
    BOOL success = (inShares < m_shares);
    if (YES == success)
    {
        m_cash = m_cash + (double)inShares*inPrice;
        m_shares -= inShares;
        m_ numberTransactions++;
    }
    return (success);
}

- (NSUInteger)getNumberTransactions
{
    return (m_numberTransactions);
}

@end
```

As the Model for `StockMarketer`, the `StockAccount` class acts as a book-keeper for the user while she performs simple stock trades.

Creating the View component

This app will build and run but will only show you a blank window, because you haven't yet added the View that will provide information to and receive inputs from the user. The code you implemented earlier is the Model part of MVC; now you're going to add the View. You can see what the end result will look like in Figure 6-7.

1. **Select** `MainMenu.xib` **in Project navigator and select the Window in the Interface Builder Dock. Click the View button to show the Utilities if necessary.**

Figure 6-7: The View that your stock account app will display.

2. **Drag a Label from the Object Library and drop it onto the window in the upper-left corner. Set its text to** Cash:.

3. **Drag a Label from the Object Library and drop it onto the window to the right of the Cash: label. Set its text to** $0.00.

4. **Drag a Label from the Object Library and drop it onto the window below the Cash: label. Set its text to** Shares:.

5. **Drag a Label from the Object Library and drop it onto the window to the right of the Shares: label. Set its text to** 0.

6. **Drag a Label from the Object Library and drop it onto the window below the Shares: label. Set its text to** Share Price:.

7. **Drag a Label from the Object Library and drop it onto the window to the right of the Share Price: label. Set its text to** $0.00.

8. **Drag a Label from the Object Library and drop it onto the window below the Share Price: label. Set its text to** Portfolio Value:.

9. **Drag a Label from the Object Library and drop it onto the window to the right of the Portfolio Value: label. Set its text to** $0.00.

10. **Drag a Label from the Object Library and drop it onto the window below the Portfolio Value: label. Set its text to** Number of Shares to Buy/Sell:.

11. **Drag a Text Field from the Object Library and drop it onto the window to the right of the Number of Shares to Buy/Sell: label.**

12. **Drag a Label from the Object Library and drop it onto the window below the Number of Shares to Buy/Sell: label. Set its text to** Total # of Transactions:.

13. **Drag a Label from the Object Library and drop it onto the window to the right of the Total # of Transactions: label. Set its text to** 0.

14. **Drag a Button from the Object Library and drop it onto the window at the bottom-left corner. Set its text to** Buy.

15. **Drag a Button from the Object Library and drop it onto the window at the bottom-right corner. Set its text to** Sell.

16. **Build the app.**

    Make the labels you added to show numeric values — such as 0 or $0.00 — large enough to display large values for the number of shares, the total amount of cash, and so on. I recommend making the labels about half the width of the window.

    You can run your app, and it will show the window you just created, but the View and the Model aren't communicating yet.

Implementing a Controller

You're now two-thirds done with your implementation of an MVC-based app: you've created a Model (StockAccount) and you've created a View (the components in the window). Now you need to create the last piece, the Controller class and object to perform the communications between the Model and the View.

1. **Select the** StockMarketer **group in Project navigator and choose File ➪ New ➪ New File from the menu.**

2. **Create an** NSObject **subclass and name it** StockAccountController.

    This will be your Controller class.

3. **Select the** `MainMenu.xib` **item in Project navigator.**

4. **Drag an Object from the Object Library and drop it into the Interface Builder Dock below the Font Manager object. Click the Show the Utilities View button if necessary.**

5. **Select the Object in the Interface Builder Dock and click the Show the Identity inspector button in the Utilities view. In the Custom Class pane, set the Class to** `StockAccountController` **in the drop-down menu.**

6. **Click the Show the Assistant Editor button.**

   You're going to use the Assistant to link the UI components to the Controller.

7. **In the Jump Bar at the top of the Assistant Editor, click the** `StockMarketerAppDelegate.h` **menu and select** `StockAccountController.h` **instead.**

   The Assistant defaults to the `StockMarketerAppDelegate` class, so you have to change it.

8. **Control-drag from the $0.00 Label next to the Cash: Label into the Assistant editor to a point just above the** `@end` **directive. In the pop-up window, set the Name to** `m_cash` **and click the Connect button.**

9. **Repeat Step 8 for the 0 Label next to the Shares: Label and set its Name to** `m_shares`.

10. **Repeat Step 8 for the $0.00 Label next to the Share Price: Label and set its Name to** `m_sharePrice`.

11. **Repeat Step 8 for the $0.00 Label next to the Portfolio Value: Label and set its Name to** `m_portfolioValue`.

12. **Repeat Step 8 for the Text Field next to the Number of Shares to Buy/ Sell: Label and set its Name to** `m_sharesToTrade`.

13. **Repeat Step 8 for the 0 Label next to the Total # of Transactions: Label and set its Name to** `m_totalTransactions`.

14. **Control-drag from the Buy Button into the Assistant Editor to a point right above the line containing the** `@end` **directive. In the pop-up window, choose Action from the Connection drop-down menu and set the Name to** `buyShares`. **Click the Connect button.**

15. **Repeat Step 14 for the Sell Button and set the Name to** `sellShares`.

16. **In the Assistant Editor, add the** purple **code from Listing 6-3.**

17. **Select** `StockAccountController.m` **in the Project navigator and add the** purple **code from Listing 6-4.**

18. **Build your app.**

You've added your Controller class, and connected it to its UI components. Your Controller can now accept the user's buy and sell orders and tell the Model what to do. Then the Controller will take information from the Model and update the View.

Listing 6-3: The contents of StockAccountController.h

```
//
//   StockAccountController.h
//   StockMarketer
//
//   Created by Karl Kowalski on 4/24/11.
//   Copyright 2011 Kowalski Software Enterprises.
//   All rights reserved.
//

#import <Foundation/Foundation.h>

#import "StockAccount.h"


@interface StockAccountController : NSObject
{
@private

    NSTextField *m_cash;
    NSTextField *m_shares;
    NSTextField *m_sharePrice;
    NSTextField *m_portfolioValue;
    NSTextField *m_sharesToTrade;
    NSTextField *m_totalTransactions;
    StockAccount *m_stockAccount;
}

@property (assign) IBOutlet NSTextField *m_cash;
@property (assign) IBOutlet NSTextField *m_shares;
@property (assign) IBOutlet NSTextField *m_sharePrice;
@property (assign) IBOutlet NSTextField *m_portfolioValue;
@property (assign) IBOutlet NSTextField *m_sharesToTrade;
@property (assign) IBOutlet NSTextField *m_totalTransactions;
- (IBAction)buyShares:(id)sender;
- (IBAction)sellShares:(id)sender;
- (void)updateDisplay;
@end
```

Listing 6-4: The source code for the Controller

```
//
//   StockAccountController.m
//   StockMarketer
//
//   Created by Karl Kowalski on 4/24/11.
//   Copyright 2011 Kowalski Software Enterprises.
//   All rights reserved.
//

#import "StockAccountController.h"


@implementation StockAccountController

@synthesize m_cash;
@synthesize m_shares;
@synthesize m_sharePrice;
@synthesize m_portfolioValue;
@synthesize m_sharesToTrade;
@synthesize m_totalTransactions;

- (id)init
{
    self = [super init];
    if (self) {
        // Initialization code here.
        m_stockAccount = [[StockAccount alloc] init];
    }

    return self;
}

- (void)dealloc
{
    [m_stockAccount release];
    [super dealloc];
}

- (IBAction)buyShares:(id)sender
{
    NSUInteger numberShares = [[m_sharesToTrade stringValue]
            intValue];
    NSString* sharePriceString = [[m_sharePrice stringValue]
            stringByReplacingOccurrencesOfString:@"$"
            withString:@""];
    double sharePrice = [sharePriceString doubleValue];
```

(continued)

Listing 6-4 *(continued)*

```objc
    BOOL result = [m_stockAccount purchaseShares:numberShares
            atPrice:sharePrice];
    if (NO == result)
    {
        NSAlert* alert = [[NSAlert alloc] init];
        [alert addButtonWithTitle:@"OK"];
        [alert setMessageText:@"You don't have enough cash to
            buy that many shares!"];
        [alert setAlertStyle:NSCriticalAlertStyle];
        [alert runModal];
        [alert release];
    }
    [self updateDisplay];
}

- (IBAction)sellShares:(id)sender
{
    NSUInteger numberShares = [[m_sharesToTrade stringValue]
            intValue];
    NSString* sharePriceString = [[m_sharePrice stringValue]
            stringByReplacingOccurrencesOfString:@"$"
            withString:@""];
    double sharePrice = [sharePriceString doubleValue];
    BOOL result = [m_stockAccount sellShares:numberShares
            atPrice:sharePrice];
    if (NO == result)
    {
        NSAlert* alert = [[NSAlert alloc] init];
        [alert addButtonWithTitle:@"OK"];
        [alert setMessageText:@"You don't have that many
            shares you can sell!"];
        [alert setAlertStyle:NSCriticalAlertStyle];
        [alert runModal];
        [alert release];
    }
    [self updateDisplay];
}

- (void)updateDisplay
{
    [m_sharePrice setStringValue:@"$10.00"];
    double cash = [m_stockAccount getCash];
    NSUInteger shares = [m_stockAccount getShares];
    NSUInteger transactions = [m_stockAccount
            getNumberTransactions];
    double portfolioValue = 10.0 * (double)shares;
    [m_cash setStringValue:[NSString
            stringWithFormat:@"$%.2f", cash]];
```

```
    [m_shares setStringValue:[NSString
          stringWithFormat:@"%d", shares]];
    [m_portfolioValue setStringValue:[NSString
          stringWithFormat:@"$%.2f", portfolioValue]];
    [m_totalTransactions setStringValue:[NSString
          stringWithFormat:@"%d", transactions]];
}

@end
```

You need to perform one more sequence of steps before the app is all connected — you have to connect the application delegate class `Stock MarketerAppDelegate` to the `StockAccountController` to ensure it updates its UI components right before the app displays its window. To do this, follow these steps:

1. **Select** `StockMarketerAppDelegate.h` **in the Project navigator.**

2. **Add the** purple **code from Listing 6-5 into** `StockMarketerAppDelegate.h`.

   You're adding a reference to the `StockAccountController` object so that the `StockMarketerAppDelegate` object can access it.

3. **Select** `StockMarketerAppDelegate.m` **in the Project navigator.**

4. **Add the** purple **code from Listing 6-6 into** `StockMarketerAppDelegate.m`.

5. **Build and run your StockMarketer app.**

   You can now trade shares of stock, and the total number of shares your account will increase or decrease to reflect each purchase and sale. Your cash reserves will rise and fall, and the current stock price will be randomly adjusted with each transaction.

Listing 6-5: The StockMarketerAppDelegate.h file's contents

```
//   StockMarketerAppDelegate.h
//   StockMarketer
//
//   Created by Karl Kowalski on 4/24/11.
//   Copyright 2011 Kowalski Software Enterprises.
//   All rights reserved.
//

#import <Cocoa/Cocoa.h>
```

(continued)

Listing 6-5 *(continued)*

```
#import "StockAccountController.h"

@interface StockMarketerAppDelegate : NSObject
        <NSApplicationDelegate>
{
    IBOutlet StockAccountController* m_controller;
@private
    NSWindow *window;
}

@property (assign) IBOutlet NSWindow *window;

@end
```

Listing 6-6:   The source code for the app delegate

```
//
//  StockMarketerAppDelegate.m
//  StockMarketer
//
//  Created by Karl Kowalski on 4/24/11.
//  Copyright 2011 Kowalski Software Enterprises.
//  All rights reserved.
//

#import "StockMarketerAppDelegate.h"

@implementation StockMarketerAppDelegate

@synthesize window;

- (void)applicationDidFinishLaunching:(NSNotification *)
        aNotification
{
    // Insert code here to initialize your application
    [m_controller updateDisplay];
}

@end
```

You've now implemented an MVC pattern within a Cocoa app. The Model keeps track of the amount of cash available for transactions and the total number of shares, as well as the number of transactions; the View provides a display of the information contained within the Model and the UI components for a user to make changes; and the Controller sits between these two pieces of the app. You could add more features to the Model — for instance, you might want to keep track of each individual transaction and store the set in an NSArray. The beauty of using the MVC design pattern is that you can use the same View and Controller with an updated Model and provide a separate View and Controller to make use of the additional features of the updated Model.

Adding a Preferences Window

Many of the apps you use provide a way for you to modify aspects of the apps' behaviors to suit your preferred style. Xcode comes with its own preferences panel, which you can display by selecting Xcode⇨Preferences from the menu bar. Figure 6-8 shows what the Xcode 4 Preferences Panel looks like.

Figure 6-8: Xcode's font preferences, where you can express your choice of text display.

Your app can display its own Preferences Panel, if you want to give your users a way to customize the presentation of information your app manages. For example, you could provide your users with a means to set the fonts your app uses to display text information to a size that makes the data easier to see — this is especially helpful for those of us who are getting on in years. It's much easier for me to increase the size of the displayed text than it is for me to remember where my glasses are.

You're going to add a very simple preferences panel to the StockMarketer app. There will be only one preference the user can set: the color of the amount shown for the Portfolio Value label.

1. **Select the StockMarketer folder in Project navigator and choose File⇨New ⇨New File from the menu bar.**

2. **Create a subclass of** `NSWindowController`, **and name it** `PreferencesController`.

3. **Select** `PreferencesController.h` **in Project navigator and modify its contents to include the** purple **code shown in Listing 6-7.**

4. **Save your changes.**

Listing 6-7:   A PreferencesController object manages an NSColorWell

```
//
//   PreferencesController.h
//   StockMarketer
//
//   Created by Karl Kowalski on 4/24/11.
//   Copyright 2011 Kowalski Software Enterprises.
//   All rights reserved.
//

#import <Cocoa/Cocoa.h>


@interface PreferencesController : NSWindowController
            <NSWindowDelegate>
{
    IBOutlet NSColorWell* m_textColor;
@private

}

- (NSColor*)getTextColor;

@end
```

5. **Select** `PreferencesController.m` **in Project navigator and modify its contents to include the** purple **code shown in Listing 6-8.**

The `PreferencesController` class does only as much as it needs to do.

6. **Save your changes.**

Listing 6-8:   The implementation of the PreferencesController is very simple

```
//
//   PreferencesController.m
//   StockMarketer
//
//   Created by Karl Kowalski on 4/24/11.
//   Copyright 2011 Kowalski Software Enterprises.
//   All rights reserved.
//

#import "PreferencesController.h"


@implementation PreferencesController

- (id)init
{
    if (nil == [super initWithWindowNibName:@"Preferences"])
    {
        return (nil);
    }
    return (self);
}

- (id)initWithWindow:(NSWindow *)window
{
    self = [super initWithWindow:window];
    if (self) {
        // Initialization code here.
    }

    return self;
}

- (void)dealloc
{
    [super dealloc];
}

- (void)windowDidLoad
{
    [super windowDidLoad];

    // Implement this method to handle any initialization
    // after your window controller's window has been
    // loaded from its nib file
    if (nil != [self window])
    {
```

(continued)

Listing 6-8 *(continued)*

```
        // set us to get notified when the window closes
        [[self window] setDelegate:self];
    }
}

-   (NSColor*)getTextColor
{
    NSColor* textColor = [m_textColor color];
    return (textColor);
}

@end
```

Your app now contains a `PreferencesController` class that will manage the contents and display of a Preferences Panel. The next step is to add the XIB file that the `PreferencesController` is going to load.

1. **Choose File ➪New ➪ New File from the menu bar. Choose the User Interface item from the left column and the Window template, as shown in Figure 6-9. Click the Next button.**

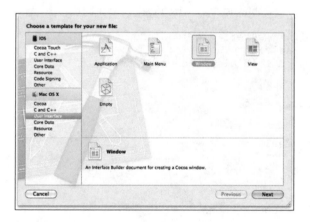

Figure 6-9: Creating a new XIB component for the project.

2. **Save the file as** `Preferences.xib`**.**

   Xcode will create a new XIB file and add it to your project. The `Preferences.xib` file will be shown in Interface Builder, with a window already added to the Dock. The name of this file is very important, as this is the filename that Cocoa will be asked to load when your `PreferencesController` is created within your app.

3. **Show the Utilities view if necessary. Select the** `File's Owner` **object from the Dock and then open the Identity inspector. Set the object's class to** `PreferencesController`.

   The `File's Owner` object is a reference to the object for which the XIB file was loaded. Your app's `App Delegate` class will create and maintain that object.

4. **Drag an** `NSColorWell` **from the Object Library into the window in** `Preferences.xib`.

   I also added a Label to mine so I'll remember what the color change is going to affect.

5. **Select the window and open the Attributes inspector. Change the window's title to Preferences.**

6. **Control-drag from the File's Owner to the** `NSColorWell`.

   Since you set the File's Owner object to be a `PreferencesController` class, there should be one Outlet for you to connect.

7. **Control-drag the File's Owner to the window.**

   The `PreferencesController` has an `IBOutlet` named window, and you have to connect this to the window object in the XIB file.

8. **Save your changes.**

9. **Select** `StockMarketerAppDelegate.h` **in the Project navigator and modify its contents to match the code found in Listing 6-9.**

   You're adding a `PreferencesController` as an `IBOutlet` member variable. The new lines are in purple.

10. **Save your changes.**

Listing 6-9: The App Delegate class for your project will maintain a reference to a PreferencesController

```
//
//   StockMarketerAppDelegate.h
//   StockMarketer
//
//   Created by Karl Kowalski on 4/24/11.
//   Copyright 2011 Kowalski Software Enterprises.
//   All rights reserved.
//
```

(continued)

Listing 6-9 *(continued)*

```
#import <Cocoa/Cocoa.h>

#import "StockAccountController.h"
#import "PreferencesController.h"

@interface StockMarketerAppDelegate : NSObject
            <NSApplicationDelegate>
{
    IBOutlet StockAccountController* m_controller;
    IBOutlet PreferencesController* m_prefsController;
@private
    NSWindow *window;
}

@property (assign) IBOutlet NSWindow *window;

- (IBAction)showPreferences:(id)inSender;

@end
```

11. **Select** `StockMarketerAppDelegate.m` **in the Project navigator and modify its contents to match the code found in Listing 6-10.**

    You're implementing the code to create the `PreferencesController` and display it when needed. The original version of `StockMarketer` `AppDelegate.m` did not include a `dealloc` method, so you're adding one now to clean up the `PreferencesController` the app delegate now creates within the `showPreferences:` method. As usual, the new lines are in purple.

12. **Save your changes.**

Listing 6-10:   The implementation of the showPreferences: method to display the Preferences window

```
//
//  StockMarketerAppDelegate.m
//  StockMarketer
//
//  Created by Karl Kowalski on 4/24/11.
//  Copyright 2011 Kowalski Software Enterprises.
//  All rights reserved.
//
```

```
#import "StockMarketerAppDelegate.h"

@implementation StockMarketerAppDelegate

@synthesize window;

- (void)applicationDidFinishLaunching:(NSNotification *)
        aNotification
{
    [m_controller updateDisplay];
}

- (IBAction)showPreferences:(id)inSender
{
    if (nil == m_prefsController)
    {
        m_prefsController = [[PreferencesController alloc]
            init];
    }
    [[m_prefsController window] makeKeyAndOrderFront:self];
}

- (void)dealloc
{
    [m_prefsController release];
    [super dealloc];
}

@end
```

13. **Select** MainMenu.xib **in the Project navigator.**

14. **Click the StockMarketer menu to reveal all the menu items. Control-drag from the Preferences menu item to the App Delegate object in the Dock and connect it with the** showPreferences: IBAction.

15. **Save your changes.**

    Now when you select the Preferences menu item while the app is running, the Preferences window will appear.

16. **Build and run your app.**

    When you select StockMarketer⇨Preferences, you should see the display similar to that in Figure 6-10.

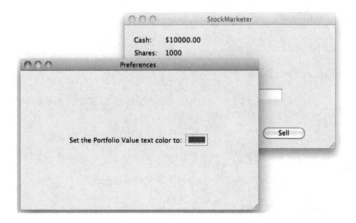

Figure 6-10: A Preferences window is displayed when you select
StockMarketer➪Preferences.

The last piece to this process is to change the color of the text label when
the preferences window has closed. In `PreferencesController.m`, the
`windowDidLoad` method set the `PreferencesController` as its window's
delegate. Cocoa will now notify the `PreferencesController` when its
window has been closed, so that the `PreferencesController` can tell the
appropriate Label in the `StockAccountController` to change its color.
To do this, you're going to implement *notifications* in the `StockMarketer`
project.

Using notifications

You've already implemented some notifications in StockMarketer: the
`PreferencesController`, as a result of being set as the delegate of its
window, has been set up to receive notifications from the window when certain events occur. When the user closes the `PreferencesController`'s
window, Cocoa will transmit an `NSNotification` which will be picked up
by the `PreferencesController` in its `windowWillClose:` method. You'll
create this method and implement code to broadcast a notification out to any
other object that's listening for it.

1. **Add the following code to** `PreferencesController.m`:

```
- (void)windowWillClose:(NSNotification*)inNotification
{
    [[NSNotificationCenter defaultCenter] postNotificationName:@"changePort
        folioColor" object:[self getTextColor]];
}
```

2. Build your app to ensure the code change compiles with no errors.

Now when the Preferences window is closed, the `Preferences Controller` will post a notification. Nobody's listening yet, but you'll change that next.

3. Select `StockAccountController.h` **in the Project navigator. Add the following two lines of code at the end of the file, before the line containing** `@end`**:**

```
- (void)setPortfolioLabelColor:(NSColor*)inColor;
- (void)handleColorNotification:(NSNotification*)inNotification;
```

4. Save your changes.

5. Select `StockAccountController.m` **in the Project navigator and add the implementation of the** `setCashLabelColor:` **and** `handleColor Notification:` **methods from the following code:**

```
- (void)setPortfolioLabelColor:(NSColor*)inColor
{
    if (nil != inColor)
    {
        [m_portfolioValue setTextColor:inColor];
        [m_ portfolioValue setNeedsDisplay:YES];
    }
}

- (void)handleColorNotification:(NSNotification*)inNotification
{
    [self setPortfolioLabelColor:[inNotification object]];
}
```

6. Add the following line to the `init` **method, immediately following the line that initializes the** `m_stockAccount` **member variable:**

```
[[NSNotificationCenter defaultCenter] addObserver:self selector:@
    selector(handleColorNotification:) name:@"changePortfolioColor"
    object:nil];
```

7. Build and run the app.

You see the main window; after selecting StockMarketer⇨Preferences, you see the Preferences window appear. When you select a color and close the Preferences window, the color of the "Portfolio Value" label changes, as shown in Figure 6-11.

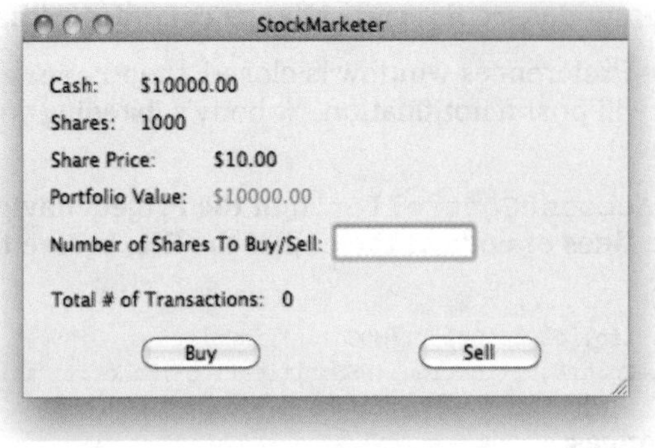

Figure 6-11: A colorized Portfolio Value label.

Notifications provide a helpful way of communicating within your app, especially between a Model and its Controller, and a Controller and its View. You can set up any object to listen for any notification of a particular name, coming from a particular object or — as in the example — from any object in the application. You can even set up to listen for any notification, period — but this will cause your object's notification handler to get called for every notification, and there are a lot of them.

TIP Keep in mind that the delegate methods sometimes are implemented as responses to notification broadcasts. It's better to narrow the focus of your notification recipients to specific messages or to messages coming from a specific object.

Chapter 7

Drawing Advanced Views

. . . .

. . . .

The Xcode Interface Builder Editor's palette of UI components provides you with the tools you need to create a great many different types of apps. The standard Apple components give you a large collection of buttons, sliders, and views to choose from so you can offer your users the best way to interact with your app — whether your app takes information from your users or delivers it to them. Using just the standard components, you can make quality applications that users enjoy using. But why stop there? You can modify the appearance of many of the components to make them look new and unique while still retaining the same functionality.

Often, however, you'll discover that the standard components just aren't enough. That's when you'll need to start rolling your own, custom-designed components. You won't be just adding a new look to old tools, you'll be creating new ones that your app uses to express information in ways that the standard Apple components don't. Custom components and views can add life to your apps and make them stand out from the rest, especially if your new components make your app more powerful or easier to use — which makes for a better user experience.

In this chapter, I show you how to create your own custom views where your code takes complete control over how its contents are drawn. In addition, I cover some interesting and fun animations that your app can display for your user.

Okay, sometimes I slip up and use the word "widget" instead of "component". The two are interchangeable for the purposes of this chapter. I forget at what exact point the term *widget* came to mean "component used in a user interface" but it has stuck. Don't be surprised if you end up using it yourself.

Reviewing Apple's Component Collection

I'm going to list some of the standard Apple UI components as provided by the IB Editor in Xcode 4. Here's a list of the widgets you can place on an app's screen:

- Push Button
- Disclosure Triangle
- Help Button
- Round Button
- Label
- Text Field
- Secure Text Field
- Text Field with Number Formatter
- Combo Box
- Date Picker
- Wrapping Label
- Wrapping Text Field
- Text View
- Check Box
- Pop Up Button
- Segmented Control
- Radio Group
- Stepper
- Horizontal Slider
- Vertical Slider
- Circular Slider
- Circular Progress Indicator

✔ Table View

✔ Browser

✔ Custom View

✔ Tab View

✔ Box

✔ Web View

✔ QuickTime Movie View

✔ PDF View

Quite a list — and you can make quite a range of different apps using just these ordinary widgets. However, the more apps you make, the sooner you discover that you have to create a few types of views yourself. The basic widgets don't provide (for example) the following:

✔ **Graphing View:** For my DiabeticPad app, it would be useful to display a graph of the sugar levels against time. Apple's components don't come with a view that can take two sets of numeric values and graph one against the other. So I've had to create my own.

✔ **Movie View:** Apple provides a QuickTime Movie View as part of its standard set, but what about other types of video formats? If your app is going to display videos of a format that QuickTime doesn't support, you'll have to devise your own view to display it.

✔ **Non-uniform Geometric Shapes:** The easiest object to draw on the screen is a rectangle, followed closely by a circle. But a jigsaw-puzzle app that uses rectangular puzzle pieces would be too easy to solve. You'd need to create arbitrary geometric shapes for the user to fit together into the puzzle picture — and you'd have to create each shape as a custom view in your app.

Understanding Cocoa's Views

Before I show you how to create your own custom view for your app, here's a rundown of the important details of how Cocoa views work in a Macintosh application. In Figure 7-1, you can see a window containing several of the basic UI widgets; see the same widgets listed in Cocoa's view hierarchy.

With the exception of an NSWindow, all items displayed on-screen are subclasses of the NSView class.

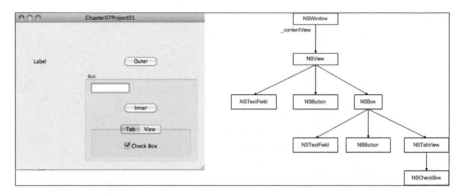

Figure 7-1: A window containing subviews representing the Cocoa View hierarchy.

- ✔ The top level of the hierarchy: the NSWindow. An NSWindow is not itself a view object, as it's not a subclass of NSView. However, the NSWindow is at the top of the view hierarchy because it is the topmost container of all the other views in your app.

- ✔ The NSWindow's _contentView member variable. This is a private member variable of type id, and is used to maintain a reference to an NSView object that will contain the UI components placed in the window.

- ✔ The NSButton "Outer" and the NSTextField "Label" and the NSBox "Box". These items are all subviews of the _contentView of the NSWindow.

- ✔ The empty NSTextField, the NSButton "Inner", and the NSTabView are all subviews of the NSBox.

- ✔ The NSCheckBox is the only subview of the NSTabView.

Each of the UI components in the Apple palette is a subclass of NSView. This means two things:

- ✔ Each NSView component can be a subview of an NSView.

- ✔ An NSView can itself contain NSView objects as subviews. Certain subclasses such as NSControl or any of its subclasses of NSView prevent this behavior.

A view that contains subviews is called the *parent* view of the *child* subviews it contains. So in Figure 7-1 you will see that the NSBox is the parent view of the NSTabView, which is itself the parent of the NSCheckBox. In addition, the NSBox is a child view of the _contentView. You could call the _contentView the "grandparent" of the NSTabView but I think that's taking the metaphor a little too far.

Your custom view classes will inherit basic functionality from NSView —
including the following:

- **A method to draw itself:** drawRect:. The Cocoa framework calls this
  method when the app needs to redraw the contents of your view. You'll
  see this happen when your app with your custom view is "uncovered" —
  that is, when another window placed on top of your view is moved away.
  You can also trigger a redraw event programmatically by executing
  [myCustomView setNeedsDisplay:YES];.

- **Resizing according to the settings in the Interface Builder Editor Size
  inspector.** Your custom view subclass will take care of drawing its contents, but you can set how the view will resize by using the Size inspector. That's because your view is just an NSView at heart, and you won't
  need to adjust any of that code.

- **Subview management.** If your custom view subclasses NSView you'll
  get all the subview-management functionality for free. Adding and
  removing subviews, drawing subviews — all of this is handled for you
  automatically.

Nearly all of what you do in your custom NSView subclasses takes place in
the drawRect: method. So now is a good time to nail down the basics of
drawing things on a screen.

Drawing on the screen

Your Macintosh display is a big rectangle, filled with tiny dots called *pixels*.
On modern screens such as my main development iMac, you'll find millions
of pixels, ready to do your bidding as you command them to display the
colors you want your app to show. When your app is drawing on the screen,
your app is telling the OS to tell the graphics hardware to set the colors of
various pixels. Your app is not setting the colors directly; instead, it's providing instructions to the graphics hardware. But to ensure that those instructions aren't gibberish, here's a short course in how to speak *Graphics*.

Mac OS X uses a graphics engine called *Quartz*, which provides the classes
and methods your app will use to draw on Mac monitors.

The first thing to keep in mind about Quartz and Macintosh drawing is: *The
coordinate system of a Mac display has its origin in the bottom-left corner of
the screen, with the x-axis increasing to the right, and the y-axis increasing
upward.*

If you've programmed on other platforms, or with Macs prior to OS X, you
may be used to having the display coordinate system's origin in the top-
left corner, with the y-axis increasing as you go down. Personally, I find

Quartz's coordinate system easy to use and *very* easy to think with, probably because it's how I learned geometry and coordinate systems in 10th grade. (It did take a while to stop thinking in terms of the earlier Mac coordinate system.)

Points

Quartz provides the `NSPoint` structure for you to use when you're working with points in the coordinate system. The following is how Quartz defines an `NSPoint`:

```
struct CGPoint
{
  CGFloat x;
  CGFloat y;
};

typedef CGPoint NSPoint;
```

As you can see, an `NSPoint` is not an Objective-C class, it's just a plain C-type struct. So you don't have to `alloc` or `init` it, and you don't have to `release` it when you're finished. You must declare it just as you would any other variable or structure in your code:

```
NSPoint myCoordinate;
```

The `CGFloat` variable type is one of the primitive C types: if you're creating a 64-bit app, Xcode defines this variable type as a `double`; otherwise it's defined as a `float`. For this chapter I'll assume you're writing 64-bit apps; you won't see any difference in behavior for the examples I present.

If you're going to be writing an app that depends on highly precise graphs, say for 3-D modeling, you'll want to ensure that your app is 64-bit in order to get the precision of a `double` value used for graphic calculations with `NSPoints`.

You can assign values to an `NSPoint` in your code in two ways:

```
NSPoint aSetPoint;
aSetPoint.x = 100.0;
aSetPoint.y = 200.0;
NSPoint aMadePoint = NSMakePoint( 100.0, 200.0 );
```

Although they're not required, I highly recommend adding the decimal-point values to the end of any constant numbers you use. I'm pretty sure that the Xcode compiler will automatically convert numbers without decimal points to double values correctly — but keep in mind that the numbers my code is dealing with are not integers (as they would have been in the pre-OS X coordinate system).

Rectangles

Now you move into two-dimensional space. Rectangles are used everywhere in drawing things on the Mac screen. So Quartz provides another structure, NSRect, to carry rectangle information around in a convenient package. Not surprisingly, the NSRect structure contains an NSPoint as one of its components.

Since a rectangle is 2-dimensional, an NSRect has a second component, an NSSize structure:

```
struct
{
  CGFloat width;
  CGFloat height;
} CGSize;

typedef CGSize NSSize;

struct CGRect
{
  CGPoint origin;
  CGSize size;
};

typedef CGRect NSRect;
```

And once more, there are two ways to fill an NSRect with values:

```
NSRect aFixedRect;
aFixedRect.origin.x = 100.0;
aFixedRect.origin.y = 200.0;
aFixedRect.size.width = 125.0;
aFixedRect.size.height = 256.0;

NSRect aMadeRect = NSMakeRect( 100.0, 200.0, 125.0, 256.0 );
```

You can find the origin and size of an NSRect by treating it just like a C-type struct:

```
CGFloat rectOriginX = aRect.origin.x;
CGFloat rectOriginY = aRect.origin.y;
CGFloat rectWidth = aRect.size.width;
CGFloat rectHeight = aRect.size.height;
```

You'll get used to NSRects and NSPoints pretty quickly as you write more custom views — or if you decide to put together views on the fly, instead of setting them up with the Interface Builder Editor in an XIB file.

Colors

The last basic topic you'll need to learn before I show you how to draw is the care and feeding of colors. Quartz provides you with the NSColor class — no more structs! — to give you an easy way to use colors within your app.

There are two different approaches you can use to create and work with colors in your app: convenience colors and . . . inconvenience. (Just kidding — the other approach is device-dependent. Read on.)

Using convenience colors

You'll find that the quickest and easiest way to create an NSColor object is by using one of the preset colors that come as class methods in the NSColor class. For instance, if you wanted a bright red color, you can write code like this:

```
NSColor* myRedColor = [NSColor redColor];
```

And you'll find that there are many other basic colors, as shown in Table 7-1.

Table 7-1	Convenience Colors
Preset NSColor Name	**Color on the screen**
blackColor	Black
blueColor	Blue
brownColor	Brown
clearColor	Clear/transparent
cyanColor	Light blue
darkGrayColor	Dark gray
grayColor	Medium gray
greenColor	Green
lightGrayColor	Light gray
magentaColor	Pinkish-purple color
orangeColor	Orange
purpleColor	Purple
redColor	Red
whiteColor	White
yellowColor	Yellow

If you look through `NSColor.h`, the header file that describes the Objective-C class `NSColor`, you'll discover even more convenience colors that Cocoa uses for UI components such as a window's frame or a table view's header.

Using device-dependent colors

If your app wants full control over the colors that it will display, you'll find that the convenience colors just aren't enough. In this case, your app will have to create its own colors more explicitly instead of depending on what Cocoa has pre-built.

The `NSColor` class comes with three different ways to create your own colors:

- ✔ **Device-dependent (device) color:** This approach depends on the colors a particular device can display. A *device color* represents the best color that a specific monitor will show. This means the color may not be the same on a MacBook as it is on an iMac or on a third-party monitor. Put two different monitors next to each other, showing the same colored image, and you'll notice that they aren't showing colors exactly the same way.

  I'm writing this chapter using two monitors on a Windows machine next to my development iMac, and all three monitors show the same color differently.

- ✔ **Device-independent (calibrated) color:** For certain graphics professions, the computer hardware and printer manufacturers created hardware and software systems to calibrate their equipment so that their users would see same color displayed, to the greatest degree possible, no matter which type of device was used. Graphics professionals want to be sure that the concert poster they designed on their high-resolution iMac is printed with the precise colors they chose. The calibration is responsible for adjusting the displayed color on different devices to account for the differences in the hardware.

- ✔ **Named color:** The use of named colors is beyond the scope of this book.

You'll be using the device-dependent approach to creating specific colors in your apps. And you'll find it pretty easy to do:

```
NSColor* redColor = [NSColor colorWithDeviceRed:1.0 green:0.0
        blue:0.0 alpha:1.0];
NSColor* greenColor = [NSColor colorWithDeviceRed:0.0
        green:1.0 blue:0.0 alpha:1.0];
NSColor* purpleColor = [NSColor colorWithDeviceRed:1.0
        green:0.0 blue:1.0 alpha:1.0];
```

Just in case you haven't been exposed to colors from a programming perspective, I'll go over the basic ideas involved in the code just given. For device-dependent colors, each color you want to create is built from four separate values:

- ✔ Red
- ✔ Green
- ✔ Blue
- ✔ Alpha

This set of four values is sometimes called an *RGB value*. Sometimes you'll see it in print as an *RGBA value*, but both terms are equivalent.

You probably already know that red, green, and blue are the primary colors of visible light, and that combinations of each of these can generate all of the colors of the spectrum including white (all 1.0's) and black (all 0.0's). The alpha value represents *transparency*. Setting this value to 1.0 means that the color is 100% opaque. Setting this value to 0.0 means that the color is 100% transparent — and instead, the color of whatever is visually behind the item being drawn is shown. With an alpha value somewhere between 0.0 and 1.0, the color being drawn will be fainter than fully opaque.

In some apps (and online) you'll see RGBA values listed as a set of integers, each one ranging from 0 to 255. Cocoa uses floating-point values between 0.0 and 1.0, so you have to convert any color value you see listed as (127, 63, 159, 255) to (0.50, 0.25, 0.625, 1.0). One easy way to convert each integer value to floating-point is to add 1 to the value and then divide by 256. So the values just given would change as follows:

```
127 + 1 = 128/256 = 0.50
63 + 1 = 64/256 = 0.25
159 + 1 = 160/256 = 0.625
255 + 1 = 256/256 = 1.0
```

There's a minor problem with this handy numerical technique, however — 0 should translate to 0.0 — but in this example, it translates to 0.00390625. The simplest solution would be to treat zero as a special case, and avoid the math. (Whew. Close one.)

Finally, in Cocoa, you use colors in your custom drawings by setting the color of the graphics pen when your app is executing its `drawRect:` method. A *graphics pen* is the code-activated tool that Cocoa uses to draw within `NSViews`. The pen has certain attributes you can manipulate, such as its color or the width in pixels of the lines it draws. To change the color of the graphics pen to the color purple in the code snippet just given, here's all you have to do:

```
[purpleColor set];
```

After your app executes this line of code, everything that gets drawn will be in purple. In the examples that follow you'll get a better idea of how your app can make color displays within your code.

Creating a Custom View

I'm going to walk you through the steps needed to set up a custom view so you can learn how to create your own app-specific views. You're going to create a simple project that consists of one view that will function as a workbench for the different drawing you'll do.

1. **Launch Xcode and choose File⇨New⇨Project, as shown in Figure 7-2.**

   You won't need a Document-Based Application or Core Data, and you definitely don't need Unit Tests. Be sure to save the project in an appropriate location.

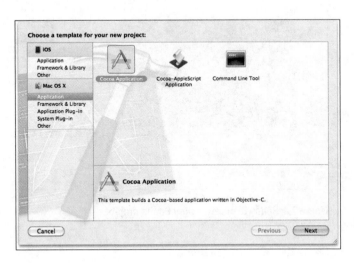

Figure 7-2: Ready to create a new Cocoa project.

2. **Select** `MainMenu.xib` **from the Project navigator to open the file with the Interface Builder Editor.**

3. **Select the Window object in the Interface Builder Editor Dock.**

4. **Show the Utilities view.**

   You can use this view to work with the object palette.

5. **Drag a Custom View from the object palette and drop it onto the window.**

   You may want to resize it so it takes up more space to make the drawings within the custom view more obvious. I chose to obey Apple's blue guidelines at all four sides, leaving a margin of space around the view.

6. **With the Custom View object still selected, show the Size inspector.**

7. **Set the Autosizing options so that all the sizing red bars are lit.**

   Doing so locks the position of the Custom View object in the window and resizes it when the window is resized. Figure 7-3 shows what this should look like.

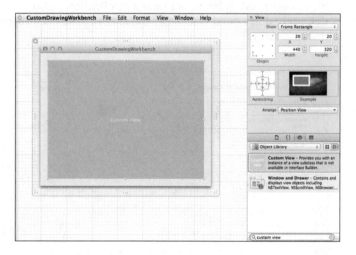

Figure 7-3: Ready to create a new Cocoa project.

8. **Show the Identity inspector.**

9. **Set the Custom Class to** `WorkbenchView` **by typing it into the combo-box.**

You will create this class next.

10. **Right-click the folder containing your project's code modules, and select New File.**

11. **Create a new class,** WorkbenchView, **and make it a subclass of** NSView.

12. **Save your changes.**

You now have a custom view, named WorkbenchView, which gets created when your app is launched and displays its main window.

If you build and run your app now, you won't see it — because right now it doesn't do any drawing. Xcode did add the drawRect: method to your class, in anticipation of how you're going to make use of the WorkbenchView — Xcode presumes that as a subclass of NSView, drawing is going to happen. This class will serve as the scratch pad for the different kinds of graphics drawing you do as you go through this chapter.

Drawing

Your custom view doesn't do any drawing yet, so let's change that. When I'm putting together a custom view, I usually like to know where the edges of the view are. I find it useful to draw a rectangle at the edge of the view, so that

- ✓ I can see where the application is placing my view.

- ✓ I know when something I've drawn has been drawn correctly, fully within the view.

Each NSView subclass has a specific rectangle of space, within which any drawing it does will occur. Sometimes your app will make calculations about where it should draw next, and sometimes those calculations will tell Cocoa to draw outside the rectangle — even though your calculations should have made it draw only *within* the rectangle. When I added the custom WorkbenchView to my project's window, I didn't resize it to fill the entire window.

So now let's draw a rectangle to show where the edges are.

1. **Select** WorkbenchView **in the Project navigator.**

2. **Enter the code from Listing 7-1 into the** drawRect: **method.**

3. **Save your changes.**

4. Build and run your app.

You should see the result shown in Figure 7-4. If you resize your window, you'll see that the border resizes just as the window does, keeping the margin constant.

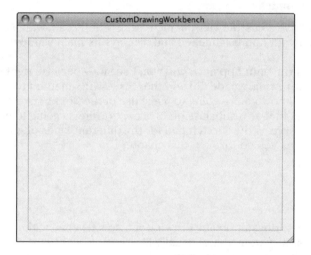

Figure 7-4: The edges of your custom NSView on display.

The code you just implemented consists of two lines, which do the following:

- The code sets an NSColor convenience color, red, to be used for drawing.

- An NSBezierPath object is told to draw the incoming NSRect by executing a method called strokeRect:. The dirtyRect input parameter is the rectangle within which Cocoa wants your custom view to draw. For the WorkbenchView, this parameter contains the size and origin of the bounds of the WorkbenchView.

When your custom view's drawRect: method is invoked, it's because Cocoa has been told that some part of the custom view's rectangle requires redrawing. This can happen because your code called the setNeeds Display: method on you custom view object with an input value of YES. Another way to invoke this method is to remove some other view from in front of your custom view, revealing the contents of your view — and possibly requiring them to be redrawn. For instance, if your custom view is drawing a sequence of colors on a schedule, it will have to redraw the current color if you open a mail message using Apple Mail and then close it after you respond to the message. The `drawRect:` method (see Listing 7-1) handles all the situations when Cocoa needs your app to draw the contents of a custom view.

Listing 7-1:   Creating a red border around your custom view

```
- (void)drawRect:(NSRect)dirtyRect
{
    // Drawing code here.
    [[NSColor redColor] set];
    [NSBezierPath strokeRect:dirtyRect];
}
```

Drawing with Beziér paths

To get a handle on paths, just draw on your extensive knowledge of playing connect-the-dots. A *path* is simply a collection of points that represent a line, or a series of connected lines. If the connected lines end up back at the starting point, the path is a now a shape. Cocoa gives you the `NSBezierPath` class to do all the drawing in your app.

Okay, I lied a little bit: The `NSBezierPath` class isn't the *only* way to do drawing in your app. You can also use the OpenGL library, but that's better suited for drawing and manipulating 3-D shapes. Sorry I didn't mention that, but *most* of your drawing will be done using `NSBezierPath`. It's a better tool for this particular job.

The `NSBezierPath` class comes with several class methods you can use directly to draw shapes on the user's display within your custom view:

- `fillRect:(NSRect)`. For a given `NSRect`, draw the rectangle filled with the current color.

- `strokeRect:(NSRect)`. For a given `NSRect`, draw the rectangle outline with the current color.

- `strokeLineFromPoint:(NSPoint) toPoint:(NSPoint)`. Draw a line from the first point to the second with the current color.

In addition to these methods, you can use the following `NSBezierPath` convenience methods to create an `NSBezierPath` object of a particular type:

- `bezierPathWithRect:(NSRect)`. This method gives you an `NSBezierPath` object that is initialized for drawing or filling the rectangle you pass in as an input parameter.

- `bezierPathWithOvalInRect:(NSRect)`. This method gives you an `NSBezierPath` object that is initialized for drawing or filling an ellipse within the rectangle you pass into it.

- `bezierPathWithRoundedRect:(NSRect) xRadius:(CGFloat) yRadius:(CGFloat)`. You can create an `NSBezierPath` object that is initialized for drawing or filling a rectangle that has rounded corners (such as some standard buttons you see in Xcode). You have to provide the vertical (`yRadius`) and horizontal (`xRadius`) distances for the rounded corners.

In order to make the returned `NSBezierPath` object actually draw these rectangles or the oval on the display, you must use one of the following methods on the object:

- `stroke`. This will cause the `NSBezierPath` object to draw outline of the oval or rectangle using the current graphics pen color and width.

- `fill`. This method will cause the `NSBezierPath` object to fill in the entire oval or rectangle using the current graphics pen color.

You can use the methods I've shown here to create simple rectangles and ovals and draw them on the display. Here's an example that creates a blocky kind of vehicle in `WorkbenchView`. All the code is written within the `drawRect:` method; all you have to do is rewrite `drawRect:` using the code from Listing 7-2.

Listing 7-2:   Drawing my family car with Cocoa

```
- (void)drawRect:(NSRect)dirtyRect
{
    CGFloat rectWidth = dirtyRect.size.width;
    CGFloat rectHeight = dirtyRect.size.height;
    // use 60% of the width as our body width
    // use 20% of the height for the height of the body
    CGFloat carWidth = 0.60*rectWidth;
    CGFloat carHeight = 0.20*rectHeight;
    CGFloat carXPos = 0.20*rectWidth;
    CGFloat carYPos = 0.40*rectHeight;
```

```
NSRect bodyRect = NSMakeRect( carXPos, carYPos, carWidth,
     carHeight );
[[NSColor brownColor] set];
[[NSBezierPath bezierPathWithRoundedRect:bodyRect
     xRadius:5.0 yRadius:5.0] fill];
// now create the wheels for our car
// front wheel
CGFloat wheelDiameter = 0.50 * carYPos;
CGFloat frontWheelXOffset = 0.25*carWidth; // front axle
     pos
CGFloat frontWheelRectXPos = carXPos + frontWheelXOffset
     - 0.50 * wheelDiameter;
CGFloat frontWheelRectYPos = carYPos - wheelDiameter;
NSRect frontWheelRect = NSMakeRect( frontWheelRectXPos,
     frontWheelRectYPos, wheelDiameter, wheelDiameter
     );
// black tires
[[NSColor blackColor] set];
// draw outer part
[[NSBezierPath bezierPathWithOvalInRect:frontWheelRect]
     fill];
// draw inner part
[[NSColor whiteColor] set];
frontWheelRect.origin.x += 10.0;
frontWheelRect.origin.y += 10.0;
frontWheelRect.size.width -= 20.0;
frontWheelRect.size.height -= 20.0;
[[NSBezierPath bezierPathWithOvalInRect:frontWheelRect]
     fill];
// back wheel
CGFloat backWheelXOffset = 0.75*carWidth;
CGFloat backWheelRectXPos = carXPos + backWheelXOffset -
     0.50*wheelDiameter;
NSRect backWheelRect = NSMakeRect( backWheelRectXPos,
     frontWheelRectYPos, wheelDiameter, wheelDiameter);
[[NSColor blackColor] set];
// draw outer part
[[NSBezierPath bezierPathWithOvalInRect:backWheelRect]
     fill];
// draw inner part
[[NSColor whiteColor] set];
backWheelRect.origin.x += 10.0;
backWheelRect.origin.y += 10.0;
backWheelRect.size.width -= 20.0;
backWheelRect.size.height -= 20.0;
[[NSBezierPath bezierPathWithOvalInRect:backWheelRect]
     fill];
// now the top part
```

(continued)

Listing 7-2 *(continued)*

```
        CGFloat topRectXPos = carXPos + 0.45*carWidth;
        CGFloat topRectYPos = carYPos + carHeight;
        CGFloat topRectWidth = 0.45* carWidth;
        CGFloat topRectHeight = carHeight;
        NSRect carUpper = NSMakeRect( topRectXPos, topRectYPos,
              topRectWidth, topRectHeight );
        [[NSColor orangeColor] set];
        [NSBezierPath fillRect:carUpper];
        // windshield
        NSPoint windshieldBase;
        windshieldBase.x = topRectXPos - carHeight;
        windshieldBase.y = topRectYPos;
        NSPoint windshieldTop;
        windshieldTop.x = topRectXPos;
        windshieldTop.y = topRectYPos + topRectHeight;
        [NSBezierPath strokeLineFromPoint:windshieldBase
                toPoint:windshieldTop];
        // and the antenna
        NSPoint antennaBase;
        antennaBase.x = carXPos + 0.92*carWidth;
        antennaBase.y = topRectYPos;
        NSPoint antennaTop;
        antennaTop.x = carXPos + 1.04*carWidth;
        antennaTop.y = 0.95*rectHeight;
        [[NSColor darkGrayColor] set];
        [NSBezierPath strokeLineFromPoint:antennaBase
                toPoint:antennaTop];
        CGFloat knobXPos = antennaTop.x - 5.0;
        CGFloat knobYPos = antennaTop.y - 5.0;
        NSRect knobRect = NSMakeRect(knobXPos, knobYPos, 10.0,
                10.0);
        [[NSColor blackColor] set];
        [[NSBezierPath bezierPathWithOvalInRect:knobRect] fill];
}
```

Figure 7-5 shows you what the family car looks like when drawn using the
WorkbenchView.

The code in Listing 7-2 should seem pretty straightforward. Everything is nice
sharp lines and corners, with a couple of circles and the rounded-corner rectangle thrown in.

TIP

You could easily write a stick-figure game using just the code given here and some of the ideas from Chapter 9 on background operations.

Figure 7-5: Time for a ride!

You can also draw non-rectangular shapes (such as, say, a triangle, a pentagon, or any geometric shape drawn from connected lines). Listing 7-3 contains code to create an arbitrary shape, close it, and fill it with a light blue color. Figure 7-6 shows what the app draws on the user's screen.

Listing 7-3: A non-uniform two-dimensional shape drawn as a series of points

```
- (void)drawRect:(NSRect)dirtyRect
{
    CGFloat rectWidth = dirtyRect.size.width;
    CGFloat rectHeight = dirtyRect.size.height;
    [[NSColor cyanColor] set];
    NSPoint p00, p01, p02, p03, p04, p05, p06, p07, p08, p09,
            p10;
    p00.x = 0.10*rectWidth;
    p00.y = 0.50*rectHeight;
    p01.x = 0.25*rectWidth;
    p01.y = 0.40*rectHeight;
    p02.x = 0.30*rectWidth;
```

(continued)

Listing 7-3 *(continued)*

```
    p02.y = 0.48*rectHeight;
    p03.x = 0.45*rectWidth;
    p03.y = 0.31*rectHeight;
    p04.x = 0.75*rectWidth;
    p04.y = 0.45*rectHeight;
    p05.x = 0.55*rectWidth;
    p05.y = p04.y;
    p06.x = p05.x;
    p06.y = 0.70*rectHeight;
    p07.x = p04.x;
    p07.y = p06.y;
    p08.x = p03.x;
    p08.y = 0.90*rectHeight;
    p09.x = p02.x;
    p09.y = 0.65*rectHeight;
    p10.x = 0.20*rectWidth;
    p10.y = 0.70*rectHeight;
    NSBezierPath* objPath = [NSBezierPath bezierPath];
    [objPath moveToPoint:p00];
    [objPath lineToPoint:p01];
    [objPath lineToPoint:p02];
    [objPath lineToPoint:p03];
    [objPath lineToPoint:p04];
    [objPath lineToPoint:p05];
    [objPath lineToPoint:p06];
    [objPath lineToPoint:p07];
    [objPath lineToPoint:p08];
    [objPath lineToPoint:p09];
    [objPath lineToPoint:p10];
    [objPath closePath];
    [objPath fill];
}
```

Here's where math and art come together: If you can calculate points on a coordinate system, you can draw any object you can sketch. The NSView is your canvas, and your app can draw and color any kind of shape you need to display.

Drawing text

In addition to drawing lines, rectangles, and ovals, Cocoa provides you with the capability to display text in your views. You need only two items to draw text on the screen:

    ✔ An `NSString` object containing the text you want to draw.

    ✔ An `NSPoint` containing the location where you want the text drawn.

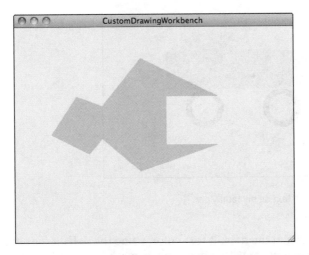

Figure 7-6: You can draw a path from one point to the next and create a solid object.

Use the following procedure to draw text on your custom view:

1. **Create an `NSString` object with the text you want to display.**

   I've decided to add some graffiti to my family car.

   ```
   NSString* graffitiString = @"Orange Rider";
   ```

2. **Choose the location where you want the text to be drawn and set an `NSPoint` with the x and y values:**

   ```
   NSPoint graffitiPoint;
   graffitiPoint.x = carXPos + 0.05*rectWidth;
   graffitiPoint.y = carYPos + 0.05*rectHeight;
   ```

3. **Draw the text using the `NSString drawAtPoint:withAttributes:` method:**

   ```
   [graffitiString drawAtPoint:graffitiPoint withAttributes:nil];
   ```

In Figure 7-7 shows you the result of these instructions, if you add them to the end of the code in Listing 7-2.

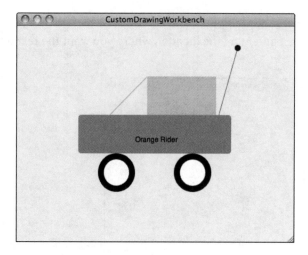

Figure 7-7: Drawing text on my family car.

The text is drawn in the default text color, using the default font. It looks like I wrote on my family car with a black magic marker. I want big letters, and colored bright white so the family car will stand out. To make this happen, you add some attributes to the text string when it draws. Fortunately, the `withAttributes:` parameter offers you the capability to do just that. The parameter that the method expects is an `NSDictionary`, so you'll need to create one and put the text attributes you want to see into it. You'll actually be creating an `NSMutableDictionary`, since you'll want to be changing its contents between the time you create it and the time you use it.

Here are the steps you follow:

1. **Create an** `NSMutableDictionary` **variable in the code.**

   I also `autorelease` it, so I don't have to remember to `release` it after I'm done.

   ```
   NSMutableDictionary* textAttrs = [[[NSMutableDictionary alloc] init]
           autorelease];
   ```

2. **Add an** `NSFont` **object to define what font to use:**

   ```
   [textAttrs setObject:[NSFont fontWithName:@"Helvetica" size:32]
           forKey:NSFontAttributeName];
   ```

3. **Add an** `NSColor` **object to define what color the text should be:**

   ```
   [textAttrs setObejct:[NSColor whiteColor] forKey:NSForegroundColor
           AttributeName];
   ```

4. **Set the** withAttributes: **parameter to be the** NSMutable
   Dictionary **you created:**

```
[graffitiString drawAtPoint:graffitiPoint withAttributes:textAttrs];
```

Now the car is nicely labeled, as you can see in Figure 7-8.

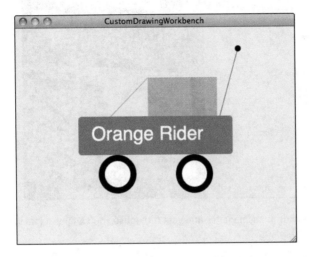

Figure 7-8: Now everyone in town will know when I'm riding around.

You can find more attribute types in the header file NSAttributedString.h.
You'll find this file in the Project navigator by opening the Frameworks folder
in your project, then opening Other Frameworks, and finally the AppKit.
framework and its Headers folder.

Drawing images

In addition to letting you draw shapes and lines, Cocoa gives you a class,
NSImage, which you can use to draw images on your views. NSImage
will read in image data from an image file within your project. You can
easily add an image file to your project simply by dragging the file from
the Finder into the Project navigator in Xcode. In Figure 7-9, you can see
the result of my doing this with a photo of another Dummies book, named
BlackBerryForDummies.JPG.

Figure 7-9: Drag and drop an image file into your project so you can pull it into your code.

When you want to draw this image in your custom view, you follow these steps:

1. **Create an** `NSImage` **using the image file:**

   ```
   NSImage* myImage = [NSImage imageNamed:@"BlackBerryForDummies.JPG"];
   ```

2. **Draw the image in the view by using the** `drawInRect:fromRect:ope ration:fraction:` **method:**

   ```
   [myImage drawInRect:dirtyRect fromRect:NSZeroRect
           operation:NSCompositeCopy fraction:1.0];
   ```

   The `drawInRect:fromRect:operation:fraction:` method operates like this:

   - The image will be drawn within the rectangle specified by the parameter passed as `drawInRect:`.

     This is the view's rectangle passed into the `drawRect:` method.

   - The `fromRect:` parameter specifies which part of the image's own rectangle to draw.

     By specifying this parameter as `NSZeroRect`, you're telling the graphics code to draw the entire image.

   - The `operation:` parameter indicates the type of drawing operation to use.

By choosing NSCompositeCopy, you are telling the graphics code to copy the image.

- The fraction: parameter specifies the amount of transparency to use, with 1.0 being fully opaque and 0.0 fully transparent. Figure 7-10 shows a half-transparent image, midway between those values.

Figure 7-10: A half-opaque image of my previous Dummies book.

You can now display images in your apps, anywhere you can draw them.

Animating Views

Now comes the fun part. Everything you've done so far has been pretty static, drawing lines and shapes and text and images. It's time to add some motion. The Cocoa framework includes features that give you the opportunity to provide your displays with animation. This package of features is called *Core Animation*, similar in its scope to the Core Data part of Cocoa. You can use it to implement very simple animations such as motions across your views, or even more complicated transitions. I'm going to show you the simplest of these, just to introduce the basic concept. (Reader, meet concept. Concept, meet reader.) Here are the steps:

1. **Create a new Project using Xcode.**

   As in the previous examples, you only need a basic project with no Core Data.

2. **Add a new File to the project.**

   This will be an `NSView` subclass named `AnimationView`.

3. **Select the** `MainMenu.xib` **file from the Project navigator.**

4. **Add one Custom View to the window.**

   I recommend enlarging the view as large as you prefer.

5. **Using the Size inspector, set all the Autosizing options to on.**

6. **Using the Identity inspector, set the Class to** `AnimationView`.

7. **Save your changes.**

   You've now got a window which will create and add an `AnimationView` as its main subview.

8. **Select** `AnimationView.h` **from the Project navigator.**

   Modify the code to match that shown in Listing 7-4.

Listing 7-4: The methods and member variables of the AnimationView class

```
//
//  AnimationView.h
//  BasicAnimation
//
//  Created by Karl Kowalski on 4/10/11.
//  Copyright 2011 Kowalski Software Enterprises.
//  All rights reserved.
//

#import <Cocoa/Cocoa.h>

#import <QuartzCore/QuartzCore.h>

@interface AnimationView : NSView
{
    NSImageView* m_imageView;
@private

}

-   (void)animateView;

@end
```

9. **Save your changes.**

   Your `AnimationView` class now has a new method and a new member variable.

10. **Add an image to your project.**

    I've added the `BlackBerryForDummies.JPG` file once more.

11. **Select `AnimationView.m` from the Project navigator.**

    Modify the code to match that shown in Listing 7-5.

Listing 7-5: The implementation of the AnimationView

```
//
//  AnimationView.m
//  BasicAnimation
//
//  Created by Karl Kowalski on 4/10/11.
//  Copyright 2011 Kowalski Software Enterprises.
//  All rights reserved.
//

#import "AnimationView.h"


@implementation AnimationView

- (id)initWithFrame:(NSRect)frame
{
    self = [super initWithFrame:frame];
    if (self)
    {
        // set image view to the lower left corner
        NSRect imageRect = NSMakeRect(0.0, 0.0, 121.0, 162.0
            );

        m_imageView = [[NSImageView alloc]
            initWithFrame:imageRect];
        [m_imageView setImageScaling:NSScaleToFit];
        [m_imageView setImage:[NSImage imageNamed:@"BlackBerr
            yForDummies.JPG"]];
        [self addSubview:m_imageView];
        // start animation in 3 seconds
        [self performSelector:@selector(animateView)
            withObject:nil afterDelay:3.0];
        [self performSelector:@selector(animateView)
            withObject:nil afterDelay:7.0];
    }
```

(continued)

Listing 7-5 *(continued)*

```
    return self;
}

-   (void)animateView
{
    if ([m_imageView frame].origin.y < 0.50*[self frame].
        size.height)
    {
        NSPoint upperRight;
        upperRight.x = [self frame].size.width - [m_imageView
            frame].size.width;
        upperRight.y = [self frame].size.height - [m_
            imageView frame].size.height;
        [[m_imageView animator] setFrameOrigin:upperRight];
    }
    else
    {
        NSPoint lowerLeft = CGPointMake( 0.0, 0.0 );
        [[m_imageView animator] setFrameOrigin:lowerLeft];
    }
}


- (void)dealloc
{
    [super dealloc];
}

- (void)drawRect:(NSRect)dirtyRect
{
    // Drawing code here.
}
```

12. **Save your changes.**

13. **Build and run your app.**

    You should see the image you imported into your project move from the lower-left corner to the upper-right, and then back again a few seconds later.

Congratulations — you've just animated an image in your view! The process, all in `AnimationView.m`, went like this:

1. During the initialization of `AnimationView`, you created an `NSImage View` containing the `NSImage` from the image file you added to your project.

   The size of the `NSImageView` was a scaled-down size of my `BlackBerryForDummies.jpg` image.

2. You told the `AnimationView` to execute a specific selector, `animate View`, three seconds later.

3. You told it to do it again seven seconds later, four seconds after the first time.

   Initialization was then complete.

4. In the `animateView` method, you checked for whether the origin of the `NSImageView` was above or below the center point of the view:

   • If it was below, you created an `NSPoint` that would place the `NSImageView` up into the upper-right corner.

   • If it was above, you created an `NSPoint` that placed the view back down in the lower-left corner.

5. You invoked the `setFrameOrigin:` method of the `animator` part of the `NSImageView`.

   This is the agent that handles the animation of the `NSImageView`.

Every `NSView` object comes with a basic animation object called *animator*. You can use this object to perform operations on the `NSView`, only the animator will spread the operations out over time. In the example just given, the animator was told to set the origin of the `NSImageView`'s frame to be either the lower-left (if it was already in the upper-right) or the upper-right (if it was currently in the lower-left). The upper-right origin was calculated to be the upper-right of the `AnimationView` minus the width/height of the `NSImageView`, so that the entire image would be bound to the limits of the `AnimationView`.

This is the most basic animation you can do with an `NSView` subclass. Now you can put together apps that do more than just draw — you can make your apps dance. The world of app animation is now at your fingertips.

Part III
Focus on the User

In this part . . .

Your app's primary purpose is to provide your users with a means of improving their lives. If your app is making users' lives better, more users will buy your app. This part gives you the foundation of code to support your users while they use your app. You'll first discover how to store the data your users provide to your app to make sure that your app retains the important data in the best way possible. You'll also learn how to keep your users in control of your app, even when your app is doing something lengthy and laborious. And the last chapter of this part introduces you to delivering printed and PDF document output for your users to share.

Chapter 8

Maintaining Your Users' Data

*Y*our app is going to take all kinds of input from the users who download it. Additionally, your users will expect your app to maintain this data because that's what computers do. Your app has to keep track of the important pieces of information that your users provide.

Apple provides a number of options for storing and retrieving any data that your app may need to store. Your app may not have to store every action a user takes, but if necessary, you can do that, too, up to the limits of available storage space. In this chapter, I show you the options you have for storing data, giving you the information you'll use to decide the best approach for keeping your users' information safe and sound. I also give you an example of how to output your app's data to a generic text format, so that your users can make use of their data in other applications.

Analyzing the Data

Your app will likely use a variety of data, for all the different activities your app allows users to perform. A word-processing app can maintain the following pieces of information for an author writing a chapter in a book:

✔ Strings of alphanumeric text, ordered in paragraphs

✔ Text formatting information

✔ Images

✔ Footnotes

✔ Hyperlinks

Your app has to manage the important data your users enter into your app. My application is a logbook that helps diabetics record the important information they need to manage their condition. This data includes

- The date and time of the log entry
- The blood glucose level value, if any
- The insulin dosage, if any
- The amount of carbohydrates to be consumed, if any
- The amount of exercise, if any
- Any notes to help a health care provider better understand what's happening

This data is the bare minimum of information that a diabetic log should contain, and so this data will dictate the structure of the Objective-C class to maintain this data. This chapter shows how to organize the data your app will manage and how to save this data to and retrieve this data from storage.

Storing the Data

You're going to create an app in this chapter similar to my DiabeticPad app that allows users to enter data into a software version of a diabetic's logbook. Your app will provide an interface for users to enter their data and store it first in memory while the app is running and save it into a file of their choosing on their Mac. When your app is launched again, it will read data from their file into memory so it's ready for your users to add more log entries and review and edit what they've entered previously. Your first task is to create an app to support the data entry, storage, and retrieval goals:

1. **Launch Xcode and click the Create a new Xcode project button on the opening screen.**

2. **Select Application from the Mac OS X pane and Cocoa Application as the project template and click the Next button.**

3. **Give the project a name. Make sure the Create Document-Based Application option is unchecked, and make sure the Use Core Data option is unchecked. Click the Next button.**

   I've used DiabeticPad as the name for my app.

4. **Choose an appropriate location for Xcode to store this project, and click the Create button.**

   Xcode will create a basic project with an app delegate class ready for you to add data classes to.

Now you've got a basic project to use for the next section, where you'll add a class to hold the basic information for each entry in the logbook.

Creating a data class

Create your own class for this data storage as follows:

1. **In the Project navigator, right–click the DiabeticPad folder icon and choose New Group.**

   A new folder named "New Group" appears as a subfolder under the DiabeticPad folder. I named mine Data. I added this new Group because I prefer to arrange modules that belong together within some sort of container inside the project. Note, however, that Xcode does not create an actual folder in the file system.

2. **Right-click the new folder and choose New File.**

   The process of creating a new class within the project begins, and Xcode organizes the project with the header and source files for the class grouped in the Data folder.

3. **Select Cocoa from the left pane under Mac OS X.**

4. **Select Objective-C class from the top-right pane and then click Next, as shown in Figure 8-1.**

Figure 8-1: Creating a new class for your project.

5. Select NSObject **for the Subclass Of field and then click Next.**

Your new data class will be a subclass of NSObject because it's just a basic data class and doesn't need additional features or functionality. Xcode asks you to name your new class, where to store it in the file system, and which Group it should be placed in.

6. Keep the defaults, change the name to DPData.m, **and then click Save.**

The main Xcode project window appears (as shown in Figure 8-2), and the DPData header and source files are both selected in the left pane. The source file contents display in the text editor, so you're ready to begin editing these files.

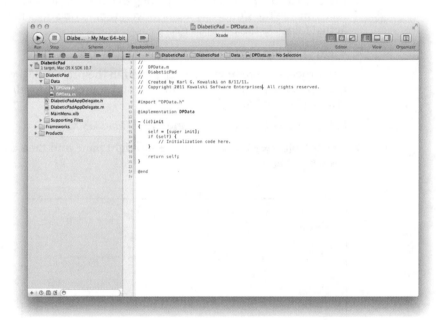

Figure 8-2: Xcode displays the new class you just created.

The two files that Xcode created are fairly empty. Because this class is a subclass of NSObject, Xcode can add little else automatically — that's your job. You will add the purple lines shown in Listing 8-1 to the class header file, DPData.h:

Listing 8-1:   The DPData.h file for the diabetic logbook

```
////  DPData.h
// DiabeticPad
//
// Created by Karl Kowalski on 1/21/11.
// Copyright 2011 Kowalski Software Enterprises.
// All rights reserved
//
#import <Foundation/Foundation.h>

@interface DPData : NSObject <NSCoding>
{
    // the following items are the class member variables
@private
    NSDate* m_timestamp;
    NSUInteger m_bgLevel;
    NSUInteger m_carbs;
    NSString* m_exercise;
    NSString* m_notes;
    NSMutableArray* m_insulins;
}

@property(readwrite,copy) NSDate* m_timestamp;
@property(readwrite) NSUInteger m_bgLevel;
@property(readwrite) NSUInteger m_carbs;
@property(readwrite,copy) NSString* m_exercise;
@property(readwrite,copy) NSString* m_notes;
@property(readwrite,copy) NSMutableArray* m_insulins;

- (void)initialize;
// sets
// NSCoding methods
- (id)initWithCoder:(NSCoder*)inCoder;
- (void)encodeWithCoder:(NSCoder*)inCoder;

@end
```

The last member variable, m_insulins, is declared a pointer to an object of the class NSMutableArray. This class will handle the storage of NSString objects that represent an insulin type and the amount of insulin of that type. In DiabeticPad, I use NSString objects to hold this information, and the actual representation of this data is up to the app's user.

Notice the NSCoding protocol declaration on the @interface line. This declaration tells Xcode that this class will implement *archiving*. Archiving is the process of putting the data contained in this object into a form that is easy to store in a file. I've never tried to find out what the archived version of my data looks like; I just trust that Mac OS X will do the right thing and I've never been disappointed. Mac OS X expects that a class declaring itself to support the NSCoding protocol will provide two methods, initWithCoder and encodeWithCoder, and I've added them to the end of the list of methods in the DPData class.

The source code module that represents a logbook entry is shown in Listing 8-2.

Listing 8-2:   The contents of DPData.m, the source code for diabetic log data

```
//
//  DPData.m
//  DiabeticPad
//
//  Created by Karl Kowalski on 1/21/11.
//  Copyright 2011 Kowalski Software Enterprises.
//  All rights reserved.
//

#import "DPData.h"


// these are the key strings for archiving
NSString* ARCHIVE_DPDATA_NOTES = @"dpdata_notes";
NSString* ARCHIVE_DPDATA_BGLEVEL = @"dpdata_bglevel";
NSString* ARCHIVE_DPDATA_TIMESTAMP = @"dpdata_timestamp";
NSString* ARCHIVE_DPDATA_INSULINS = @"dpdata_insulins";
NSString* ARCHIVE_DPDATA_CARBS = @"dpdata_carbs";
NSString* ARCHIVE_DPDATA_EXERCISE = @"dpdata_exercise";

@implementation DPData

@synthesize m_timestamp;
@synthesize m_carbs;
@synthesize m_exercise;
@synthesize m_notes;
@synthesize m_bgLevel;
@synthesize m_insulins;

- (id)init
{
    self = [super init];
    if (self)
    {
      // perform any needed initialization
      [self initialize];
    }
```

```
    return (self);
}

- (void)initialize
{
    // initialize the timestamp to now
    m_timestamp = [NSDate date];
    // initialize the other objects to their default values
    m_bgLevel = 0;
    m_notes = @""; // empty string for notes
    m_carbs = 0;
    m_exercise = @""; // empty string for exercise
    // since there are no insulin dosages to report,
    // no need to setup anything
}

- (id)initWithCoder:(NSCoder*)inCoder
{

    // since we're being called with an NSCoder
    // that means we're being UNarchived
    // so we do not call initialize
    m_timestamp = [inCoder decodeObjectForKey:ARCHIVE_DPDATA_
            TIMESTAMP];
    m_notes = [inCoder decodeObjectForKey:ARCHIVE_DPDATA_
            NOTES];
    m_bgLevel = [inCoder decodeIntegerForKey:ARCHIVE_DPDATA_
            BGLEVEL];
    m_insulins = [inCoder decodeObjectForKey:ARCHIVE_DPDATA_
            INSULINS];
    m_exercise = [inCoder decodeObjectForKey:ARCHIVE_DPDATA_
            EXERCISE];
    m_carbs = [inCoder decodeIntegerForKey:ARCHIVE_DPDATA_
            CARBS];
    return (self);
}

- (void)encodeWithCoder:(NSCoder*)inCoder
{

    // send the data into the NSCoder for archiving
    [inCoder encodeObject:m_timestamp forKey:ARCHIVE_DPDATA_
            TIMESTAMP];
    [inCoder encodeObject:m_notes forKey:ARCHIVE_DPDATA_
            NOTES];
    [inCoder encodeInteger:m_bgLevel forKey:ARCHIVE_DPDATA_
            BGLEVEL];
    [inCoder encodeObject:m_insulins forKey:ARCHIVE_DPDATA_
            INSULINS];
    [inCoder encodeObject:m_exercise forKey:ARCHIVE_DPDATA_
            EXERCISE];
```

(continued)

Listing 8-2 *(continued)*

```
    [inCoder encodeInteger:m_carbs forKey:ARCHIVE_DPDATA_
        CARBS];
}

- (void)dealloc
{
    if (nil != m_timestamp)
    {
        [m_timestamp release];
    }
    if (nil != m_notes)
    {
        [m_notes release];
    }
    if (nil != m_insulins)
    {
        [m_insulins release];
    }
    if (nil != m_exercise)
    {
        [m_exercise release];
    }
    [super dealloc];
}
@end
```

This class, DPData, is the basic block of information that the DiabeticPad app will maintain for my users. A DPData object will carry the information for a logbook entry, which users may create to record any of the following situations:

- A blood glucose measurement
- An insulin injection
- A meal
- Pre-exercise information
- Any information regarding health that might be useful to record

Records in the logbook will be maintained within a collection of DPData objects while the application is running. Between runs, my application will have to store this data within the file system of the Macintosh the app is running on. My users are effectively making a recording of their diabetic health over time so they and their health care professionals can review this information later. Your app may do something as simple as keep track of a player's high score in a maze game or maintain accounting records for a quick-and-easy bookkeeping application. Almost all apps accept some form of input from their users. Users expect the app to keep a record of this input, and they rarely enjoy typing information into your app more than once.

The DPData class

The logbook information listed above can be found as `member` variables within the `DPData` class. If you look at the header file again in Listing 8-1, you will find the following data types:

- `NSDate`, for the date and time of the logbook entry.

- `NSUInteger`, for the blood glucose level.

    Glucose meters display this value as a positive number. I chose to use a data type that represents an unsigned (always zero or greater) integer. I also used this to hold the value for carbohydrates in an upcoming meal.

- `NSMutableArray`, to store `NSString` objects that represent the insulin type and dosage amount.

    A diabetic can inject one or more different types of insulin at once, and it is important to keep track of both the kind of insulin and the amount. The user will add this information as a string of text, such as "Regular Insulin 12 units" or "R12," whatever is most preferable for them.

- `NSString`, for any text notes. An `NSString` can hold nearly an unlimited amount of text but the user interface of my app restricts the amount of text to a manageable 1,024 characters. Additionally, I use an NSString to hold information about any exercise.

Why that number? I didn't want to restrict the user to some overly small amount, like 256 characters, which would limit the entry to 2–3 sentences. I don't believe users will write a book's worth of information, but I prefer they have a decent amount of space to put down any information that might be useful. The app only stores the characters that a user enters, so no memory is wasted.

The `DPData` class also provides methods that allow for the getting and setting of these values. This is accomplished through the use of the `@property` and `@synthesize` directives.

The DPData class supports the archiving and un-archiving of its data:

- ✔ When it's time to store my app's data in a more permanent form, such as onto the Mac's hard drive or other permanent storage, the application will archive the data into a stream of bytes that can then be written into a file on the disk.

- ✔ When the application launches and wants to get the information from the file, the un-archiving process is executed.

The NSCoder object provides methods that allow basic data types, such as integers and floating-point numbers, to be encoded and decoded. Best of all, classes such as NSString and NSArray implement the NSCoding protocol themselves, and you can see that my code simply hands those member variables into the NSCoder object.

Storing data in files

Mac OS allows apps to keep users' data in files. Nearly every application running on a Macintosh uses files to store information so that the information is available the next time the app runs. Your users might keep their computers, and your app, running 24 hours a day, seven days a week; therefore, your app would never need to store its data in a file because the information would always be present in memory. However, the app or the computer will eventually shut down, and your users are expecting the information they entered to be ready to go the next time they launch your app.

The first version of my DiabeticPad app stores the logbook records in a single file. Using one file to store all the data makes it very easy for users to make copies of the file and keep the records stored as a backup, such as burning it onto a writable disc. The one limitation with using a single file to store all the data is that the larger the file becomes, the longer it takes to read all the data into memory when the app starts up. I discuss ways of alleviating this problem in this section and the next.

Storing and retrieving data

I cover the process that stores the information first, so you know what to expect when I cover the process that retrieves that information. I find it easier to visualize the process of un-archiving if I know how data is archived.

I decided I didn't want to *require* a user to save the information because usability studies have convinced me the best way to ensure that the information is saved is to just do it, and users will be able to delete any information they later decide is unwanted. I provide a Save menu item, but the data is saved when the user quits my application, too.

When the user closes my app or chooses File⇨Save, the application behaves as follows:

1. The app uses the NSKeyedArchiver class, providing it with the NSArray that contains all the available DPData objects. An NSKeyedArchiver class is a subclass of NSCoder and is the repository for all of the data to be written into a file.

   The NSKeyedArchiver class comes with a class method (so there's no need to allocate an NSKeyedArchiver object) that takes in any NSObject subclass. The result is an NSData object containing all the data from all the DPData objects.

2. The app creates a file in the file system, at a location the user specifies.

3. The app writes all the data in the NSData object into the file. The app closes the file when the last byte is written.

Figure 8-3 shows this process visually.

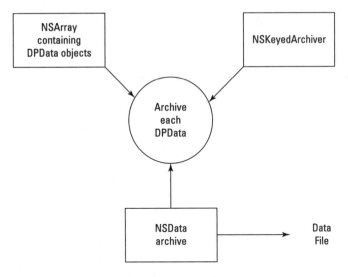

Figure 8-3: Data flowing from the app to a file.

I decided I didn't want to require a user to find the file that stores all the information. Most users will only want to use one data file for all their log readings. I provide an Open menu item in case they want to review a different set of data. However, when a user launches my app or tells my app what file to open, the application behaves as follows:

1. The app checks for whether the expected data file is available.

   If the app cannot find this file, no further action is taken. The app creates a new file when it's time to save.

2. The app attempts to read the data from the file.

   The entire contents of the file are read into an NSData object.

3. Using the NSData object, the app creates the array of DPData objects using the NSKeyedUnarchiver class.

   Like the NSKeyedArchiver class, the NSKeyedUnarchiver class comes with a class method for retrieving information from an NSData object and returning the original object — the NSArray containing the DPData objects — that was used in the archive process above. The NSKeyedUnarchiver reads the NSData object filled with the contents of the data file and then returns an NSArray object containing all the DPData objects that were stored when the file was created. Figure 8-4 shows a visual representation of this data retrieval process.

In Figure 8-5 you can see the general flow of operations the app executes when reading data from a file and writing data out to a file.

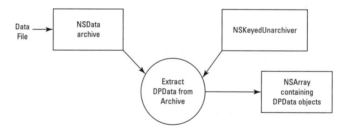

Figure 8-4: Data flowing from a file into the app.

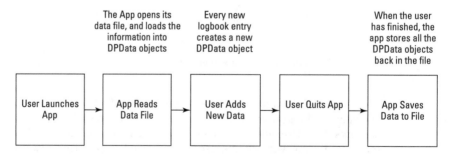

Figure 8-5: Flow of operations an app follows for reading and writing data with files.

Slowing down the app

As I mention above, reading all the data in from one file when the app starts up and then writing it all back out to one file when the app finishes takes more and more time as more and more logbook entries are added each day. I normally add at least seven entries each day, two each for breakfast, lunch, and dinner, and one more before bed (sometimes more if my day isn't normal). Information like this is helpful for my health care professionals and me to understand what's happening. Seven readings a day is approximately 2,500 readings per year. The file just keeps getting bigger. Current Mac hardware can support reading and writing this amount of data fairly rapidly, so the need to speed things up is not desperate. However, you should always consider how well your app will handle larger amounts of data. For example, I could extend this app to record the logbook data of multiple users in a clinic or a research lab.

The following are some ways to manage this problem:

✓ **Store the data in multiple files.** This reduces the amount of time it takes to read and write the data because individual files are smaller than one file containing everything.

This is the easiest to implement. The disadvantage to this approach is that the user is required to specify which file to read in. The app can name the separate files using the date and provide a visual interface showing the dates for which information was recorded. This approach requires more effort for implementing the code and more code, which means increased potential for errors to sneak in.

✓ **Store the data in one file, but load the data in a lazy fashion.** For instance, the app could write the data into the file with the most recent data at the beginning and then load the most recent ten items for the user to interact with. When the user wants to see older logbook entries, the app can load another ten. This loads the data based on the user's search through the records; if the user is only interested in adding another logbook entry, only the first ten entries need to be read in.

This approach requires writing the data back out to the single file, which makes the app more complicated.

✓ **Store the data in one file, but load it as a background process.** The user operates under the illusion that the app is responsive to their control while the process retrieves all the available records similar to the original approach.

This approach causes the app to take a long time to write the data back to the file.

✓ **Use Core Data to manage the information.** Apple provides the Core Data framework to assist in developing applications that manage sets of user data.

The best way to manage data in a Macintosh app is to use the Cocoa framework known as Core Data.

Using Core Data to store information

Many applications perform the following operations:

- ✔ Maintaining an array of objects that group data
- ✔ Writing the data for those objects to a file for storage
- ✔ Reading the data from the file storage
- ✔ Recreating the objects in memory

The DiabeticPad app follows this same pattern. Someone at Apple decided to provide a framework within Mac OS to make this generalized set of operations easier for developers to implement, so that these kinds of apps can be made quickly so you can spend your development time wisely on features and functionality that are more important.

Cocoa includes a framework called Core Data that allows you to give your app the capabilities of data management similar to those provided by apps that rely on databases. A *database* is a set of data that contains records of information stored in tables. A *record* is a collection of different pieces of information bundled together (such as the set of member variables that make up DPData objects). A set of records in a database is a *table*. Using Core Data allows you to set up a description of the record that you want Core Data to maintain, and Core Data does the grunt-level work for storing and retrieving the structure of the information you describe. Core Data may use a database to support the needs of your application, but you don't have to worry about how Core Data does the job.

Cocoa also provides the Core Data framework to iOS, so you can take what you learn here to develop Core Data apps for iOS too.

A database holds data, plain and simple. For the DiabeticPad app, this data is in several tables, which consist of rows and columns like a spreadsheet, as shown in Figure 8-6. The columns represent individual data values, called *fields,* which contain a specific type of data. Each row of fields in the table is called a *record* of data. Core Data provides a set of classes that enable your app to manage and manipulate this data very easily.

Record #	Timestamp	Blood Glucose	Carbs	Exercise	Insulin Dosages	Notes
1	1/27/11 7:31	149	36	none	Humalog 7	
2	1/27/11 9:30	112				
3	1/27/11 11:30	207	40		Humalog 9	
4	1/27/11 13:41	188				
5	1/27/11 17:23	101			Humalog 10	
6	1/27/11 19:33	219				Large Dinner
7	1/27/11 23:01	322			Lantus 28	Very high!

Figure 8-6: The logbook entries of DiabeticPad can be visualized as records in a spreadsheet.

A CoreData version of DiabeticPad

A Mac application built to use Core Data is a little different from a regular application — a few extra classes are necessary to support the interaction between the Core Data components and the visual interface for displaying and manipulating the data stored by your application. You need to start a new project with the Core Data framework enabled to gain its benefits:

1. **In Xcode, choose File⇨New ⇨New Project.**

   The New Project Assistant screen displays.

2. **Select Application under Mac OS X in the left pane, select Cocoa Application in the top-right pane, and then click Next.**

3. **Set the Product Name to** `CoreDataDiabeticPad` **to distinguish it from the app that doesn't use Core Data.**

4. **Check the Create Document-Based Application and Use Core Data checkboxes.**

5. **Set the Document Class to** `CoreDataDiabeticPadDoc,` **set the Document Extension to be dpdoc, and then click Next.**

6. **Select a location for your new project and Click the Create button.**

   Xcode creates the project for you, which should look similar to that shown in Figure 8-7.

You can see some of the differences between a Core Data–based app and a normal Document-based app.

   ✔ A new file, `CoreDataDiabeticPadDoc.xcdatamodeld`, is added to the project and is visible in the Project navigator.

   Here you tell Core Data about the information it's responsible to maintain.

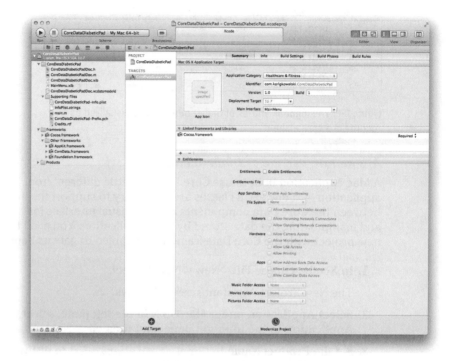

Figure 8-7: The beginnings of a beautiful Core Data experience.

> ✔ Inside `CoreDataDiabeticPadDoc.h`, the class `CoreDiabeticPadDoc` inherits from a parent class called `NSPersistentDocument` instead of `NSDocument`.
>
> `NSPersistentDocument` is a subclass of `NSDocument`, so your app gets all the same features and behaviors available in that class.
>
> ✔ The inclusion of `CoreData.framework` in your project's Frameworks group.
>
> A Core Data application uses this library of code to perform operations on Core Data–based classes.

When I started writing the Core Data–based version of DiabeticPad, I really enjoyed working with the model file, `CoreDataDiabeticPadDoc.xcdatamodeld`, because the Xcode editor is very easy to use. Luckily, the CoreDataDiabeticPadDoc app only has one type of record, but apps that are more complex can make use of Core Data's ability to create real relational databases complete with records in one table referencing records in another.

Creating the DiabeticPad logbook record

The only record in DiabeticPad is used to hold the same data used in the `DPData` class in the beginning of this chapter. The Core Data classes will take care of the following interactions with the records it will store:

- ✔ Creating new log entries
- ✔ Updating log entries with data
- ✔ Deleting log entries
- ✔ Archiving the log entries to a file
- ✔ Retrieving the log entries from a file

I use *record* to refer to the grouping of log entry data; Core Data uses the term *entity* when referring to the representation of the data in the data model. Your next task is to give Core Data and your app a model of the data your app will be working with. Here's how to create the logbook entry entity for the CoreData DiabeticPad app.

1. **Select the** `CoreDataDiabeticPadDoc.xcdatamodeld` **item in the Project navigator.**

   The CoreData entity editor appears, with an empty display, as shown in Figure 8-8.

2. **Click the Add Entity button at the bottom of the screen.**

   An entry appears below the ENTITIES label.

3. **Rename the entry to** `LogEntry`.

   All entity objects must begin with an uppercase letter.

4. **In the Attributes panel, click the + button.**

   An attribute called `attribute` with `Undefined` as its type is created.

5. **Rename this attribute** `timestamp` **and set its type to** Date.

   You've created the timestamp attribute for the logbook entry entity.

6. **Add the attributes listed in Figure 8-9.**

   The creation of the logbook entry entity is complete.

That was almost too simple. Of course, you're not finished yet. You need to link this entity into your user interface to give your users something to work with.

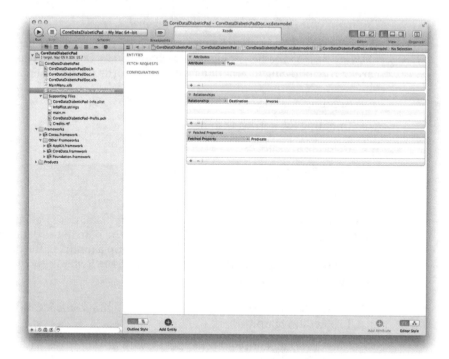

Figure 8-8: Ready to create an entity in a Core Data data model.

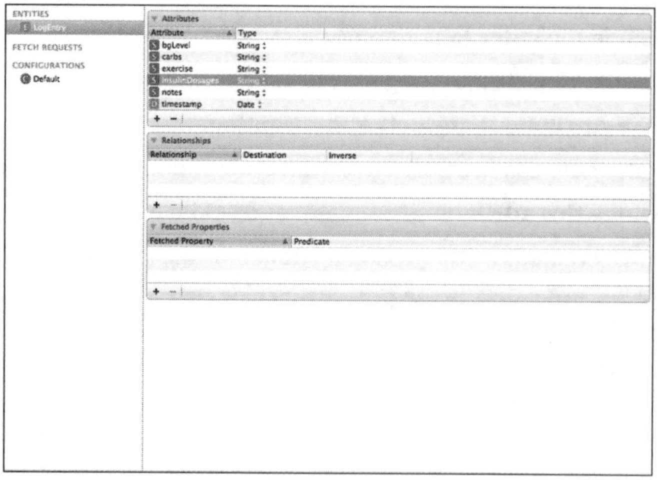

Figure 8-9: The complete attributes of the logbook entry entity.

Creating the CoreDataDiabeticPad user interface

After you create the structure of a CoreData entity, you need to add the UI components that support a user interface that allows your users to

- Create new entries
- Navigate through existing entries
- Edit entries
- Delete entries

Here's how:

1. **Select** `CoreDataDiabeticPadDoc.xib` **from the Project navigator and show the Utilities view, if it's not already visible.**

2. **Remove the default "Your document contents here" label.**

   You won't need this. Figure 8-10 shows CoreDataDiabeticPad's document window in Interface Builder.

3. **From the Object Library, drag an Array Controller object onto the object pane to the left of the window.**

   This creates an instance of the Array Controller when the XIB file is loaded. The Array Controller is used to manage the objects held in the CoreData in-memory storage.

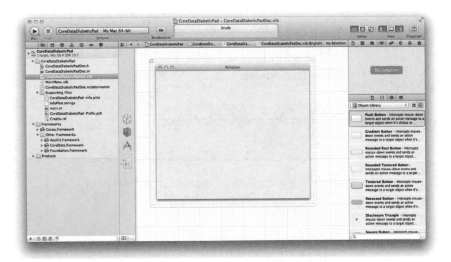

Figure 8-10: The CoreDataDiabeticPadDoc.xib file in Interface Builder.

4. **Click the Show Bindings inspector button. Click the disclosure triangle next to the Managed Object Context item in the Parameters pane. Click the Bind to: checkbox and select File's Owner from the drop-down menu.**

Figure 8-11 shows the Parameters section of the Bindings inspector for the Array Controller. In this step you are binding the Array Controller object that gets created when the XIB file for the Document window is created, to the File's Owner object associated with this XIB file. In this case, the File's Owner will be a `CoreDataDiabeticPadDoc` object.

In the next steps, you have these UI components to add to the window:

- Text Fields to input and edit according to the information in each logbook record

- Labels to describe the data presented in the Text Fields

- Buttons to add, remove, and use to navigate through the records maintained by the app

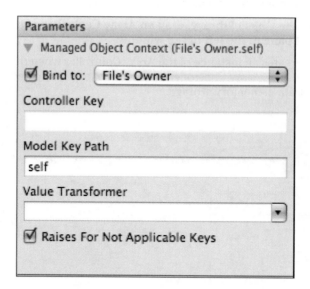

Figure 8-11: Use the Bindings inspector to bind your Array Controller to the NSPersistentDocument object that is the owner of this XIB file.

5. **Drag a Label from the Object Library and drop it onto the window. Change the Label's text to Date & Time: and position it as shown in Figure 8-10.**

6. **Drag a Text Field from the Object Library and drop it onto the window to the right of the Date & Time: Label, as shown in Figure 8-10.**

7. **Repeat Steps 5 and 6 for the Labels and Text Fields corresponding to Blood Glucose, Carbohydrates, Exercise, Insulin Dosage, and Notes.**

   I have placed the components in my window as shown in Figure 8-12. I made the Notes Text Field larger than the others to allow users to see a larger amount of text, since the Notes will usually hold more information.

8. **Drag a Button from the Object Library and drop it onto the window. Position the button in the upper-right corner and change its text to** Add New.

9. **Drag a Button from the Object Library and drop it onto the window. Position the button in the lower-right corner and change its text to** Next.

10. **Drag a Button from the Object Library and drop it onto the window. Position the button in the lower-left corner and change its text to** Previous.

11. **Drag a Button from the Object Library and drop it onto the window. Position the button halfway between and slightly above the Previous and Next Buttons. Change its text to** Remove.

   Your window should look similar to that shown in Figure 8-12. You've added the UI components for entering and editing data for a logbook record, and next you're going to connect these components to data and actions in your app.

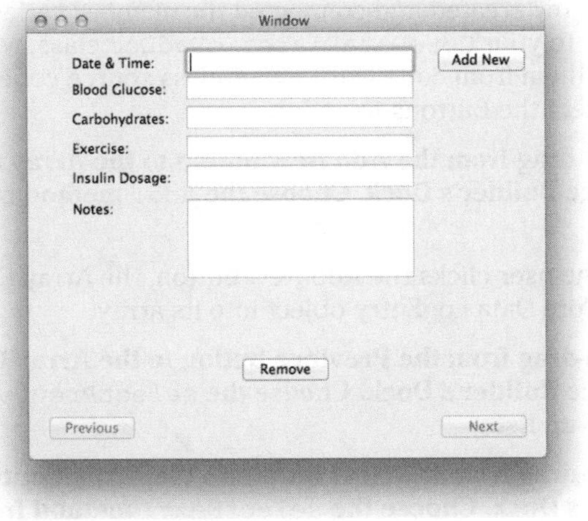

Figure 8-12: The document window that displays for the user's diabetic logbook entries.

12. **Click the Show the Assistant editor button to display the**
CoreDataDiabeticPadDoc.h **file alongside Interface Builder.**

13. **Control-drag from the Text Field next to Date & Time into the**
CoreDataDiabeticPadDoc.h **file in the Assistant editor to a point**
between the closing brace } and the @end **directive. In the pop-up**
window, set the Name to m_timestamp **and click the Connect button.**

14. **Repeat Step 13 for the Blood Glucose, Carbohydrates, Exercise,**
Insulin Dosage, and Notes Text Fields.

    I set the names to m_bgLevel, m_carbs, m_exercise, m_insulin
    Dosages, and m_notes, respectively. These names are similar to those
    you entered for the attributes of the LogEntry entity in the Core Data
    model.

15. **Control-drag from the Previous Button into the** CoreDataDiabetic
PadDoc.h **file in the Assistant editor to a point between the closing**
brace } and the @end **directive. In the pop-up window, set the Name**
to m_previous **and click the Connect button.**

16. **Control-drag from the Next Button into the** CoreDataDiabetic
PadDoc.h **file in the Assistant editor to a point between the closing**
brace } and the @end **directive. In the pop-up window, set the Name to**
m_next **and click the Connect button.**

17. **Control-drag from the Remove Button into the**
CoreDataDiabeticPadDoc.h **file in the Assistant editor to a point**
between the closing brace } and the @end **directive. In the pop-up**
window, set the Name to m_remove **and click the Connect button.**

    You've now created and connected the member variables for your
    window to your CoreDataDiabeticPadDoc class, which allows you to
    modify them from code within your class source code. Your next task is
    to connect the Buttons to actions.

18. **Control-drag from the Add New button to the Array Controller in**
Interface Builder's Dock. Choose the add: **method from the pop-up**
list.

    When the user clicks the Add New button, the Array Controller will add
    a new Core Data LogEntry object into its array.

19. **Control-drag from the Previous button to the Array Controller in**
Interface Builder's Dock. Choose the selectPrevious: **method from**
the pop-up list.

20. **Control-drag from the Next button to the Array Controller in Interface**
Builder's Dock. Choose the selectNext: **method from the pop-up list.**

21. **Control-drag from the Remove button to the Array Controller in Interface Builder's Dock. Choose the** `remove:` **method from the pop-up list.**

    Now your window's UI components are connected to your app and to the Array Controller that will be created when the document window is displayed. You now need to set the bindings of the Text Fields to display the data available from the current logbook entry in the Array Controller. Follow Steps 22-27.

22. **Select the Date & Time text field in the window and click the Show the Bindings inspector button. Click the disclosure triangle next to Value in the Value pane. Click the Bind To: checkbox and select Array Controller from the drop-down menu. Enter** `timestamp` **into the Model Key Path field.**

23. **Select the Blood Glucose text field in the window. In the Bindings inspector, click the Bind To: checkbox and select Array Controller from the drop-down menu. Enter** `bgLevel` **into the Model Key Path field.**

24. **Select the Carbohydrates text field in the window. In the Bindings inspector, click the Bind To: checkbox and select Array Controller from the drop-down menu. Enter** `carbs` **into the Model Key Path field.**

25. **Select the Exercise text field in the window. In the Bindings inspector, click the Bind To: checkbox and select Array Controller from the drop-down menu. Enter** `exercise` **into the Model Key Path field.**

26. **Select the Insulin Dosage text field in the window. In the Bindings inspector, click the Bind To: checkbox and select Array Controller from the drop-down menu. Enter** `insulinDosages` **into the Model Key Path field.**

27. **Select the Notes text field in the window. In the Bindings inspector, click the disclosure triangle next to the Data parameter. Click the Bind To: checkbox and select Array Controller from the drop-down menu. Enter** `notes` **into the Model Key Path field.**

    All UI components that display information about a logbook entry are now bound to data in the Array Controller's selected LogEntry. Next, you bind buttons to the Array Controller so that the buttons are enabled or disabled depending on the selected LogEntry in the Array Controller.

28. **Select the Remove button in the window. In the Bindings inspector, click the disclosure triangle next to the Enabled parameter in the Availability pane. Click the Bind To: checkbox and select Array Controller from the drop-down menu. Enter** `canRemove` **in the Controller Key field.**

29. **Select the Previous button in the window. In the Bindings inspector, click the disclosure triangle next to the Enabled parameter in the Availability pane. Click the Bind To: checkbox and select Array Controller from the drop-down menu. Enter** `canSelectPrevious` **in the Controller Key field.**

30. **Select the Next button in the window. In the Bindings inspector, click the disclosure triangle next to the Enabled parameter in the Availability pane. Click the Bind To: checkbox and select Array Controller from the drop-down menu. Enter** `canSelectNext` **in the Controller Key field.**

Your Next, Previous, and Remove buttons are now enabled or disabled based on the selected item from the Array Controller. For instance, if the selected logbook entry is the very first in the set, the Previous button will be disabled; if the selected entry is the very last in the set, the Next button will be disabled. And if there are no entries in the Array Controller, the Remove button will be disabled.

One more step is needed: binding the Array Controller object to the File's Owner object so that the Array Controller knows where to find the bindings for the UI components. Each UI component is looking to the Array Controller for its information; you have to set the Array Controller to retrieve that information from the File's Owner. You do so in Step 31.

31. **Select the Array Controller in the Interface Builder Dock. In the Bindings inspector, click the disclosure triangle next to the Managed Object Context parameter in the Parameters pane. Click the Bind To: checkbox and select File's Owner from the drop-down menu. Set the Model Key Path to** `managedObjectContext`.

You get a look at what a *managed object context* is in the next sequence of steps. For now, setting this value is all that matters.

All the elements of the user interface are now ***bound*** to the Core Data entity that is currently selected within the Array Controller.

Some of the layout decisions I made include these:

- ✔ All the text fields were sized identically, except for the Notes field.
- ✔ The Previous button is on the left, which is usually "the Past."

✔ The Next button is on the right, which is usually "the Future."

✔ The Add New button is in the upper right, separated from the other buttons so that there's less chance of a mistake.

✔ The Remove button is below the data, but above the Previous and Next buttons, to ensure less chance of clicking it accidentally.

You need to do one more thing to get this sample application running correctly: modify some of the code in `CoreDataDiabeticPadDoc` to force the Array Controller to bind to the *Managed Object Context* owned by the `CoreDataDiabeticPadDoc` object. A Managed Object Context is responsible for managing a collection of data objects within a Core Data application. In the `CoreDataDiabeticPad` application, the `CoreDataDiabeticPadDoc` object comes with a reference to an `NSManageObjectContext` object, which is where you'll connect your Array Controller to provide it with logbook objects to control. To set your app's Array Controller to manage the set of LogEntry entities, follow these steps:

1. **Select** `CoreDataDiabeticPadDoc.xib` **in the Project navigator. Click the Show the Assistant editor button to display the Assistant if necessary.**

2. **Control-drag from the Array Controller object in the Interface Builder Dock into the** `CoreDataDiabeticPadDoc.h` **file in the Assistant editor, to a point just before the end brace }. Set the Name to** `m_` `arrayController` **in the pop-up window and click the Connect button.**

   Your `CoreDataDiabeticPadDoc.h` file should look similar to the code shown in Listing 8-3. And you've now connected the Array Controller object created for the window to the `NSArrayController` object in the `CoreDataDiabeticPadDoc` object.

3. **Select** `CoreDataDiabeticPadDoc.m` **in the Project navigator.**

   You can click the Show the Standard editor to remove the Assistant editor and give yourself lots of space to code.

4. **Add the code in** purple **shown in Listing 8-4.**

5. **Build your app.**

When you implement the `windowControllerDidLoadNib:` method, its code will tell the `NSArrayController` object to use the `CoreData` `DiabeticPadDoc`'s `NSManagedObjectContext` object as the source of the objects to be used in the array. In addition, the `NSArrayController` will perform a *fetch* operation through its managed object context object to retrieve the entities stored by Core Data.

Listing 8-3:   CoreDataDiabeticPadDoc.h with an NSArrayControllerObject reference

```
//
// CoreDataDiabeticPadDoc.h
// CoreDataDiabeticPad
//
// Created by Karl Kowalski on 3/19/11
// Copyright 2011 Kowalski Software Enterprises.
// All rights reserved.
//

#import <Cocoa/Cocoa.h>

@interface CoreDataDiabeticPadDoc : NSPersistentDocument
{
@private
    NSTextField *m_timestamp;
    NSTextField *m_bgLevel;
    NSTextField *m_carbs;
    NSTextField *m_exercise;
    NSTextField *m_insulinDosages;
    NSTextField *m_notes;
    NSButton *m_previous;
    NSButton *m_next;
    NSButton *m_remove;
    IBOutlet NSArrayController* m_arrayController;
}
@property (assign) IBOutlet NSTextField *m_timestamp;
@property (assign) IBOutlet NSTextField *m_bgLevel;
@property (assign) IBOutlet NSTextField *m_carbs;
@property (assign) IBOutlet NSTextField *m_exercise;
@property (assign) IBOutlet NSTextField *m_insulinDosages;
@property (assign) IBOutlet NSTextField *m_notes;
@property (assign) IBOutlet NSButton *m_previous;
@property (assign) IBOutlet NSButton *m_next;
@property (assign) IBOutlet NSButton *m_remove;

@end
```

Listing 8-4:   CoreDataDiabeticPadDoc.m using its NSArrayControllerObject reference

```
//
// CoreDataDiabeticPadDoc.m
// CoreDataDiabeticPad
//
// Created by Karl Kowalski on 3/19/11
```

```
// Copyright 2011 Kowalski Software Enterprises.
// All rights reserved.
//

#import "CoreDataDiabeticPadDoc.h"

@implementation CoreDataDiabeticPadDoc

@synthesize m_timestamp;
@synthesize m_bgLevel;
@synthesize m_carbs;
@synthesize m_exercise;
@synthesize m_insulinDosages;
@synthesize m_notes;
@synthesize m_previous;
@synthesize m_next;
@synthesize m_remove;

- (id)init
{
    self = [super init];
    if (self)
    {
        // Add your subclass-specific initialization here
    }
    return (self);
}

- (NSString*)windowNibName
{
    // Xcode's comments removed
        return @"CoreDataDiabeticPadDoc";
}

- (void)windowControllerDidLoadNib:(NSWindowController *)
        aController
{
    [super windowControllerDidLoadNib:aController];
    // get our Document's Managed Object Context
    NSManagedObjectContext* moc = [self
        managedObjectContext];
    // check that we got it before using it
    if (nil != moc)
    {
        // set the Array Controller to use the MOC
        [m_arrayController setManagedObjectContext:moc];
        // set the AC to use LogEntry entities
        [m_arrayController setEntityName:@"LogEntry"];
        NSError* anError = nil;
```

(continued)

Listing 8-4 *(continued)*

```
        // tell the AC to retrieve all the stored entities
        BOOL result = [m_arrayController fetchWithRequest:nil
            merge:YES error:&anError];
        if (YES == result)
        {
            // success, select the first item
            result = [m_arrayController setSelectionIndex:0];
        }
    }
}

@end
```

That's all that's needed to sync the Array Controller with the Managed Object Context.

The Managed Object Context is the tip of a very large programmatic iceberg. For instance, it manages the data being created, stores the data internally, and handles saving this data to and reading this data from files. If you're going to use Core Data for your apps, I recommend reviewing Apple's documentation for both Core Data and Cocoa Bindings. I also recommend searching the Internet for references to this information. For instance, the solution that led to the code in Listing 8-4 came as a result of entering "bind array controller to managedobjectcontext" into Google.

Implementing your own array controller class in Xcode

After you finish the user interface display for the logbook data managed by CoreData, it's time to put the finishing touches on the app. You're going to create a subclass of `NSArrayController` and use it in place of the Array Controller you added to the XIB file. Your app will be able to customize the behavior of the array controller that manages all of the Core Data objects representing each logbook entry. In this example, you'll override the `newObject` method of `NSArrayController` so that you can preset the timestamp to the current date and time when the user adds a new logbook entry. In normal use of my DiabeticPad app, a user will create a new entry for a blood glucose reading right when they make one.

Here's what you do:

1. **Select File⇨New ⇨New File to display the New File assistant.**

2. **Select Cocoa and the Objective-C class template and click Next.**

3. **Enter** NSArrayController **into the Subclass of field and click Next.**

4. **Save the class as** LogBookEntryArrayController **and select the** CoreDataDiabeticPad **group. Click the Save button.**

   Xcode will add two files to your project.

5. **Clean the project by selecting Product⇨Clean, and then Build the project.**

   This is just a precaution to make sure that all the editors are now aware of the new class you've just added.

6. **Select the** CoreDataDiabeticPadDoc.xib **file in the Project navigator to display Interface Builder. Click the Show the Utilities view if necessary.**

7. **Select the Array Controller object in the Interface Builder Dock. Click the Show the Identity inspector button. In the Custom Class section, select** LogBookEntryArrayController **from the drop-down menu as shown in Figure 8-13.**

8. **Build the project.**

9. **Select the** LogBookEntryArrayController.m **file for editing.**

   You're going to modify how it creates new objects.

10. **Add the code shown in Listing 8-5.**

    This code ensures that a timestamp is created using the current date and time, which is usually what a user wants to see when they enter new log data.

11. **Build once more to make sure Xcode doesn't find any problems.**

Listing 8-5:   The newObject method now also sets the current date and time

```
- (id)newObject
{
    // call the superclass method to initiate
    id aNewObj = [super newObject];
    NSDate* rightNow = [NSDate date];
    // set the timestamp attribute to the current date and
    // time
    [aNewObj setValue:rightNow forKey:@"timestamp"];
    return (aNewObj);
}
```

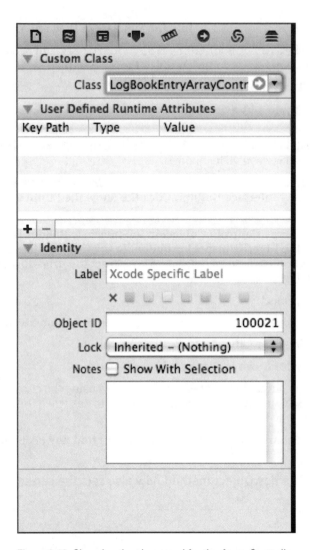

Figure 8-13: Changing the class used for the Array Controller to one of your own devising.

The method you've just added to LogBookEntryArrayController is going to intercept every newObject: message sent to the controller, such as when the user clicks the Add New button. The parent class's method newObject is called first to create the new entry. After that, this new code sets the entry's timestamp attribute to the current date and time. Note that this only happens when a user tells the app to create a new logbook entry; entry objects created when the app tells Core Data to load the entries from storage won't have their timestamps reset.

The application is now fully functional for the following operations:

✔ Creating new logbook entries

✔ Deleting logbook entries

✔ Retrieving the data stored in an entry

✔ Saving the entire set of data into a file

✔ Loading the set of data from a previous file

Users can create new files as they choose and separate their logbooks by any time period they want. Core Data allows them to store the files in any of these formats:

✔ **XML:** This format is easy to read, and you can see how the CoreData library stores the information about both the entity objects that the user creates and the database structure itself.

The XML format is the easiest to deal with.

✔ **Binary:** This format is unreadable for most humans, but it makes for a smaller file size.

✔ **SQLite:** A library of software that developers can incorporate into their applications to provide database features and functionality. Core Data can create files as SQLite databases so that other apps can interact with the database using SQLite as well. This format is unreadable for most humans, too.

Maintaining User Preferences

Many apps come with options for managing the different features of using the application. A browser app might include the following choices (and more) for a user:

✔ The font style and size for standard text

✔ The default search engine

✔ The home page to open when the browser is launched

✔ Whether to accept cookies

Figure 8-14 shows my Appearance settings when I use Safari on my Macintosh, and this is one of the smallest of the Preference displays for Safari.

Figure 8-14: Preference options used to configure how Safari does things for me.

My selection of my preferred options is called "preferences," and each of your users will have their own set of expectations and desires for your app to fulfill, even for simple things. You are not required to deliver what your users want, but they will happily leave you for someone else whose app caters to their preferred way of doing things. Therefore, you want to look over your application and decide what, if anything, can be better stored as a user's preference. In this section, I show you how to retain user's preferences using the classes that Apple provides for the job.

Your users' preferences are not normally stored with each data set that is saved into the file system. Your app could do this, and in the very ancient days of Macintosh programming, that's what developers sometimes did. However, if your users' preferences change, old files storing the preferences they selected would not reflect today's choices. Generally, preferences are choices users make regarding the overall behavior of your app, and not the specific behavior of your app for a particular set of data. The set of preferences for Safari cover a wide range of choices Safari users make when they expect the browser to behave in a particular fashion. One of the most important is how Safari should behave with respect to user privacy and security. This is precisely the type of information that should be stored in a preferences container, and this information is used for each website I browse to.

Apple provides a very simple class, NSUserDefaults, to support setting and retrieving all the preferences you may need to store and keep track of for your users. Most applications can get by with using the simple NSUserDefaults methods, including

⊮ **Getting the shared** NSUserDefaults **instance.** Your app will need to gain access to the object owned by the OS that permits access to the defaults database for your application.

⊮ **Storing user preferences.** The NSUserDefaults class provides methods that permit you to create, by name, the preferences stored in the NSUserDefaults data storage.

⊮ **Getting stored preferences.** You can retrieve preferences, if any, that your app has stored in the past.

Listing 8-6 shows sample code that retrieves the user's preferences when the app starts, and a second method that's executed when the application is about to exit.

Listing 8-6: Storing and retrieving optional preferences of DiabeticPad users

```
// default storage path
NSString* DEFAULT_STORAGE_PATH = "~/Library/Application
        Support/DiabeticPad";

// member variables from header
//
// NSString* m_defaultStorageFolder;
// path to store data files
// NSInteger m_bloodGlucoseLowValue;
// value to indicate too low
// NSInteger m_bloodGlucoseHighValue;
// value to indicate too high
//

- (void)initialize
{
    // get the global user defaults
    NSUserDefaults* prefs = [NSUserDefaults
        standardUserDefaults];
    // retrieve, if available,
    // the default log storage location
    m_defaultStorageFolder = [prefs stringForKey:@"logbook
        StoragePath"];
    // use the default if it's not stored
    if (nil == m_defaultStorageFolder)
    {
        m_defaultStorageFolder = [DEFAULT_STORAGE_PATH
        stringByExpandingTildeInPath];
    }
```

(continued)

Listing 8-6 *(continued)*

```
    m_bloodGlucoseLowValue = [prefs
        integerForKey:@"lowBGLevel"];
    m_bloodGlucoseHighValue = [prefs
        integerForKey:@"highBGLevel"];
}

- (void)storeUserPreferences
{
    NSUserDefaults* prefs = [NSUserDefaults
        standardUserDefaults];
    if (nil == m_defaultStorageFolder) // just in case
    {
        m_defaultStorageFolder = [DEFAULT_STORAGE_PATH
        stringByExpandingTildeInPath];
    }
    [prefs setObject:m_defaultStorageFolder
        forKey:@"logbookStoragePath"];
    [prefs setInteger:m_bloodGlucoseLowValue
        forKey:@"lowBGLevel"];
    [prefs setInteger:m_bloodGlucoseHighValue
        forKey:@"highBGLevel"];
}
```

The three member variables are retrieved from the user defaults in the `initialize` method and stored using the `storeUserPreferences` method. These preferences are

✔ **The folder in which to store the data files.** The user has the freedom to change this location from the preferences panel (see Chapter 6) or when a new file is first saved.

✔ **A value representing a blood glucose level that is considered too low.** Low values are important to note when reviewing the daily logbook entries, and users can set this value to cause the display of an entry with a blood glucose reading below the value highlighted for greater visibility.

✔ **A value representing a blood glucose level that is considered too high.** Like low values, high blood glucose readings are also important to keep track of. Setting this value displays logbook entries where the blood glucose level is higher than the value.

Your app is not limited to storing strings and basic data types (such as integers) as user preferences. You can use the NSUserDefaults class to store just about any kind of value or object that your application uses. Here are the data types your app can store as a user preference:

- ✔ Integer values.
- ✔ Floating-point values.
- ✔ Double values (higher precision floating-point numbers).
- ✔ Boolean values (true or false).
- ✔ NSString objects. String data can be pretty much anything. You can represent just about anything using some form of string.
- ✔ NSURL objects. The Safari browser preference for the default home page to be opened could be stored as an NSURL.
- ✔ NSData objects.
- ✔ NSNumber objects. Instead of the primitive types (see the first four listed above), you can create objects that hold the primitive types and store them instead. Using an NSNumber makes it easier to store sets of numbers in an NSArray or an NSDictionary. The primitive data types, such as integer values, must be contained in an NSNumber object before it can be held in a collection.
- ✔ NSDate objects.
- ✔ NSArray objects. You can store an entire array of NSObjects in user preferences. This makes it easier for your app to store a collection of different types of objects together without having to set or get each one individually.
- ✔ NSDictionary objects. An NSDictionary object can store key-value pairs of NSObjects.

If your app needs to store any other type of object, you will need to archive the object into an NSData object which can be stored as a default. The object must implement the NSCoding protocol, as shown in the section "Creating a data class" earlier in this chapter. This gives you freedom and flexibility when your app needs to store preferences for your users.

In Listing 8-6, I created an NSString called DEFAULT_STORAGE_PATH. This is the file system location of where the app will store its output data files by default. In OS X 10.7 Lion, the Library folder that this path refers to is hidden, which can cause some frustration, especially if you're trying to determine whether your app is saving data in the right place. While it's not simple to do, you can always navigate the entire file system by using Apple's Terminal app, available in Applications ⇨Utilities.

Exporting data

Because your users will only ever look at or manipulate their data by using your app, there's no need to go into any detail regarding exporting their data. Then reality sets in. As perfect as a Mac app is, your users will want access to their data in ways you've never imagined. For DiabeticPad users, I can easily envision their health care providers wanting to look at their data. And as much as I wish everyone had a Macintosh, a few medical professionals out there haven't realized just how wonderful Macs and Mac apps are. Somewhere, someday, one of my users will have to present all their data to a health care professional who's using a Windows PC. That means exporting the data.

The app data free trade agreement

No, this is not something Congress has dreamed up. Nor have Apple and Microsoft entered into a pact. Your users are using your app to record their data, but at some moment in the future, your users will want to explore that data in some fashion you haven't thought of or implemented. To do this, your users could send you feedback and then wait for you to implement more features and functionality to support their requests. Alternatively, you could just give your users the raw data in a form that allows them to manipulate it in ways you hadn't considered.

DiabeticPad stores simple records of connected pieces of information:

- Date and time
- Blood glucose level
- Carbohydrates consumed
- Exercise
- Notes
- Insulin dosage and type

Most of the records will have the first two pieces of data, and other records will contain additional data as users see fit. One of the first features missing from DiabeticPad is a graph of the blood glucose levels over time. I left this out intentionally; I did not want to spend the time and effort needed to do the basic job necessary to accommodate this kind of viewing of the data because there are applications on the market designed by professionals and refined over years of sales that can do the same job. Moreover, those applications will import the data from my app, too, if the data is formatted properly. And that's the underlying concept in this section: the data your app exports is going to be imported by someone else's app. If you know or can guess what app your users are most likely to use with the exported data, you can help them immensely by determining the best way to deliver their information.

Exporting data from DiabeticPad

DiabeticPad has a pretty simple set of data records, and my expectation is that my users will want to import the data into a spreadsheet. That's a relatively safe bet, and so DiabeticPad was written to export data into a text file where the data values are separated by commas. This format is called Comma Separated Values (CSV). All the major spreadsheet applications available can import this type of text file and convert it to their own preferred format.

Figure 8-15 shows the Export panel a user sees when they choose File⇨ Export from the menu in DiabeticPad. The file is saved using the code in Listing 8-7.

Figure 8-15: Users can move their data from the internal storage to a file that a spreadsheet app can import.

Listing 8-7: **MyDocument method that saves logbook records in CSV format**

```
- (IBAction)handleExportToCSV:(id)inSender
{
    // assumption: this method is in a
    // subclass of NSPersistentDocument
    NSSet* managedObjects = [self.managedObjectContext
            registeredObjects];
    NSEnumerator* enumer = [managedObjects objectEnumerator];
    NSMutableData* outputData = [[NSMutableData alloc] init];
    id object; // placeholder
    NSDateFormatter* formatter = [[[NSDateFormatter alloc]
            init] autorelease];
    // set a readable date/time format
    [formatter setDateFormat:@"yyyy-MM-dd HH:mm"]
    NSString* columnHeaders = @"Date/Time, Blood Glucose,
            Carbs, Exercise, Insulin Dosages, Notes\n";
    [outputData appendBytes:[columnHeaders UTF8String]
            length:[columnHeaders length]];
    while (object = [enumer nextObject])
    {
        NSDate* timestamp = [object
            valueForKey:@"timestamp"];
        NSString* bloodGlucose = [object
            valueForKey:@"bgLevel"];
        NSString* carbs = [object valueForKey:@"carbs"];
        NSString* exercise = [object
            valueForKey:@"exercise"];
        NSString* insulinDosages = [object
            valueForKey:@"insulinDosages"];
        NSString* notes = [object valueForKey:@"notes"];
        NSString* dateString = [formatter
            stringFromDate:timestamp];
        // check all objects for nil or zero-length values
        if (nil == notes)
        {
            notes = @"";
        }
        if (nil == bloodGlucose)
        {
            bloodGlucose = @"0";
        }
        if (nil == carbs)
        {
            carbs = @"0";
        }
        if (nil == exercise)
        {
            exercise = @"0";
        }
```

```
        NSString* outputString = [NSString stringWithFormat:
            @"%@,%@,%@,%@,%@,%@,\n", dateString, bloodGlucose,
            carbs, exercise, insulinDosages, notes );
        [outputData appendBytes:[outputString UTF8String]
            length:[outputString length] ];
    }
    [self writeDataToFile:outputData];
    [outputData release];
}
```

The new method added to export the data as a CSV file works by looping over all the available Core Data entity objects and appending their data as text into an NSMutableData object. The data object is then passed to the method used to write the data to the user-selected file. The details of the method's operations are as follows:

1. Get the set of all the objects maintained by the Core Data store.

   If the app is not using Core Data to store its logbook entries, the collection object used to store the entries would be retrieved instead.

2. Create the NSMutableData object to hold the text for output to the file.

3. Create an NSDateFormatter object that will be used to properly format the NSDate object representing the timestamp entity into a readable form.

4. Create a text string containing the column headers and then append the text to the NSMutableData object.

5. For every entity in the set, do the following

   a. Get the individual objects for each of the entity attributes maintained by Core Data.

      Each attribute is held by the Core Data entity in a subclass of NSObject; the strings are NSString objects, the timestamp is an NSData object, and the integers are NSNumber objects.

   b. Convert all the attribute objects into strings.

      For instance, the NSDate object used for the timestamp is converted to an NSString object by the NSDateFormatter object.

   c. Put all the attribute objects in order into one string, separating the values by commas and adding a newline character (\n) at the end.

   d. Append the text to the end of the NSMutableData object.

6. After all the entities have been processed, deliver the NSMutableData object to the method that will output the text data to the user's file.

Each record in the app's storage is accessed and processed to turn it into a text string that can be written to a text file. If your app is managing all its objects, such as a DPData object as mentioned earlier in the chapter, you could create a method for the DPData class that outputs an NSString object that's ready to be appended by an NSMutableData object. This would make the above code less busy; you would do all the checks on the validity of the data within the DPData method before delivering the NSString representing its contents. As in most programming efforts, there's always a way to improve things.

Importing data

Your users may also have the data your app can use stored in a neutral format such as CSV exported from some other app. One of the blood glucose monitoring devices I use allows its data to be exported to a CSV format so other apps such as DiabeticPad can import the data. Importing data from other apps requires some investigation: You need to know what's in the exported file and how it's organized before you can implement code to read the information and use it in your app. Since CSV is a text-based format, Apple's TextEdit app will show you what's inside any CSV file you want your app to import.

I'll use the CSV file created by DiabeticPad in the previous section as an example for importing a file. The code shown in Listing 8-8 will read data from the file at the path specified in the method's input parameter and create Core Data objects from the records in the file.

Listing 8-8: MyDocument method to import logbook records stored as CSV

```
- (BOOL)importFromCsv:(NSString*)inFilePath
{
    BOOL success = YES;
    if (nil != inFilePath)
    {
        NSError* error = nil;
        NSString* csv = [NSString stringWithContentsOfF
            ile:inFilePath encoding:NSUTF8StringEncoding
            error:&error];
        if (nil != csv)
        {
            // split input into separate records,
            // one per line
            NSArray* csvLines = [csv componentsSeparatedBy
            String:@"\n"];
```

```
NSEnumerator* lineEnumer = [csvLines
objectEnumerator];
NSString* csvRecord = nil;
BOOL firstLine = YES;
while (csvRecord = [lineEnumer nextObject])
{
    if (YES == firstLine)
    {
        // first line is column headers
        firstLine = NO;
        continue;
    }
    // each csvRecord contains its data
    // separated by commas
    NSArray* dataArray = [csvRecord
componentsSeparatedByString:@","];
    // we know the ordering, since we created it
    // everything comes in as a String first
    NSString* timestampString = [dataArray
objectAtIndex:0];
    NSString* bgLevelString = [dataArray
objectAtIndex:1];
    NSString* carbsString = [dataArray
objectAtIndex:2];
    NSString* exerciseString = [dataArray
objectAtIndex:3];
    NSString* insulinDosagesString = [dataArray
objectAtIndex:4];
    NSString* notesString = [dataArray
objectAtIndex:5];
    // have all we need to make a data record
    // use the array controller to create a
    // new object
    NSObject* arrayObject = [m_arrayController
newObject];
    // set the data to that object
    [arrayObject setValue:bgLevelString
forKey:@"bgLevel"];
    [arrayObject setValue:carbsString
forKey:@"carbs"];
    [arrayObject setValue:exerciseString
forKey:@"exercise"];
    [arrayObject setValue:insulinDosagesString
forKey:@"insulinDosages"];
    [arrayObject setValue:notesString
forKey:@"notes"];
    // need to convert the timestamp string
    // to NSDate
```

(continued)

Listing 8-8 *(continued)*

```
                    // for CSV data we created, we know the
                    // format; for unknown data, you have
                    // to investigate
                    NSDateFormatter* formatter
            = [[[NSDateFormatter alloc]
            initWithDateFormat:@"yyyy-MM-dd HH:mm"
            allowNaturalLanguage:NO] autorelease];
                    NSDate* timestamp = [formatter dateFromString
            :timestampString];
                    [arrayObject setValue:timestamp
            forKey:@"timestamp"];
                }
        }
        else
        {
            // error occurred during read
        }
    }
    return (success);
}
```

At this point, you can create and manage the data objects that your app uses on behalf of your users, and your app can output the data in a form that other applications can pick up and process in ways that your app doesn't have to implement. For instance, one of the medical professionals I work with likes to view my blood glucose readings as a graph. DiabeticPad can export all the readings into a spreadsheet so my health care provider can see all the readings and the points where I injected insulin to keep the blood glucose in a tolerable range.

Chapter 9

Working in the Background

*E*very current Macintosh comes with several CPUs, each of which can perform independently of the others. The minimalist MacBook contains an Intel Core 2 Duo CPU; the beefiest Macintosh Pro comes with two separate six-core Intel CPUs (and yes, I dream about that one). OS X is written with multitasking in mind, and the apps you run on your Mac can take advantage of multiple CPUs without your having to tell them to do so. So iTunes is downloading tonight's video while playing its theme song, your e-mail app is retrieving the latest messages from your office while you're writing, and your web browser is displaying the new messages from your friends at your favorite social-networking site, while you're translating some German.

Your Mac app can use all the CPUs on the machines where your users install it. Normally, your app will operate on just one CPU, submitting its programming instructions to the processor. But you can enhance your app's performance, even while running on just one CPU, if you set up some of your code to operate in the *background*. Although your Mac can run multiple apps all at the same time, your app can achieve something similar by performing different tasks at the same time. A Mac application that executes different tasks concurrently achieves this by launching different *threads,* each of which represents one task. In this chapter, you find out about the threads that your app can create with Cocoa and OS X, and you see how to exploit them to make your app more accommodating for your users.

Understanding Basic Threads

Hang on; you're about to receive a crash course in threads. I cover the basic concepts you need to know to get started and to overcome any fear of using them, but a complete explanation is outside the scope of this book. You can easily find quite a few online and written resources to fill in any gaps.

An *application* is a set of instructions that sits in your computer's memory. The instructions are fed one at a time to the computer's central processing unit (CPU). The CPU can execute only one instruction at a time. As CPUs have gotten faster and faster, however, it has become possible for one CPU to execute two or more sets of instructions practically simultaneously. Today, CPUs come with multiple cores, each of which functions as an independent CPU that can access the memory and the devices attached to the computer. Modern OSes, such as OS X, juggle the different sets of instructions to be executed together, either giving each set a short period of time to operate on one CPU or lining up each set to be executed separately on multiple CPUs. A *thread* is one of those sets of instructions.

By using threads, a developer can create an app that performs multiple actions simultaneously in the background while the user is viewing the app's display. The user can interact with the UI of your app even while the app is waiting for data to download (a common occurrence with the networked apps of today). Your users will believe that they are in control of your app, even though your app is operating in the background, performing tasks that can take noticeable amounts of time; your app's UI will remain responsive to the users' commands. If your app doesn't use threads to perform data access in the background, your users will be left staring at an unchanging display, unable to interact with the app (and possibly even the computer itself) until your code returns to interactive execution after the data is retrieved or fails to be retrieved. This experience is not a very pleasant one for your users.

Three Cocoa classes provide your app the ability to execute code in the background of Mac OS X:

- ✔ NSTimer: An NSTimer allows you to schedule code to be executed at some point in the future. An alarm-clock app would use an NSTimer to wake up a napping user at a specific time or after a set amount of time. Your app can also schedule the code to repeat the operation after a certain amount of time.

- ✔ NSTask: An NSTask is an object your app creates to execute a completely separate application. Your app has access to all the other apps that run on the user's Macintosh, and your app can launch these other apps to perform various operations, assuming that your app has privileges to do so. Instead of building your app complete with a user guide, for example, you can host all that information on a website. When a user selects the User's Guide menu item from your app's Help menu, your app can launch the Safari web browser with the URL to your online guide.

✔ NSThread: You use an NSThread when your app is going to process information or perform operations in the background without involving the user. If your app takes pictures using the Mac's camera and then provides a variety of images that are stretched, rotated, or blurred, your app can use NSThread objects to process each image in a different way. One NSThread could perform only stretch operations, and so on.

OS X is based on Unix and comes with the standard Unix C-language thread model: POSIX threads, also known as *pthreads*. If you're coming from a Unix or Linux OS, you can make use of pthreads in your app, just like you would in a C-language application, because Objective-C can compile C code for your app to use. So if you have a library of image-processing software that your app can't live without, for example, you can incorporate the C-code into your app and use it just as your C-language apps do. Also, in case you were wondering, the underlying implementation for threads in Mac OS X is based on the POSIX threads API.

Your app will use the preceding classes for all the background operations you want to perform. These operations generally fall into two categories:

✔ **Fire and forget:** This kind of operation is the easier of the two to implement and the simpler to understand. Your app will initialize a fire-and-forget thread to perform a specific set of instructions, launch it, and let it do its work. When the thread has completed its job, it just stops. One example of an operation that's suited for this type of thread is code that writes information to a file or a network repository.

✔ **Call me when you're done:** You'll find this operation to be the kind that you implement most often. Your users direct your app to perform a lengthy operation, such a searching an online food forum for interesting recipes containing garlic and pesto, after which your app reports back some information about the results of the operation. This type of operation requires some sort of callback mechanism to be set up for the thread to execute after it finishes doing its job. Fire-and-forget operations are easy to create, but in a lot of cases, they also require a means of reporting information back to the user. In the preceding example, what happens if the thread can't write to the file or connect to the network repository?

Knowing when to use a thread

For apps that have a visual interface, you use a thread to perform an operation in the background in only one situation:

> When the operation that your app intends to execute will take too much time away from your app's paying attention to your users' actions.

For your apps that don't have a visual interface, you use a thread to perform operations that can be almost completely self-contained. For example, a web-server app creates a separate thread for every incoming request to retrieve a page from the site, so that each request is processed separately and isn't delayed while a prior request is still completing.

Your users are busy. They use their computers to make themselves more productive and more efficient in doing their daily tasks. Today's Macs have multiple processors that are also very fast and come with an operating system that enables multiple apps to execute at the same time. Your users will browse the web, read and write e-mail, check their calendars, listen to music, and also run your app. Your users expect your app to behave like a butler, running around to perform chores for them. Further, users will expect your app to do multiple chores, like a mansion full of butlers waiting for orders. If I send one butler out to find all the garlic-and-pesto vegetarian recipes, I may want to send another one out to find all the five-star-rated bruschetta-and-pepper-jack-cheese recipes. I don't want to wait for the first butler to finish before I send out the second. That would just waste my time.

So, how much time is "too much"? You may not like this answer: It depends. Also, you may have to wait for feedback from your users before you can determine whether you should run a particular operation as a background thread. My own preference is to not leave users waiting, so if something I want my app to do doesn't finish really quickly (within a few tenths of a second), that's something I want to put in a separate thread and run in the background.

Here are some types of operations for which you may want to consider implementing your app's code as a background thread:

- **Hardware operations:** Your app will have to use the hardware on your users' computers to perform some operations. Your app may play music or display videos for your users. Both of these operations, and many others, require your app to move information from storage to a speaker (for sounds) or the display (for videos). If your app puts the code required to do these operations in a thread separate from the main body of your app, the performance of users' computers will improve, and the users will feel more in control of your app and their machines.

✔ **Network operations:** More and more information is available out on the Internet, and users are sending out requests for this information and retrieving it in greater amounts. But accessing the Internet is always a chancy process; you can never be sure whether the service your app needs to connect to is free to handle your request. Your app's request could end up in a queue, waiting for the service to finish the earlier 500 requests before it can handle yours. Even if your app is simply trying to connect to another computer or mobile device on your local network, your app can still find itself waiting for the results. You should definitely place all code that connects your app to the Internet into a thread that runs independently of the app's main thread.

✔ **Scheduled operations:** A calendar app like Apple's iCal can display reminders when a scheduled appointment is imminent. Users can set iCal to remind them of appointments at a specific time ahead of the appointment, leaving them free to concentrate on more important tasks, knowing that the trusty Macintosh will remind them when appropriate. You should place any code that will execute at a specific moment in a thread to run in the background.

✔ **Repeated operations:** Your app might display a clock that displays a sweep second hand, such as the one shown in Figure 9-1. Users expect the clock to be changing its display once per second — maybe more frequently if your app is being used for Olympic tryouts or, less frequently, if the app is being used to count down the remaining shopping days before an anniversary. No matter how often your app updates its time display, you need to put the update code inside a thread.

Figure 9-1: An example of a clock requiring display updates every second.

Heavy calculation operations: Certain types of applications perform intense mathematical calculations involving hundreds of equations. The financial and scientific communities create and use apps of this type to find answers to complex problems. If the solution to a problem can be reduced to a repeatable sequence of steps, that sequence can be written as a thread and executed independently of your app's main thread.

Thread rules to keep in mind

You will find that threads are easy to handle as long as you keep them simple and focused on the one task they are programmed to do. As a rule, I try to keep a thread's code no larger than one screen's worth of executable statements. This makes it easy to see everything a thread is going to do and encourages me to refrain from making a thread do too much. The following sections provide a few other rules to keep handy when you're implementing your app's threads.

Calling back to the thread's origin

One part of your application will launch the thread. Usually, this occurs somewhere within the main event thread of the application — the thread that's responsible for intercepting user inputs and delivering the data to the appropriate code in your app. Your user has ordered your app to perform some action, but this will take too much time to complete. In addition, the action your app performs to satisfy the user's request will require a result to be returned to the user when the thread has finished. Because this thread is separated from the main event thread and the rest of your app's code, your thread requires some mechanism to return data to your app.

The best way to accomplish this is to provide an object that will execute a method when the thread is started, usually passed into the thread in its initializer method. The NSThread class provides an initialization method that accepts a target object and a method for the code to execute on the target object. You set up the target object to perform the long-duration activity in its selected method, and as a result, the data is available within that object when the activity has completed. You can provide both success and failure methods to this object, to give it a way to tell the user that the activity completed successfully or explain why the activity resulted in failure. You can see in Listing 9-1 that the LongDurationActivity creates an NSThread object to perform a really long task and then reports its results to the user, who's looking at the screen.

Listing 9-1:   The class LongDurationActivity uses an NSThread to perform lengthy calculations

```
@implementation LongDurationActivity

- (void)launchActivity
{
    NSThread* activityThread = [[NSThread alloc] initWithTarget:self selector:
            @sel(lengthyActivity:) argument:nil];
    [activityThread start]; // start the thread
}

- (void)lengthyActivity:(id)inArgument
{
    BOOL activityIsSuccessful = NO;
    NSString* failureMessage = nil;
    // pseudo-code
    // within this method will be lots of calculations,
    // downloads, processing, etc.
    // the BOOL will be set to YES if everything works
    // and if something goes wrong, the failureMessage
    // will be set appropriately
    if (YES == activityIsSuccessful)
    {
        [self activitySuccess];
    }
    else
    {
        [self activityFailure:failureMessage];
    }
    [NSThread exit]; // tell the current thread (us) that we've finished
}

- (void)activitySuccess
{
    // update the screen with the results of the
    // calculations
}

- (void)activityFailure:(NSString*)inMessage
{
    // handle the error, display the message
    // to the user to explain what happened
}

@end
```

The code in Listing 9-1 is the simplest way to create and use an NSThread. Your app creates the thread object, hands it the object to use when calling the method for the thread to execute, and then sets it off. The thread's code will execute and call either the activitySuccess or activityFailure: method. At the very end of the code, the NSThread class method exit is called on the current thread, which removes the thread from the application memory space so it's no longer hanging around.

Synchronization

You'll discover that the biggest challenge is keeping your thread's operations synchronized with the other code running in your app. For an app that launches multiple threads to retrieve the ten best rates on hotels in Berlin for the week including July 4, for example, you'll want to ensure that the display of the top ten rates is kept in sync with the arrival of new data. Your app should provide visual feedback to the user that the butlers are doing their jobs.

You can reduce the likelihood of running into thread synchronization issues by keeping your use of threads to a minimum and also by making your thread code short and simple. But even if you're careful, thread synchronization problems can still arise. You'll find that nearly all problems of thread synchronization involve two separate threads both attempting to modify and use the same resource. This situation is called a *race condition*. Fortunately, the Cocoa framework provides a simple solution: the NSLock. You temporarily lock a section of code within the thread that executes it to prevent other threads from attempting to execute the same section of code at the same time.

Listing 9-2 shows two separate methods in a class. One method uses a lock (incrementWithLock), and the other doesn't (incrementWithoutLock). The only difference between the two methods is that the first one will execute the critical section of code guarded by the lock for the thread that has locked it only until the lock is removed at the end of the method. In the second method, the following problem can occur if multiple threads attempt to execute the method:

- Thread A executes the method incrementWithoutLock.

- The CPU starts to perform the sequence of steps to increment the value of the m_count variable contained by this object.

- Just before the increment is added, however, the OS pauses Thread A's execution and allows Thread B to resume its operations.

- Thread B is also executing incrementWithoutLock.

↙ The CPU performs the entire sequence of steps to increment the value of the m_count variable. Thread B is completed, and the OS resumes Thread A's execution.

↙ Because the resumption of Thread A's operations also resets the values of everything Thread A had in memory when it was interrupted, including the value of m_count right before Thread A was paused, the value of m_count is returned to exactly what it was before Thread B incremented it, eliminating Thread B's result as though it never happened. If both threads had used incrementWithLock instead, the problem would not have happened. Thread A would have secured the right to execute the code to increment m_count through the NSLock object, and Thread B would have to wait for the unlocking before executing.

Listing 9-2:   The difference between a method with a lock and one without

```
@interface ThreadLockTest
{
    int m_count;
}
- (void)incrementWithLock;
- (void)incrementWithoutLock;

@end

@implementation ThreadLockTest

- (void)incrementWithLock
{
    NSLock* locker = [[NSLock alloc] init];
    [locker lock];
    m_count++;
    [locker unlock];
    [locker release];
}

- (void)incrementWithoutLock
{
    m_count++;
}

@end
```

Although the example in Listing 9-2 is very simplified and its resolution is fairly simple, as your app becomes more complex and starts using more threads, you'll encounter more difficulty in tracking down this kind of problem.

Locks are one way of reducing the chance that one thread will violate the same data another thread is trying to use. Your app does pay a price for using locks, however: Depending on how many times you're locking down access to sections of your code, your app may suffer some performance penalties. Be careful in spreading locks around your code, and always try to fully understand the nature of the problem before rushing to lock another section of your code. I recommend reviewing Apple's Threading Programming Guide, available at

```
http://developer.apple.com/library/mac/#documentation/Cocoa/Conceptual/
                Multithreading/Introduction/Introduction.html
```

Deadlocks

You may encounter situations in which one thread in your app is waiting for access to a resource such as a file, but that resource is locked by another thread, and this second thread is waiting to access a resource that's unfortunately locked by the first thread. Think of two children on a playground, each holding a different color ball; neither will hand the other his ball before receiving the one held by the other. This situation is called a *deadlock*. Neither thread can continue because each is waiting for the other to finish.

The best solution to this problem is to keep your threads' operational code to a minimum: Each thread should have only one task that it should be able to complete independently of any other thread. The best way to do this is to make sure that your app always executes only one thread apart from the main event thread.

I hope that I haven't scared you away from using threads. A thread is a powerful tool that provides a solution to executing long-running tasks while giving users a sense that they're still in control of your app.

Using Threads to Schedule Events

Single-event scheduling is the easiest kind of threading. You won't have to create a new class to handle the execution; you simply do the following:

1. **Create a method in your class to be executed at some moment in the future.**

2. **Call the Cocoa method** performSelector:withObject:after Delay: **on that class with that method selector.**

That's all that you need to do for this very simple example.

Setting up and executing a scheduled one-time event

The following example demonstrates how to set up and schedule an event — namely, displaying a text string — to execute a user-entered number of seconds (1–60) in the future. Follow these steps:

1. **Launch Xcode.**

2. **Create a new project.**

   You don't need the project to be document-based, and it won't use Core Data. Just a simple window is all you need. I chose to name mine `OneTimeEvent`, which creates one class (`OneTimeEventAppDelegate`) to support the interaction between my code and the user interface.

3. **Select the `MainMenu.xib` file in the Project Navigator. Show the Utilities panel if it's not visible.**

   Xcode displays the contents of `MainMenu.xib` using Interface Builder.

4. **Select the Window object from Interface Builder's Dock if it's not visible.**

   You're going to add UI components to your app's window so you can see the app in action — and it should look like the window shown in Figure 9-2. If you're comfortable working with Interface Builder, you can create the interface to match Figure 9-2 on your own — in which case, you can skip ahead to Step 14.

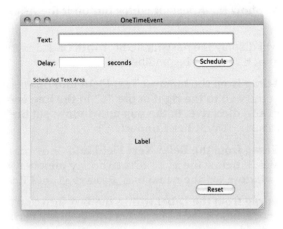

Figure 9-2: The main window of the OneTimeEvent app.

5. Drag and drop a Label from the Object Library. Set its text to Text.

6. Drag and drop a Text Field from the Object Library and place it next to the Text Label. Resize the Text Field horizontally to extend to the edge of the window.

7. Drag and drop a Label from the Object Library and place it below the Text Label. Set its text to Delay.

8. Drag and drop a Text Field from the Object Library and place it next to the Delay Label.

9. Drag and drop a Label from the Object Library, place it to the right of the Delay Label, and set its text to Seconds.

10. Drag and drop a Button from the Object Library and place it next to the Seconds Label. Set its text to Schedule.

11. Drag and drop a Box from the Object Library and place it below the Delay Label. Set its text to Scheduled Text Area. Resize the Box to take up the rest of the window's area.

12. Drag and drop a Button from the Object Library and place it near the lower-right corner of the Box. Set its text to Reset.

13. Drag and drop a Label from the Object Library and place it within the Box. Resize the Label so it occupies the full width of the Box.

    That completes all the visual elements this app will need. Your next task is to connect the components to the OneTimeEventAppDelegate.

14. Click the Show the Assistant editor button if the Assistant editor is not open.

    Xcode will display the Assistant editor with OneTimeEventApp Delegate.h ready to be modified.

15. Control-drag from the topmost Text Field into OneTimeEvent AppDelegate.h to the right of the "{" in the line containing the @interface directive. In the pop-up window, set the name to m_textToDisplay. Click Connect.

16. Control-drag from the Delay Text Field into OneTimeEventApp Delegate.h below the m_textToDisplay member variable. In the pop-up window, set the name to m_delayValue. Click Connect.

17. Control-drag from the Label within the Box into OneTimeEventApp Delegate.h below the m_delayValue member variable. In the pop-up window, set the name to m_displayLabel. Click Connect.

> Be careful. You need to be sure you're dragging from the Label, and not the Box.

18. Control-drag from the Schedule Button into OneTimeEventApp Delegate.h **right above the** @end **directive. In the pop-up window, set the connection type to Action and set the name to** schedule Event. **Click Connect.**

19. Control-drag from the Reset Button into OneTimeEventApp Delegate.h **right above the** @end **directive. In the pop-up window, set the connection type to Action and set the name to** resetLabel. **Click Connect.**

20. Add the purple **code in Listing 9-3 to** OneTimeEventAppDelegate.h.

Listing 9-3: The contents of the header file OneTimeEventAppDelegate.h

```
//
// OneTimeEventAppDelegate.h
// OneTimeEvent
//
// Created by Karl Kowalski on 4/3/11
// Copyright 2011 Kowalski Software Enterprises. All rights reserved
//

#import <Cocoa/Cocoa.h>

@interface OneTimeEventAppDelegate : NSObject <NSApplicationDelegate> {
    IBOutlet NSTextField *m_textToDisplay;
    IBOutlet NSTextField *m_delayValue;
    IBOutlet NSTextField *m_displayLabel;
@private
    NSWindow* window;
}

@property (assign) IBOutlet NSWindow *window;

- (IBAction)scheduleEvent:(id)inSender;
- (IBAction)resetLabel:(id)inSender;
- (void)displayText;

@end
```

21. Select OneTimeEventAppDelegate.m **from the Project Navigator.**

22. Enter the purple code from Listing 9-4.

Listing 9-4: The code implementation for scheduling a single event at a later moment

```
//
// OneTimeEventAppDelegate.m
// OneTimeEvent
//
// Created by Karl Kowalski on 4/3/11
// Copyright 2011 Kowalski Software Enterprises. All rights reserved.
//

#import "OneTimeEventAppDelegate.h"

@implementation OneTimeEventAppDelegate

@synthesize window;

- (void)applicationDidFinishLaunching:(NSNotification*)aNotification
{
    // Insert code here to initialize your application
    // clear the label
    [m_displayLabel setStringValue:@""];
}

- (IBAction)scheduleEvent:(id)inSender
{
    NSTimeInterval delay = [m_delayValue doubleValue];
    // check the bounds of the value
    if (delay < 1.0)
    {
        delay = 1.0;
    }
    else if (delay > 60.0)
    {
        delay = 60.0;
    }
    // now schedule
    [self performSelector:@selector(displayText) withObject:nil
            afterDelay:delay];
}

- (IBAction)resetLabel:(id)inSender
{
    [m_displayLabel setStringValue:@""];
    [m_displayLabel setNeedsDisplay];
}
```

```
- (void)displayText
{
    NSString* displayString = [m_textToDisplay stringValue];
    if (nil == displayString || [displayString length] == 0)
    {
        // Note: the text string here is just for the example
        // A robust app would retrieve text from a separate
        // file that can be localized
        displayString = [NSString stringWithString:@"you forgot to enter a text
            string!"];
    }
    [m_displayLabel setStringValue:displayString];
    [m_displayLabel setNeedsDisplay];
}

@end
```

23. Build and run the app.

**24. Enter text into the Text field and a delay value into the Delay field,
and then Click Schedule.**

You see the text displayed on schedule, as shown in Figure 9-3.

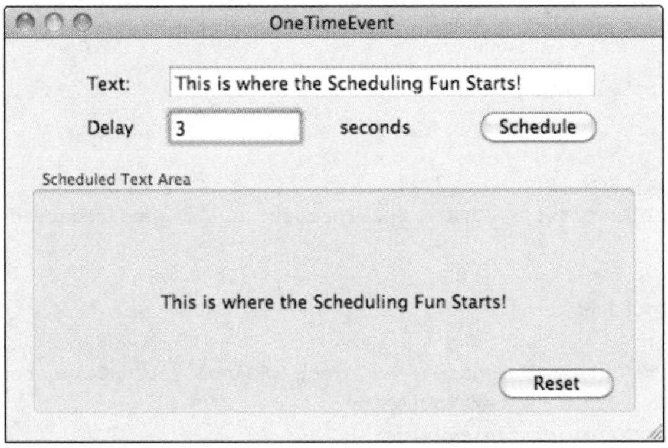

Figure 9-3: Your app can now change text labels several
seconds into the future.

The code you implemented from Listing 9-4 consists of three methods:

✔ **A method (**`scheduleEvent`**) to schedule the text-change operation:**
`scheduleEvent` checks the value of the delay and ensures that the
delay is between 1 and 60 seconds.

✔ **A method (`resetLabel`) to reset the text between scheduled events:** You could implement this method as part of the `scheduleEvent` method, but I'm a bit of a control freak, and I always want to be able to force the text label to reset itself.

✔ **A method (`displayText`) to be scheduled for future execution:** `displayText` performs a check of the text entered (or not entered) in the `Text Field` and then sets the text to be displayed appropriately.

You should feel free to play around with setting different values in the `Text Fields` to see how the app responds. If you enter **A** in the Delay field, for example, you find that the text changes 1 second later due to the delay value check that occurs in `scheduleEvent` — the `NSTextField` member variable is smart enough to convert a non-numeric value to 0.00 . You can also schedule multiple future text changes, but you have to be careful: Each event takes the text that's *currently* in the `Text Field m_textToDisplay`, so you have to change the text between the first scheduled event's occurrence and the next one. If you schedule two events to happen faster than you can change the text value, you won't see any change. You can improve the behavior of your app by modifying the code as shown in purple in Listing 9-5 and Listing 9-6.

Listing 9-5: Modifying the displayText Method to receive a parameter

```
//
// OneTimeEventAppDelegate.h
// OneTimeEvent
//
// Created by Karl Kowalski on 4/3/11
// Copyright 2011 Kowalski Software Enterprises. All rights reserved
//

#import <Cocoa/Cocoa.h>

@interface OneTimeEventAppDelegate : NSObject <NSApplicationDelegate> {
    IBOutlet NSTextField *m_textToDisplay;
    IBOutlet NSTextField *m_delayValue;
    IBOutlet NSTextField *m_displayLabel;
@private
    NSWindow* window;
}

@property (assign) IBOutlet NSWindow *window;

- (IBAction)scheduleEvent:(id)inSender;
- (IBAction)resetLabel:(id)inSender;
- (void)displayText:(id)inText;

@end
```

The change in Listing 9-5 is simple: Your method `displayText:` will now accept an object of type `id` passed to it, which will be the text to display. I chose to use an `id` object to match the object parameter type of the method `performSelector:withObject:afterDelay:` that the background thread will execute.

Listing 9-6:   Modifying the scheduleEvent method to pass a parameter to displayText

```
- (IBAction)scheduleEvent:(id)inSender
{
    NSTimeInterval delay = [m_delayValue doubleValue];
    // check the bounds of the value
    if (delay < 1.0)
    {
        delay = 1.0;
    }
    else if (delay > 60.0)
    {
        delay = 60.0;
    }
    // now schedule
    [self performSelector:@selector(displayText) withObject:[m_textToDisplay
            stringValue] afterDelay:delay];
}

- (void)displayText:(id)inText
{
    NSString* displayString = inText;
    if (nil == displayString || [displayString length] == 0)
    {
        displayString = [NSString stringWithString:@"you forgot to enter a text
            string!"];
    }
    [m_displayLabel setStringValue:displayString];
    [m_displayLabel setNeedsDisplay];
}
```

Now when you run the app and schedule multiple events, you'll see the text changing for each event as scheduled.

You can see that this app is pretty simple, yet you're already writing code for background processing. You're using the Cocoa method in `NSObject` to set a timer that will count down a fixed amount of time and then execute code. You can use this feature to create a clock or calendar app that will display an alert or play an audible sound at a specified point in the future. Another way to use this ability would be to add that kind of functionality to an app that does something else. You could add a feature to DiabeticPad that keeps track of and reminds users of their medical appointments, for example.

Using an NSTimer to schedule repeated events

You now know that scheduling single events for future execution is pretty easy and doesn't require the creation or use of a separate class; it can be done within the class you're working with. Also, you could implement code that schedules events repeatedly. You can schedule a method to be executed a minute from now and within that method schedule to be executed 60 seconds later. But the Cocoa framework provides a class that takes care of this for you: NSTimer. Because this kind of behavior is used frequently in many applications, the engineers at Apple created NSTimer to provide this functionality consistently.

The next app you're going to write demonstrates how to use an NSTimer to repeatedly change the color of a view. So let's get to it.

1. **Launch Xcode, if it's not running.**

2. **Create a new project.**

   As with the OneTimeEvent project earlier in this chapter, you don't need Core Data or a Document-based app. I named mine ColorizeTimer.

3. **Add a new class to the project, called ColorizedView.**

   This is an Objective-C class, and it will be a subclass of NSView.

4. **Select the ColorizedView.h file in the Project Navigator.**

5. **Modify ColorizedView.h to match the added purple code as shown in Listing 9-7.**

   Your app will use this class to set and draw different colors.

6. **Save your changes.**

Listing 9-7:   The ColorizedView.h header file

```
//
// ColorizedView.h
// ColorizeTimer
//
// Created by Karl Kowalski on 4/3/11
// Copyright 2011 Kowalski Software Enterprises. All rights reserved.
//

#import <Cocoa/Cocoa.h>

@interface ColorizedView : NSView
{
    NSColor* m_color;
@private
```

```
}

- (void)setColor:(NSColor*)inColor;

@end
```

7. **Select the** `ColorizedView.m` **file in the Project Navigator.**

8. **Modify** `ColorizedView.m` **to match the code shown in Listing 9-8.**

   Your code change is simply to add the code in purple from the listing.

9. **Save your changes.**

Listing 9-8:   The ColorizedView.m source module

```
//
// ColorizedView.m
// ColorizeTimer
//
// Created by Karl Kowalski on 4/3/11
// Copyright 2011 Kowalski Software Enterprises. All rights reserved.
//

#import "ColorizedView.h"

@implementation ColorizedView

- (id)initWithFrame:(NSRect)frame
{
    self = [super initWithFrame:frame];
    if (self)
    {
        // Initialization code here
        m_color = [NSColor grayColor];
    }
    return self;
}

- (void)dealloc
{
    [super dealloc];
}

- (void)setColor:(NSColor*)inColor
{
    m_color = inColor;
    // notify app that we need to redraw
    [self setNeedsDisplay:YES];
}
```

(continued)

Listing 9-8 *(continued)*

```
- (void)drawRect:(NSRect)dirtyRect
{
    // set the color to be drawn
    [m_color set];
    // draw a filled rectangle
    [NSBezierPath fillRect:dirtyRect];
}

@end
```

10. Select the `MainMenu.xib` **file in the Project Navigator. Show the Utilities view and Click the button to Show the Assistant editor.**

11. **Click the Window object in Interface Builder's Dock.**

12. **Drag and drop a Label from the Object Library to the upper-left corner of the window. Set the text of the Label to** Change Frequency.

13. **Drag and drop a Text Field from the Object Library and place it to the right of the Change Frequency Label.**

14. **Drag and drop a Label from the Object Library and place it to the right of the Text Field you just added. Set the text of the Label to** Per Minute.

15. **Drag and drop a Button from the Object Library and place it in the window below the Text Field and Labels. Set the text of the Button to** Start.

16. **Drag and drop a Button from the Object Library and place it in the window to the right of the Start Button. Set the text of this Button to** Stop.

17. **Drag and drop a Box from the Object Library and place it in the window below the two Buttons. Resize the Box to fill the remainder of the window, and set its text to** Colorizer Space.

    I obeyed the blue guides that Interface Builder provides when resizing the Box.

18. **Drag and drop a Custom View from the Object Library into the Box. Center the Custom View within the Box, and resize it to fill the Box.**

    Again, I obeyed the blue guides that Interface Builder provides when I resized the Custom View.

19. **Drag and drop a Label from the Object Library into the Custom View. Center the Label within the Custom View and set its text to** Color & Index. **Resize the Label to be as wide as the Custom View.**

    Your app's window should look similar to that shown in Figure 9-4.

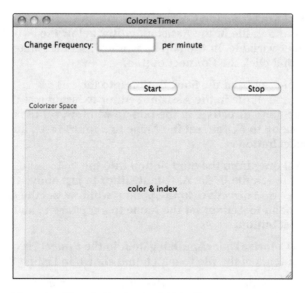

Figure 9-4: The window for the ColorizeTimer app.

20. **Select the Custom View you dropped into the Box and then Click the Show the Identity inspector button. Set the Class in the Custom Class group to** `ColorizedView`.

21. **Control-drag from the Text Field into the** `ColorizeTimerApp Delegate.h` **file in the Assistant editor to the right of the "{" at the end of the line containing the** `@interface` **directive. In the pop-up window, set the Name to** `m_frequency` **and click the Connect button.**

22. **Control-drag from the Start Button into the** `ColorizeTimerApp Delegate.h` **file in the Assistant editor below the** `m_frequency` **member variable. In the pop-up window, set the Name to** `m_start` **and click the Connect button.**

23. **Control-drag from the Stop Button into the** `ColorizeTimerApp Delegate.h` **file in the Assistant editor below the** `m_start` **member variable. In the pop-up window, set the Name to** `m_stop` **and click the Connect button.**

24. **Control-drag from the Color & Index Label into the** `ColorizeTimer AppDelegate.h` **file in the Assistant editor below the** `m_stop` **member variable. In the pop-up window, set the Name to** `m_colorLabel` **and click the Connect button.**

25. **Control-drag from the Custom View into the** `ColorizeTimerApp Delegate.h` **file in the Assistant editor below the** `m_colorLabel` **member variable. In the pop-up window, set the Name to** `m_color View` **and click the Connect button.**

26. **Control-drag from the Start Button into the** `ColorizeTimerApp Delegate.h` **file in the Assistant editor to just above the line containing the** `@end` **directive. In the pop-up window, set the Connection drop-menu to Action, set the Name to** `startTimer`, **and click the Connect button.**

27. **Control-drag from the Stop Button into the** `ColorizeTimerApp Delegate.h` **file in the Assistant editor to just above the line containing the** `@end` **directive. In the pop-up window, set the Connection drop-menu to Action, set the Name to** `stopTimer`, **and click the Connect button.**

28. **Select ColorizeTimerAppDelegate.h in the Project Navigator. Modify the contents of the file to match that shown in Listing 9-9.**

    The lines colored purple are the additions. You are adding two methods and four member variables to hold data the app will use for setting colors. Most importantly, you're adding the `#import` directive so that the compiler will know where to find the definition of a `ColorizedView`.

Listing 9-9:   The updated ColorizeTimerAppDelegate.h

```
//
// ColorizeTimerAppDelegate.h
// ColorizeTimer
//
// Created by Karl Kowalski on 4/3/11.
// Copyright 2011 Kowalski Software Enterprises. All rights reserved.
//

#import <Cocoa/Cocoa.h>
#import "ColorizedView.h"

@interface ColorizeTimerAppDelegate : NSObject <NSApplicationDelegate>
{
    IBOutlet NSTextField* m_frequency;
    IBOutlet NSButton* m_start;
    IBOutlet NSButton * m_stop;
    IBOutlet ColorizedView* m_colorView;
    IBOutlet NSTextField* m_colorLabel;

    NSTimer* m_timer;
    NSMutableArray* m_colorArray;
```

```
    NSMutableArray* m_nameArray;
    NSUInteger m_currentIndex;
@private
    NSWindow *window;
}

@property (assign) IBOutlet NSWindow *window;

- (IBAction)startTimer:(id)inSender;
- (IBAction)stopTimer:(id)inSender;
- (void)changeColorView:(NSTimer*)inTimer;
- (void)updateColor:(NSUInteger)inIndex;

@end
```

29. **Select the** `ColorizeTimerAppDelegate.m` **file in the Project Navigator.**

30. **Modify** `ColorizeTimerAppDelegate.m` **to match the code shown in Listing 9-10.**

Listing 9-10: Implementing the code for ColorizeTimerAppDelegate

```
//
// ColorizeTimerAppDelegate.m
// ColorizeTimer
//
// Created by Karl Kowalski on 4/3/11
// Copyright 2011 Kowalski Software Enterprises. All rights reserved.
//

#import "ColorizeTimerAppDelegate.h"

@implementation ColorizeTimerAppDelegate

@synthesize window;

- (void)applicationDidFinishLaunching:(NSNotification*)aNotification
{
    m_colorArray = [[NSMutableArray alloc] init];
    m_nameArray = [[NSMutableArray alloc] init];
    [m_colorArray addObject:[NSColor blueColor]];
    [m_colorArray addObject:[NSColor redColor]];
    [m_colorArray addObject:[NSColor greenColor]];
    [m_colorArray addObject:[NSColor yellowColor]];
    [m_colorArray addObject:[NSColor orangeColor]];
    [m_colorArray addObject:[NSColor purpleColor]];
    [m_nameArray addObject:@"Blue"];
    [m_nameArray addObject:@"Red"];
```

(continued)

Listing 9-10 *(continued)*

```objc
    [m_nameArray addObject:@"Green"];
    [m_nameArray addObject:@"Yellow"];
    [m_nameArray addObject:@"Orange"];
    [m_nameArray addObject:@"Purple"];
    m_currentIndex = 0;
    [m_stop setEnabled:NO];
}

- (IBAction)startTimer:(id)inSender
{
    [m_stop setEnabled:YES];
    [m_start setEnabled:NO];
    double colorChangeFrequency = [m_frequency doubleValue];
    if (colorChangeFrequency < 1.0)
    {
        colorChangeFrequency=1.0;
    }
    else if (colorChangeFrequency > 30.0)
    {
        colorChangeFrequency=30.0;
    }
    NSTimeInterval interval=60.0/colorChangeFrequency;
    m_timer = [NSTimer scheduledTimerWithTimeInterval:interval target:self
            selector:@selector(changeColorView:) userInfo:nil repeats:YES];
}

- (IBAction)stopTimer:(id)inSender
{
    [m_stop setEnabled:NO];
    [m_start setEnabled:YES];
    if (nil != m_timer)
    {
        [m_timer invalidate];
        [m_timer release];
        m_timer = nil;
    }
}

- (void)changeColorView:(NSTimer*)inTimer
{
    m_currentIndex++;
    [self updateColor:(m_currentIndex % [m_colorArray count])];
}

- (void)updateColor:(NSUInteger)inIndex
{
    [m_colorView setColor:[m_colorArray objectAtIndex:inIndex]];
```

```
      NSString* labelString = [NSString stringWithFormat:@"Color: %@, index: %d",
            [m_colorArray objectAtIndex:inIndex], inIndex];
      [m_colorLabel setStringValue:labelString
}

- (void)dealloc
{
      [m_colorArray release];
      [m_nameArray release];
      if (nil != m_timer)
      {
            [m_timer release];
      }
}

@end
```

31. Build and run your app.

When you click the Start button, the app will cycle through the colors in the m_colorArray. You can set the frequency to any value between 1 and 30 changes per minute. I suggest setting it to 30 to see it cycle through the colors very quickly.

You've now written an app that uses an NSTimer to schedule repeated display changes. You can use NSTimer to perform just about any kind of repetitive operation that your app requires to occur on a regular basis.

You can use an NSTimer or the performSelector:withObject:afterDelay: method of NSObject to accomplish a great deal of background processing of data. But at some point, you're going to need the full power of a completely separate NSThread, as you see in the next section.

Using NSThread to retrieve data from a website

There are a couple of websites I scan on a daily basis. www.nytimes.com always has interesting articles; my hometown newspaper at www.boston.com always keeps me up to date on what's happening around town; and I've always been a fan of www.dilbert.com to keep me current with the cartoon that laughs about life in a software developer's career. Also, there's always www.dummies.com, where I can check out the new books in the *For Dummies* series.

For this example, you're going to create an app that will go to the www.dummies.com website (because I won't have many copyright issues to deal with, assuming that my editors are okay with this!) and, from its main page, download all the JPEG images displayed there. Then the app will allow the user to display the images separately, one at a time.

You can find the source code for this project and all the other projects in this book at www.dummies.com/go/macintoshappdev.

The ForDummiesImages app will use an NSThread to retrieve the contents of the www.dummies.com URL and then search through all the items in the downloaded HTML for image tags ("img"). The downloaded content is assumed to be in an XML format, so the app will use Cocoa's NSXMLDocument, NSXMLElement, and NSXMLNode classes to perform the search. The NSXMLNode class provides a feature that allows you to search the XML contents using a standardized inquiry. Don't panic! You won't need to learn all the intricate details of this search process. The search for this example is pretty simple, and I'll point it out. Here are the steps:

1. **Launch Xcode, if it's not already running.**

2. **Create a new project.**

   I named mine *ForDummiesImages*.

3. **Select** MainMenu.xib **in the Project Navigator. Show the Utilities view and Click the Show the assistant editor button.**

4. **Click the Window in Interface Builder's Dock to display the app window.**

5. **Drag and drop a Button from the Object Library onto the app window. Set the Button's text to** Previous **and place the Button on the left side of the window, about halfway between the top and the bottom.**

6. **Drag and drop a Button from the Object Library onto the app window. Set the Button's text to** Next **and place the Button on the right side of the window, about halfway between the top and the bottom.**

7. **Drag and drop a Button from the Object Library onto the app window. Set the Button's text to** Start Download **and place the Button at the top of the window, about halfway between the left and right sides.**

8. **Drag and drop a Custom View from the Object Library onto the app window. Place the Custom View at the center of the window and resize it so that it fills the remaining space between the buttons.**

9. **With the Custom View still selected, Click the Show the Identity inspector button and change the Class of the Custom View to** NSImageView.

   Your window should look very similar to the one shown in Figure 9-5.

10. **Control-drag from the** NSImageView **into the** ForDummiesImages AppDelegate.h **editor to a point just after the "{" on the same line as the** @interface **directive. In the pop-up window, set the Name to** m_imageView **and click Connect.**

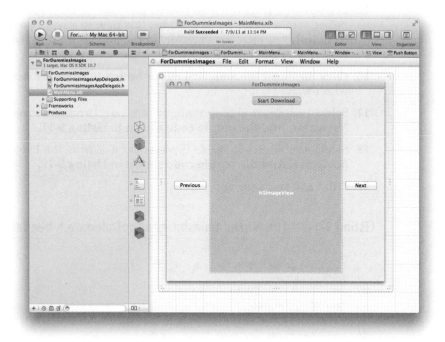

Figure 9-5: The window for displaying images downloaded from www.dummies.com.

11. **Control-drag from the Start Download Button into the** ForDummies
    ImagesAppDelegate.h **editor to a point just above the line contain-
    ing the** @end **directive. In the pop-up window, change the Connection
    to Action and set the Name to** startDownload. **Click Connect.**

12. **Control-drag from the Previous Button into the** ForDummiesImages
    AppDelegate.h **editor to a point just above the line containing the**
    @end **directive. In the pop-up window, change the Connection to
    Action and set the Name to** showPreviousImage. **Click Connect.**

13. **Control-drag from the Previous Button into the** ForDummiesImages
    AppDelegate.h **editor a second time, this time to a point just below
    the** m_imageView **member variable. In the pop-up window, set the
    Name to** m_previous **and click Connect.**

14. **Control-drag from the Next Button into the** ForDummiesImages
    AppDelegate.h **editor to a point just above the line containing the**
    @end **directive. In the pop-up window, change the Connection to
    Action and set the Name to** showNextImage. **Click Connect.**

15. **Control-drag from the Next Button into the** `ForDummiesImagesApp Delegate.h` **editor a second time, this time to a point just below the** `m_imageView` **member variable. In the pop-up window, set the Name to** `m_next` **and click Connect.**

16. **Click the Show the Standard editor button to close the Assistant window.**

17. **Select** `ForDummiesImagesAppDelegate.h` **from the Project Navigator. Add the purple code shown in Listing 9-11.**

18. **Select** `ForDummiesImagesAppDelegate.m` **from the Project Navigator. Add the purple code shown in Listing 9-12.**

19. **Build and run your app.**

Listing 9-11:   The ForDummiesImagesAppDelegate.h header file

```
//
//  ForDummiesImagesAppDelegate.h
//  ForDummiesImages
//
//  Created by Karl Kowalski on 4/3/11.
//  Copyright 2011 Kowalski Software Enterprises. All rights reserved.
//

#import <Cocoa/Cocoa.h>

@interface ForDummiesImagesAppDelegate : NSObject <NSApplicationDelegate>
{
    IBOutlet NSImageView* m_imageView;

    NSMutableArray* m_images;
    NSUInteger m_currentImageIndex;
    NSThread* m_downloadThread;
@private
    NSWindow *window;
}

@property (assign) IBOutlet NSWindow *window;

- (IBAction)startDownload:(id)inSender;
- (IBAction)showNextImage:(id)inSender;
- (IBAction)showPreviousImage:(id)inSender;
- (void)downloadImages:(id)inObject;
- (NSImage*)createImageFromUrl:(NSString*)inUrlString;

@end
```

Listing 9-12: **The implementation of the code to download images from www.dummies.com**

```
//
//  ForDummiesImagesAppDelegate.m
//  ForDummiesImages
//
//  Created by Karl Kowalski on 4/3/11.
//  Copyright 2011 Kowalski Software Enterprises. All rights reserved.
//

#import "ForDummiesImagesAppDelegate.h"


@implementation ForDummiesImagesAppDelegate

@synthesize window;

- (void)applicationDidFinishLaunching:(NSNotification *)aNotification
{
    // Insert code here to initialize your application
    m_currentImageIndex=0;
    [m_next setEnabled:NO];
    [m_previous setEnabled:NO];
}

- (IBAction)startImageDownload:(id)inSender
{
// remove any images already stored
    if (nil != m_images)
    {
        [m_images release];
    }
    m_images = [[NSMutableArray alloc] init];
    if (nil != m_downloadThread)
    {
        [m_downloadThread cancel];
    }
    m_downloadThread = [[NSThread alloc] initWithTarget:self selector:@
            selector(downloadImages:) object:nil];
     [m_downloadThread start];
}

- (IBAction)showNextImage:(id)inSender
{
    m_currentImageIndex++;
    if (m_currentImageIndex > [m_images count])
    {
        m_currentImageIndex = 0;
    }
```

(continued)

Listing 9-12 *(continued)*

```
    [m_imageView setImage:[m_images objectAtIndex:m_currentImageIndex]];
}


- (IBAction)showPreviousImage:(id)inSender
{

    m_currentImageIndex--;
    // the index will wrap around to a number
    // larger than the image count if it was
    // zero before the subtraction
    if (m_currentImageIndex > [m_images count])
    {
        m_currentImageIndex = [m_images count] - 1;
    }
    [m_imageView setImage:[m_images objectAtIndex:m_currentImageIndex]];
}


- (void)downloadImages:(id)inObject
{
    // create a release pool to clean up memory
    NSAutoreleasePool* pool = [[NSAutoreleasePool alloc] init];
    NSString* retrievalUrl = [NSString stringWithString:@"http://www.dummies.
            com"];
    NSURL* dummiesUrl = [NSURL URLWithString:retrievalUrl];
    NSError* error;
// create an XML document in memory
    NSXMLDocument* xmlDoc = [[NSXMLDocument alloc] initWithContentsOfURL:dummies
            Url options:NSXMLDocumentTidyHTML error:&error];
// get the root element
    if (nil != xmlDoc)
    {
        NSXMLElement* rootElement = [xmlDoc rootElement];
        if (nil != rootElement)
        {
            NSArray* imageNodes = [rootElement nodesForXPath:@"//img"
                error:&error];
            if (nil != imageNodes && [imageNodes count] > 0)
            {
                NSUInteger imageIndex=0;
                for (imageIndex=0; imageIndex<[imageNodes count]; ++imageIndex)
                {
                    // watch for exceptions each time through loop
                    @try
                    {
                        NSXMLElement* imageElement = [imageNodes
            objectAtIndex:imageIndex];
                        NSXMLNode* srcAttribute = [imageElement
            attributeForName:@"src"];
                        if (nil != srcAttribute)
                        {
                            NSString* srcAttributeValue = [srcAttribute
            stringValue];
```

```
                            if (nil != srcAttributeValue &&
                [srcAttributeValue rangeOfString:@"jpg"].location != NSNotFound)
                                {
                                        NSImage* dummiesImage = [self createImageFromUrl
                :srcAttributeValue];
                                    if (nil != dummiesImage)
                                    {
                                        [m_images addObject:dummiesImage];
                                    }
                                }
                        }
                    }
                @catch (NSException* except)
                {
                        // don't care, just continue
                }
            }
            if ([m_images count] > 0)
            {
                m_currentImageIndex = 0;
                [m_imageView setImage:[m_images objectAtIndex:m_
            currentImageIndex]];
                [m_imageView setNeedsDisplay:YES];
                [m_previous setEnabled:([m_images count] > 1)];
                [m_next setEnabled:([m_images count] > 1)];
            }
        }
    }
}
// clean up all auto-released memory to avoid leaks
    [pool release];}}

- (NSImage*)createImageFromUrl:(NSString*)inUrlString
{
    NSImage* image = nil;
    if (nil != inUrlString && [inUrlString length] > 0)
    {
        NSURL* imageUrl = [NSURL URLWithString:inUrlString];
        if (nil != imageUrl)
        {
            image = [[NSImage alloc] initWithContentsOfURL:imageUrl];
        }
    }
    return (image);
}


- (void)dealloc
{
    [m_images release];
    [super dealloc];
}

@end
```

You should see the first JPEG image displayed a few moments after you click the Start Download button.

Once again, the background thread is set to use a method on the object that creates it: the `ForDummiesImagesAppDelegate`. This procedure is the simplest approach to using `NSThread` objects. The class that needs to use an `NSThread` is the one that creates it and comes with the method that the `NSThread` object will execute. You can go further, such as creating a class that's a subclass of `NSThread` and thereby keeping the thread's executable code within that class. I chose not to do that in this case because the result of the thread's operation was going to set up the display of the images that it downloaded, and all that information would have to be delivered to the visual component of the app somehow. It was just easier to have the `NSThread` use the method within the `App Delegate` object itself.

The example makes use of a technology called *XPath*. XPath gives you the ability to specify a search for information within an XML document in memory — in this example, your app searched for HTML `<img>` tags, which contain links to image files. This example used XPath to perform a very simple search, but there's a whole language for XPath you can use to do much more complicated searches.

I first used the XML classes and XPath code in this example for a different project, to scan images from another website I also browse regularly. When I first ran the code using the `dummies.com` website, it crashed. Within the execution of the `for` loop in method `downloadImages:`, the call made to grab the string associated with the `"src"` attribute from the `NSXMLElement` object was throwing an exception, and I didn't know why. I placed the Objective-C exception-handling pieces around the offending code, and if an exception was thrown, the code would simply go on to the next `"img"` element and see what it contained. You can see the exception-handling block between the `@try` and `@catch` statements in the `downloadImages:` method. When I got the workaround implemented and got the code working, I took a look at the source of the web page at `www.dummies.com`. I found the first JPEG image reference and discovered an anomaly: Normally, attributes inside an XML tag should be of the form `attributeName="attributeValue"`. For this one item, an attribute didn't have double quotes around the value, which caused a problem for the XML parser within `NSXMLElement`.

Chapter 10

Printing Your User's Data

In This Chapter

▶ Getting familiar with the Cocoa printing process

▶ Fine-tuning the print settings

▶ Creating and running a print job

▶ Printing to PDF

*T*he Apple Macintosh gives you and your users a wonderfully rich inter-active experience with screens, menus, buttons, and many other visual elements users can manipulate onscreen. Your apps will use the graphics engine that Cocoa provides to draw their content on the users' monitors in clean, crisp pixels. But even though our world is becoming more virtual, some of your users will still want printed output. And that means your apps will have to deliver their content in a physical form, when appropriate. Cocoa gives you the classes and methods you need to provide your users the same pixels they see on the screen right on paper. This chapter will give you all the details for giving your users the paper copies they want.

Cocoa makes it easy for you to add printing features to your applications. The classes and methods you use to produce paper copies of your users' data are simple, and you can generate professional printing results that your users will appreciate.

Printing with Cocoa

You'll find that there's really only a small set of classes that Cocoa provides for you to achieve all your printing goals in your Mac apps. Most of these classes you'll use just to get information from your users to perform the printing of their information.

You'll use these classes to provide printing features in your apps:

- NSView: Cocoa makes printing to a page as simple for your app as drawing text and graphics to one of your app's NSViews. You learned how to command the pixels of an NSView in Chapter 7, and the same skills and techniques will work for printing as well, with only one exception: Printers are still not capable of drawing animated displays, at least not while they're in motion. Cocoa's printing code will draw onto a piece of paper the same contents displayed in an NSView on the screen.

- NSPageLayout: When a user selects File⇨Page Setup, your app uses the NSPageLayout class to display the Page Setup panel. This is the standard OS X panel users expect; your users will adjust the layout options for the pages they want to print. These options include the orientation of the page as well as the paper size and scale. When the user has selected the desired printing options, your app can retrieve these settings from an NSPrintInfo object. Note that you may encounter minor differences from one version of OS X to the next.

- NSPrintInfo: Your app will use an NSPrintInfo object to retrieve the settings that your user has selected from the Page Setup panel. Your app can use a default shared NSPrintInfo object (created for your app automatically) or create a new one. Apple recommends using a separate NSPrintInfo object for each document in a document-based app. This gives your app the capability to provide different print settings for each document.

- NSPrintPanel: Selecting File⇨Print from your app will display the standard Print panel, and this is handled by an NSPrintPanel object. Your app doesn't normally need to use this object. Similar to the Page Setup dialog, Apple may modify the appearance of this dialog, but the API your app uses to retrieve data from it will generally stay consistent.

- NSPrintOperation: Your app will create and use an NSPrint Operation to manage the process of printing. The easiest approach for your app to do printing is to use a default NSPrintOperation. Doing so provides the basic flow of operations that users have come to expect, which includes displaying an NSPrintPanel and then performing the print job.

Your app will use the classes listed above to smoothly transition a user from a screen display of their information to a printed one. The following is the sequence of steps your app will follow while executing a printing process:

1. Your app draws its information in an NSView.

What your app draws to its views, Cocoa draws on a printed page. Even if the NSView your app is going to print isn't displayed on the screen,

Cocoa can still print it. The same goes for subviews: as long as the view is a subclass of `NSView`, Cocoa can print what the view draws.

2. The user selects File⇨Page Setup.

Your app displays the Page Setup panel, giving the user the option of changing the page settings. You can see the standard Page Setup panel in Figure 10-1.

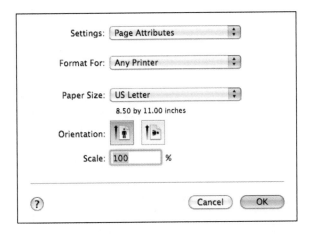

Figure 10-1: The Page Setup panel gives the user an opportunity to adjust settings for the pages in a print job.

3. The user sets options for the page layout and dismisses the panel.

Your app uses an `NSPrintInfo` object to store these settings.

4. The user selects File⇨Print to print the desired pages in hard copy.

Your app displays the Print panel, the last step before the pages are printed. Figure 10-2 shows a typical Print panel. When the user has made selections from the Print panel, he can start the print job by clicking OK.

Your app prints the view. Using the Page Setup and Print panel settings stored in an `NSPrintInfo` object, your app launches an `NSPrintOperation` that uses the `drawRect:` method of an `NSView` object to draw the view's contents on a printed page, using the same drawing code used to draw its contents on the screen.

Your app follows these steps, letting the user determine properties of the printed output and finally telling your app to print the data.

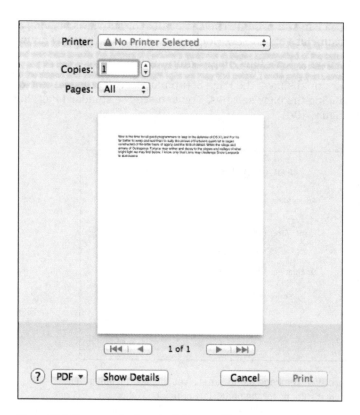

Figure 10-2: Your app displays the Print panel for users to make further adjustments and to execute the print job.

Setting up a Page

The default implementation of a window-based app does not enable the Page Setup menu, and the basic implementation of the Print menu command merely dumps a screen shot onto a printed page, as shown in Figure 10-3. If you want your app to do more than just these defaults, you'll have to do some work to get your app to behave as you prefer.

You use the following process to enable the Page Setup menu item:

1. **Launch Xcode.**

2. **Create a new basic project called** `BasicPrintApp` **and save it.**

   The project comes with an App Delegate, a window, and all the standard components that basic Cocoa apps come with.

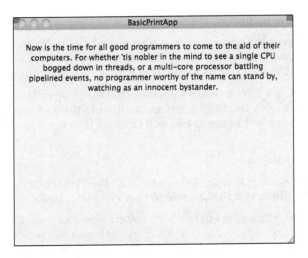

Figure 10-3: You can print from a window, but you'll just be printing the window.

3. **Add a new class to the basic project: Create** `BasicPrintView` **as a subclass of** `NSView`.

You add a new class by selecting New⇨New File from the File menu. This will start the process of creating files to represent the new class.

4. **Select.** `BasicPrintAppAppDelegate.h` **in the Project navigator, modify the file to match that shown in Listing 10-1, and then save your changes.**

The code in Listing 10-1 declares a method that your app delegate class is going to implement for itself. Doing so gives the app delegate a method to perform its own page setup, different from the default behavior. The delegate class also will contain a reference to an `NSPrintInfo` object to hold the settings that the user chooses.

5. **Click to select the** `MainMenu.xib` **file, which displays the file's contents in an Interface Builder editor.**

6. **Drag a Custom View from the Object Library in the Utilities view into the BasicPrintApp's main window.**

I prefer to maximize the size of the view up to the blue guidelines that Interface Builder shows me, and then use the Size inspector's Autosizing tool to "glue" the sides of the custom view to the sides of the window, so that the customer view will resize as the window does.

7. **In the Identity inspector, change the Class to** BasicPrintView**.**

Doing so makes the custom view you've just added an instance of your BasicPrintView, so that Cocoa will use the code you provide in BasicPrintView to perform the print operations you create.

8. **Select the App's File menu in Interface Builder to open it for editing. Control-drag from the Page Setup menu item to the** BasicPrintApp **app delegate object in the Dock, and connect it to the** pageSetup: **action.**

9. **Save your changes.**

10. **Select** BasicPrintAppAppDelegate.m **in the Project navigator. Modify the file to match the code shown in Listing 10-2.**

The code in Listing 10-2 will override any code in a parent class of BasicPrintAppAppDelegate. Your app delegate will now execute its pageSetup: method when the user selects the Page Setup menu item. In addition, the fact that the menu item is now connected to a method causes Cocoa to enable this menu item while your app is running.

11. **Save your changes.**

If you build and run the project, your app will display the standard Page Setup window when you select File➪Page Setup from the menu. And your app will also store the user's settings from the Page Setup window in the m_printInfo object for future use.

Listing 10-1:   The App Delegate header file, prepared to receive a Page Setup command from the user and store the results in an NSPrintInfo object that it maintains

```
//
//   BasicPrintAppAppDelegate.h
//   BasicPrintApp
//
//   Created by Karl Kowalski on 4/17/11.
//   Copyright 2011 Kowalski Software Enterprises.
//   All rights reserved.
//

#import <Cocoa/Cocoa.h>

@interface BasicPrintAppAppDelegate : NSObject
            <NSApplicationDelegate> {
@private
    NSWindow *window;
    NSPrintInfo* m_printInfo;
}
```

```
@property (assign) IBOutlet NSWindow *window;

-   (IBAction)pageSetup:(id)inSender;

@end
```

Listing 10-2:   The implementation of the App Delegate code needed to support Page Setup

```
//
// BasicPrintAppAppDelegate.m
// BasicPrintApp
//
// Created by Karl Kowalski on 4/17/11.
// Copyright 2011 Kowalski Software Enterprises.
// All rights reserved.
//

#import "BasicPrintAppAppDelegate.h"

@implementation BasicPrintAppAppDelegate

@synthesize window;

- (void)applicationDidFinishLaunching:(NSNotification *)
            aNotification
{
    // Insert code here to initialize your application
}


-   (IBAction)pageSetup:(id)inSender
{
    m_printInfo = [NSPrintInfo sharedPrintInfo];
    NSPageLayout* pageLayout = [NSPageLayout pageLayout];
    NSInteger response = [pageLayout runModalWithPrintInfo:
            m_printInfo];
}

@end
```

When a user selects the File➪Page Setup menu item, Cocoa determines that the action this menu item is going to execute is your `BasicPrintAppApp Delegate`'s `pageSetup:` method. This method first gets the application's default `NSPrintInfo` object and then displays a Page Setup window to get selections from the user. Your app doesn't do anything useful with this information, but you'll notice that any changes to the Page Setup are carried into the next display of the information — indicating that your app is maintaining the user's selections. Now we're going to add printing to your app.

The `NSInteger` returned from the `runModalWithPrintInfo:` message will either be `NSCancelButton` — if the user clicks the Page Setup dialog's cancel button — or `NSOKButton` — if the user clicks OK. This information is not usually required by your app, so you can safely ignore it.

Printing a Page

To add printing, you'll add another method to your project's app delegate class. Then you'll connect the Print menu item to execute that method. You'll be doing pretty basic printing by handing an `NSPrintOperation` object a reference to the app delegate's `BasicPrintView` that you want to have printed; Cocoa will take care of the rest.

1. **Select** `BasicPrintAppAppDelegate.h` **from the Project navigator, add the new code shown in purple in Listing 10-3, and save your changes.**

2. **Select** `MainMenu.xib` **from the Project navigator.**

   To keep things simple, I added a Label field to the `BasicPrintView` as shown in Figure 10-4. This is similar to the image shown in Figure 10-3, which demonstrated what the default Cocoa print operation does.

   You're welcome to add whatever text you'd like.

   As in the case with adding the `BasicPrintView` to the window, I recommend setting the Label to a maximum size as shown by the blue guidelines and also set it to resize with the window.

3. **Select the App's File menu in Interface Builder, Control-drag from the Print menu item to the** `BasicPrintApp` **app delegate object in the Dock, and connect it to the** `printView:` **action. Save your changes.**

4. **Select the Basic Print App App Delegate object in the Dock, Control-drag from the app delegate object in the Dock, and connect it to the** `BasicPrintView` **object in the window, selecting** m_printView **from the list. Save your changes.**

   You've now connected the `BasicPrintView` object that Cocoa creates when the window is generated to the application delegate, so that your app can use this view and draw its contents on a printed page.

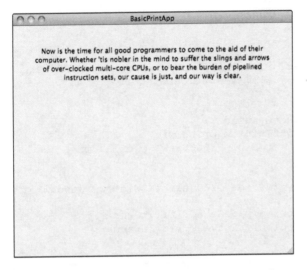

Figure 10-4: Add a text Label containing a re-wording of some famous quotation.

5. **Select** `BasicPrintAppAppDelegate.m` **from the Project navigator, add the new code shown in purple in Listing 10-4, and save your changes.**

6. **Build and run your app.**

   When you select the File⇨Print menu item, you get the standard Print panel, ready to send your view's contents to a printer or PDF file. Your app will now print the view's contents at the touch of a menu or keyboard shortcut.

Listing 10-3:   Add a reference to a BasicPrintView object and a method to handle printing

```
//
//   BasicPrintAppAppDelegate.h
//   BasicPrintApp
//
//   Created by Karl Kowalski on 4/17/11.
//   Copyright 2011 Kowalski Software Enterprises.
//   All rights reserved.
//

#import <Cocoa/Cocoa.h>
```

(continued)

Listing 10-3 *(continued)*

```objc
#import "BasicPrintView.h"

@interface BasicPrintAppAppDelegate : NSObject
            <NSApplicationDelegate>
{
@private
    NSWindow *window;
    NSPrintInfo* m_printInfo;
    IBOutlet BasicPrintView* m_printView;
}

@property (assign) IBOutlet NSWindow *window;

-   (IBAction)pageSetup:(id)inSender;
-   (IBAction)printView:(id)inSender;

@end
```

Listing 10-4:   Implement the print code

```objc
//
//  BasicPrintAppAppDelegate.m
//  BasicPrintApp
//
//  Created by Karl Kowalski on 4/17/11.
//  Copyright 2011 Kowalski Software Enterprises.
//  All rights reserved.
//

#import "BasicPrintAppAppDelegate.h"

@implementation BasicPrintAppAppDelegate

@synthesize window;

- (void)applicationDidFinishLaunching:(NSNotification *)
            aNotification
{
    // Insert code here to initialize your application
}


-   (IBAction)pageSetup:(id)inSender
{
    m_printInfo = [NSPrintInfo sharedPrintInfo];
    NSPageLayout* pageLayout = [NSPageLayout pageLayout];
```

```
        NSInteger response = [pageLayout runModalWithPrintInfo:m_
            printInfo];
    }

    -   (IBAction)printView:(id)inSender
    {
        [[NSPrintOperation printOperationWithView:m_printView]
            runOperation];
    }

@end
```

Now your app will print the text you added in the Label to a page in the printer. Your users can also save the output to a PDF file if they prefer, in order to e-mail it to anyone else they feel might like to see their information as printed by your app.

While this app is pretty simple, your own apps can deliver much more complex view-drawing code. The Cocoa framework will draw to a printer or PDF file using the same instructions as your code draws to the screen in a view's drawRect: method. Your app doesn't need to know that the end result is a piece of paper instead of some pixels on a monitor.

You can even determine in your drawRect: method whether your app is drawing to the screen. You might want to know about where your view is drawing if some of the things your view would draw on the screen wouldn't be appropriate for drawing to a piece of paper. For instance, if the user has selected some text in one of your views and then tries to print the display, you may not want the selection highlighting to be printed. The code snippet below demonstrates how to tell whether your view is about to be drawn on the screen or somewhere else:

```
-   (void)drawRect:(NSRect)inRect
{
    if ([NSGraphicsContext currentContextDrawingToScreen] ==
        YES)
    {
        // you're drawing on the screen
    }
    else
    {
        // you're not drawing on the screen
    }
}
```

Printing Straight to PDF

You now have the basic knowledge you need to move anything you can draw in an onscreen view onto a printed page. Your apps can print any view you create and follow the standard Mac app approach to create hard-copy output. But Cocoa also gives you the capability to print directly to a PDF (Portable Document Format) file. PDF has become the standard for publishing and printing documents and is also supported by almost all e-book readers. On other platforms, I have used open-source solutions for creating PDF files from within my applications. With Cocoa, it's easy to move what your app draws onscreen directly into a PDF file.

Your users can always print directly to PDF from the Print panel itself. The code you're about to add to your app provides the same feature behind the scenes, without requiring that users must select File⇨Print.

1. **Select** `BasicPrintAppAppDelegate.h` **from the Project navigator. Add the following new method declaration, right before** `@end`**:**

   ```
   - (IBAction)writeToPDF:(id)inSender;
   ```

2. **Save your changes.**

3. **Select** `MainMenu.xib` **from the Project navigator.**

   You're going to add a button that will create a PDF document from the view.

4. **Resize the** `BasicPrintView` **to make room for a button at the bottom.**

5. **Add a Button below the** `BasicPrintView`**, as shown in Figure 10-5.**

6. **Control-drag from the Button to the App Delegate method** `writeToPDF;`**.**

7. **Save your changes.**

8. **Select** `BasicPrintAppAppDelegate.m` **from the Project navigator. Implement the new method from the code shown below, right before** `@end`**:**

   ```
   - (IBAction)writeToPDF:(id)inSender
   {
       // get the view rectangle
       NSRect viewRect = [m_printView bounds];
       // now get the PDF data for the view in its rectangle
       NSData* viewData = [m_printView dataWithPDFInsideRect:viewRect];
       // now write to a file in the user's home directory
       [viewData writeToFile:[@"~/BasicPrintView.pdf"
   stringByExpandingTildeInPath] atomically:YES];
   }
   ```

9. **Build and run the app. If you click the button, you will create a PDF file named** `BasicPrintView.pdf` **in your home directory.**

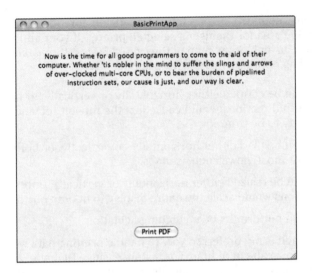

Figure 10-5: Adding a button to just print the view's contents directly to a PDF file.

You've now streamlined the users' experience — they no longer need to jump through hoops to get your screens written to a form they can move more easily. (Of course, you may *also* want to provide a way to let your users name the files more appropriately. Chapter 8 covers this.)

Printing with Multiple Pages

The preceding examples in this chapter give you the basic skills and techniques you'll need to write apps that can send their information to a printer or PDF files for users to work with. But one of the first questions I asked about printing was: What happens when what I want to print goes beyond one page?

The DiabeticPad app will require multiple pages to be printed, if my users want a printed copy of their entire history of entries. Users might also want a subset of the entire history, possibly just the most recent couple of pages' worth of data. I could provide an interface that would print whatever set of entries were on display when the user selects File⇨Print, but the user experience would suffer because most apps give users the capability to select any or all pages of a set to be printed.

The NSView class supports pagination automatically for views that are larger than the printable area for the user's selected printer. If your app's NSView subclass displays a high-detail map of the United States, for instance, you have the following options available for printing:

- The view can be clipped either horizontally or vertically, or both. Clipping both directions would cause just the top-left rectangle's worth of the display to be printed.

- The view can be tiled either horizontally or vertically, or both. This is sufficient for most views such as maps.

- The view can be resized either horizontally or vertically, or both. Resizing both directions would scale the entire display to fit onto one page.

- The view can perform its own custom pagination.

This approach is my preferred way to handle printing data whose content is unknown ahead of time. For instance, since DiabeticPad doesn't know how many entries are available to print, the printing code will have to calculate this information when a printing request comes in.

Paging your own way

Implementing a custom paging scheme can seem a bit intimidating, but it's really pretty straightforward. Your view subclass will need to override two methods of NSView:

- - (BOOL)knowsPageRange:(NSRangePointer)inRange. This method should return YES for an NSView subclass that will provide its own pagination. In addition, your subclass method must also fill in the range of pages, starting at 1, that the complete view will be divided into. A user can then select a page range from this minimum and maximum.

- - (NSRect)rectForPage:(int)inPageNumber. Your app will override this method to provide the boundaries of the rectangle to be drawn for the desired page.

To demonstrate how DiabeticPad prints out its own pages using custom pagination, I'm going to show you example code that mimics what DiabeticPad does. Although fairly simple, this app provides you with the basics for understanding how to deliver multipage printing to your apps.

1. **Launch Xcode if it isn't still running.**

2. **Create a new Document-based project with a document class named** PagedDoc, **and then save it in a convenient place.**

   Xcode create the basic set of files for a Document-based app.

3. **Select** `PagedDoc.xib` **in the Project navigator and select the Window from the Dock. Remove the** `Your document contents here` **label from the window. Save your changes.**

   This will give you an empty view in your app.

4. **Create a new file as a subclass of** `NSView`. **Call the subclass** `PagedDocView`.

   As mentioned earlier, you create a new class and its files by selecting New⇨New File from Xcode's File menu.

5. **Select** `PagedDocView.h` **from the Project navigator, modify its code to match that shown in Listing 10-5, and save your changes.**

   The new code from Listing 10-5 includes the set of member variables and the one new method, `initWithArray:`.

6. **Select** `PagedDocView.m` **from the Project navigator, modify its code to match that shown in Listing 10-6, and save your changes.**

   Listing 10-6 contains the code that the Mac executes to display your view when it's on the screen, and to print the contents of that view when the user selects the Print menu item. The initialize method — `initWithArray:` — retains a copy of the NSArray passed into the method and creates a font attribute to be used when drawing text; the `drawRect:` method draws the text to be displayed for the current page; the `knowsPageRange:` method calculates information about the printable area and sets the beginning and end of the range of possible pages; and the `rectForPage:` method remembers the current page number for use by a subsequent call to `drawRect:` and also returns the rectangular area available for drawing.

7. **Select** `PagedDoc.m` **from the Project navigator and add the purple code found in Listing 10-7.**

8. **Build and run your app.**

   The display will be empty because your app doesn't draw anything in its window — you removed the default window contents in Step 3 above. But when you print, the preview will show you the strings you passed into the view you created on the fly in the `printOperationWith Settings:error:` method.

   The default methods in the `PagedDoc.m` file are provided by Xcode as part of the Document-based app template. When you added the `print OperationWithSettings:` method to the `PagedDoc` class, you created code that Cocoa would execute that created a `PagedDocView` object and an `NSPrintOperation` object that would use it to perform multi-page printing. Cocoa will execute this code after a user selects Print from the File menu and clicks the OK button to start printing.

Listing 10-5:   The header file for the view that will be printed

```
//
//  PagedDocView.h
//  PagedDocPrint
//
//  Created by Karl Kowalski on 4/17/11.
//  Copyright 2011 Kowalski Software Enterprises.
//  All rights reserved.
//

#import <Cocoa/Cocoa.h>


@interface PagedDocView : NSView
{
    NSArray* m_stringArray;
    NSMutableDictionary* m_attributes;
    NSRect m_pageRect;
    NSInteger m_currentPage;
@private

}

-   (id)initWithArray:(NSArray*)inArray;

@end
```

Listing 10-6:   The code implemented for the view to be printed

```
//
//  PagedDocView.m
//  PagedDocPrint
//
//  Created by Karl Kowalski on 4/17/11.
//  Copyright 2011 Kowalski Software Enterprises.
//  All rights reserved.
//

#import "PagedDocView.h"


@implementation PagedDocView

-   (id)initWithArray:(NSArray*)inArray
{
    self = [super initWithFrame:NSMakeRect(0.0, 0.0, 100.0,
        100.0)];
```

```
        m_stringArray = inArray;
        [m_stringArray retain];
        m_attributes = [[NSMutableDictionary alloc] init];
        NSFont* stringFont = [[NSFont fontWithName:@"Helvetica"
                size:18.0] retain];
        [m_attributes setObject:stringFont
                forKey:NSFontAttributeName];
        return (self);
}


- (void)dealloc
{
        [m_stringArray release];
        [m_attributes release];
        [super dealloc];
}


- (void)drawRect:(NSRect)dirtyRect
{
        //  get the string to be drawn
        NSString* textString = [m_stringArray objectAtIndex:
                m_currentPage];
        if (nil == textString)
        {
            textString = [NSString stringWithFormat:@"unknown
            current index [%d] for array count [%d]",
            m_currentPage, [m_stringArray count] ];
        }
        CGSize textSize = [textString sizeWithAttributes:
                m_attributes];
        CGFloat yPos = 0.50 * m_pageRect.size.height;
        CGFloat xPos = 0.50 * (m_pageRect.size.width - textSize.
                width);
        NSRect textRect = NSMakeRect(xPos, yPos, textSize.width,
                textSize.height  );
        [textString drawInRect:textRect withAttributes:
                m_attributes];
}


-    (BOOL)knowsPageRange:(NSRangePointer)inRangePointer
{
        NSPrintOperation* currentOp = [NSPrintOperation
                currentOperation];
        NSPrintInfo* printInfo = [currentOp printInfo];
        m_pageRect = [printInfo imageablePageBounds];
        inRangePointer->location = 1;
        inRangePointer->length = [m_stringArray count];
        return (YES);
}
```

(continued)

Listing 10-6 *(continued)*

```
-   (NSRect)rectForPage:(NSInteger)inPage
{

    // Remember the current page
    m_currentPage = inPage - 1;
    return (m_pageRect);
}


-   (BOOL)isFlipped
{

    return (YES);
}


@end
```

Listing 10-7: Your document supports multi-page printing with a virtual view

```
//
//  PagedDoc.m
//  PagedDocPrint
//
//  Created by Karl Kowalski on 4/17/11.
//  Copyright 2011 Kowalski Software Enterprises.
//  All rights reserved.
//

#import "PagedDoc.h"

#import "PagedDocView.h"

@implementation PagedDoc

- (id)init
{
    self = [super init];
    if (self) {
        // Add your subclass-specific initialization here.
        // If an error occurs here, send a [self release]
        // message
        // and return nil.
    }
    return self;
}

- (NSString *)windowNibName
{
    // Override returning the nib file name of the document
```

```objc
    // If you need to use a subclass of NSWindowController
    // or if your document supports multiple
    // NSWindowControllers, you should remove this method
    // and override -makeWindowControllers instead.
    return @"PagedDoc";
}

- (void)windowControllerDidLoadNib:(NSWindowController *)
        aController
{

    [super windowControllerDidLoadNib:aController];
    // Add any code here that needs to be executed once the
    // windowController has loaded the document's window.
}

- (NSData *)dataOfType:(NSString *)typeName error:(NSError
        **)outError {
    /*
     Insert code here to write your document to data of the
            specified type. If outError != NULL, ensure that
            you create and set an appropriate error when
            returning nil.
    You can also choose to override -fileWrapperOfType:error:,
            -writeToURL:ofType:error:, or -writeToURL:ofType:
            forSaveOperation:originalContentsURL:error: instead.
    */
    if (outError) {
        *outError = [NSError errorWithDomain:NSOSStatusErrorD
            omain code:unimpErr userInfo:NULL];
    }
    return nil;
}

- (BOOL)readFromData:(NSData *)data ofType:(NSString *)
        typeName error:(NSError **)outError {
    /*
     Insert code here to read your document from the given
            data of the specified type. If outError != NULL,
            ensure that you create and set an appropriate
            error when returning NO.
    You can also choose to override -readFromFileWrapper:ofTy
            pe:error: or -readFromURL:ofType:error: instead.
    */
    if (outError) {
        *outError = [NSError errorWithDomain:NSOSStatusErrorD
            omain code:unimpErr userInfo:NULL];
    }
    return YES;
}
```

(continued)

Listing 10-7 *(continued)*

```
- (NSPrintOperation*)printOperationWithSettings:(NSDictionary
        *)inPrintSettings error:(NSError **)outError
{
    NSArray* stringArray = [NSArray arrayWithObjects:@"Page
            One", @"Page Two", @"Page Three", @"Page Four",
            @"Page Five", @"Page Six", nil];
    NSPrintOperation* printOp = [NSPrintOperation pri
            ntOperationWithView:[[[PagedDocView alloc]
            initWithArray:stringArray] autorelease]];
    return (printOp);
}

@end
```

So here's what's happening:

1. When the user selects File⇨Print for the document on display, Cocoa finds the correct document object and sends it the `printOperation WithSettings:error:` method.

2. The `PagedDoc` object creates an array of strings and uses it to create a `PagedDocView`, which is then set as the view to be printed by the `NSPrintOperation` that it creates and returns to the calling code.

3. Cocoa then executes the `NSPrintOperation`.

4. Cocoa asks the `PagedDocView` for the range of pages.

   In this case, the range is 1 to 6.

5. Cocoa displays the Print panel for the user.

   As part of this display, Cocoa asks the `PagedDocView` for the display rectangle of page 1, since that's what the Print panel will display in its preview box. Then Cocoa tells `PagedDocView` to draw the contents of the preview page's rectangle. Since `PagedDocView` remembers the page whose rectangle was just requested, the `drawRect:` method uses that page number to determine which string from the array to draw.

6. The user prints the desired pages.

7. The output, either paper or PDF, shows each page displaying its page number in the center.

That's all there is to handling the printing of multiple pages. The example above uses a *virtual* view subclass of `NSView` — the view is never displayed onscreen, but Cocoa doesn't need to know that. Cocoa just needs your view to tell it what to draw and where.

Part IV
Polishing and Supporting Your App

The 5th Wave   By Rich Tennant

"Other than this little glitch with the landscape view, I really love my iPhone."

In this part . . .

After you've put together all the parts of your Macintosh app, you'll need to make certain that it runs with no surprises. In this part, you find out how to track down and eliminate any pesky bugs that have sneaked into your code, including how to plug any memory leaks your app may have. You'll also discover how to add application and file icons to your app so that users can recognize both the app and the files it uses when looking for them in the Mac Finder or on the Dock.

When your app is ready to submit to Apple, Bonus Chapter 2 and Bonus Chapter 3 on the web site contain the steps you follow to organize all the files and data you need to upload your app to Apple's reviewers.

Chapter 11

Debugging Your App

・・

・・

*I*n an application developer's fantasy world, apps are flawlessly crafted, code is written perfectly, and users experience an awesome application that does everything exactly as it's supposed to. The data that the app stores is always crisp and fresh, and it never gets corrupted. Visuals are stunning and display perfectly on every screen attached to any Macintosh.

In the real world, however, applications don't always execute correctly. Sometimes they don't even build correctly, and the dream gets cut short before you can even build a release version. You need to find a way to fix things; you need to understand the tools that will assist you in moving closer to the dream world of a solid application.

Xcode comes with two built-in debuggers: the debugger called gdb and the new LLDB debugger. If you've ever worked with a debugger for any other platform, you'll find that Xcode provides all the tools you need to track down those pesky bugs and wash them right out of your code. Using the Xcode debugger is very easy. Debugging can be a long process, however, and can be very frustrating at times. Your application will be used by millions of users, who will ensure that every piece of code is exercised in ways that you never expected when you first wrote it. By using Xcode's debugger, you'll be able to lock down the obvious defects in your application, as well as look at all the other parts of your code with a more critical eye.

In this chapter, I show you how to use the Xcode debugger and how to use the debugger's Console window to display messages that you can include in your code.

Understanding Where Errors Happen

Xcode comes with tools and windows you can use to analyze your application while you're coding it and while it's running on a Macintosh. As you develop more Macintosh apps, you'll find errors during both of these phases. Here's a look at what defects in your code can cause for each phase:

✔ **While you're writing code:** You're going to make typing mistakes. Accept it. Sometimes those mistakes are obvious, and sometimes they're not. Xcode 4's code editor works with the LLVM compiler to find obvious typing errors and indicate where these mistakes are, without having to build your app first. And you'll find that for certain errors Xcode will display a list of available solutions for fixing the error just by clicking the error indicator. Apple calls this feature Fix-It; you can see in Figure 11-1 Xcode's Fix-It display on a typing error in an app.

Figure 11-1: Fix-It offers to replace a missing semicolon.

When Xcode compiles your Objective-C source files, it may complain about dozens (or even hundreds!) of errors when only one part of your code is actually broken. You should start your review of Xcode's complaints from the first one in its list of errors, because fixing this first one may resolve all the other messages that Xcode wants you to clear up.

✔ **While you're executing in the debugger:** The debugger is the best place to run into defects, because you can get a great deal of information about precisely where and how the error occurred. When you're running your app in the debugger, you may not always know where or when a defect is going to cause a failure that halts your app, but you can gain a better understanding if you see what's also happening nearby. It's kind of like finding out that the reason why a car crashed into a snow bank may have something to do with the kids having a snowball fight just down the street.

✓ **While your app is executing independently of Xcode:** Even though running your application in Xcode's debugger is 99 percent like running it on a Macintosh, that 1 percent difference may be enough to trip and crash your app. When you launch an app in Xcode's debugger, it does a lot of extra work to set up how the app is going to run — work that doesn't get done when your app is launched by a user or by you apart from the debugger. I've experienced problems that became apparent only when I didn't use the debugger to launch my app. In one case, the debugger was cleaning the memory (setting all the bytes to zeros) before the app was launched, which the app wasn't doing when I launched it from the Desktop. This became a problem because part of the app was checking whether a piece of memory was zero; it was when the debugger launched the app but wasn't when the app was launched normally.

Xcode displays any code syntax errors you made when you built your application, as well as warning messages about certain things you're doing in your code that the compiler isn't sure you should do. Warnings are not fatal — they won't prevent the compiler from building your app. But you should investigate warnings and remove as many as possible. Figure 11-2 shows several yellow warning indicators.

Figure 11-2: Warning, warning. Xcode isn't happy about what you've written.

You may have to click all the icons to display the warning messages:

- ✔ **On the left and right sides of line 11:** Xcode uses a small, yellow triangle icon with an exclamation point to indicate that it found something wrong with this line, and it leaves a message on the right side of the screen as well. These warnings are a quick visual indication of where Xcode believes that you may have made a mistake. On this line, Xcode is letting you know that the source file for this class don't contain implementations for all the methods declared in the header file.

- ✔ **On the left and right sides of lines 22 and 23:** You can find more information about Xcode's warnings on the lines where Xcode found a problem. If you resize the window to make it smaller, the code will be realigned within the window to accommodate the warnings flowing below each line. For these two warnings, Xcode is trying to tell you that your code isn't using the variables you declared after you assigned values to them. You may simply have forgotten to use them, or you may have used them earlier, took away the reason for using them, and forgot to remove them from the code.

- ✔ **In the activity viewer at the top of the window:** The panel tells you about warnings by displaying a yellow triangle with a number next to it that tells you how many warnings there are (three, in Figure 11-2) somewhere in your project. Clicking this little triangle displays the Issue navigator (see Figure 11-3), which gives you a little more information about the individual warnings.

- ✔ **On the right side of the window, in the Editor jump bar:** You can click the left and right arrows to move through successive warnings. Xcode will shift to and animate each message on the right side of the screen as you move to each warning.

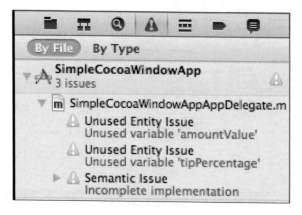

Figure 11-3: The Issue navigator is a great way to see details about the warnings and errors Xcode found in your project.

You *must* fix errors, and you *should* fix warnings. Errors make it impossible for Xcode to turn your code statements into machine language, which is why it won't build your app if it finds errors. Warnings aren't roadblocks that stop Xcode from creating your app, but you should investigate their causes because they can lead to app misbehavior.

Using Xcode's Debugger

You debug your application by launching it from within Xcode. I follow this procedure when I want to debug my apps:

1. **Click the Hide or Show the Debug Area View button in the toolbar to reveal the Debug area if it's not already visible.**

   The Debug area opens in your project window (see Figure 11-4).

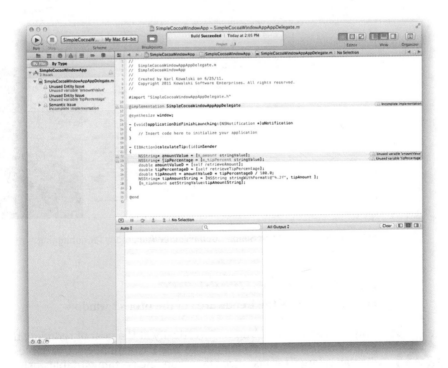

Figure 11-4: You see this window when you're ready to dive into your code line by line.

2. Click the Run button to launch your app.

You probably want to resize the project window so that you can see your app and the project window next to each other (which is one of the many reasons why bigger screens and multiple displays are better). Figure 11-5 shows you what `SimpleCocoaWindowApp` looks like next to the Project window.

If you've modified your code since the last time you launched the app, Xcode will rebuild it for you before launching. Xcode won't launch your app if there are any errors in your code, but warnings are okay, even if your app may crash as a result.

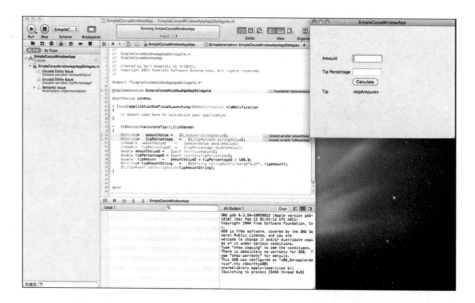

Figure 11-5: The launch of SimpleCocoaWindowApp, ready for debugging.

Navigating the Debug area

Figure 11-6 shows the Debug area of the project window.

You can resize the Debug area vertically at the cost of reducing the size of source code display. You might do this if the number of variables you want to display is large, for instance when opening certain variables using their drop-triangles to view their contents.

The window is divided into the following parts, each described in its own subsection.

Debug Bar

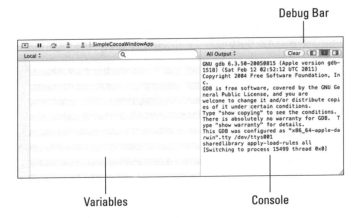

Variables   Console

Figure 11-6: The Debug area is where you can find information about the state of your application while you have it paused.

The Debug bar

The Debug bar contains controls for executing your program and for navigating your program's threads and the threads' corresponding stacks.

From left to right, the five buttons at the left end of the Debug bar let you perform the following actions:

 ✔ *Minimize the Debug area.* Minimizing the area lets you see more of the code for the module in the editor. You may want to do this if the method where the debugger stopped for a breakpoint is larger than one screen.

 ✔ *Pause or continue the application.* You can make Xcode pause your app in whatever thread is operating — usually, the main application thread. When your app is paused, the icon changes shape to indicate that clicking this button again will cause the app to continue.

 Don't confuse the Run button (at the top of the Xcode project window) with the Continue button (in the Debug bar). I did this a lot while learning Xcode. The Run button tells Xcode, "I'd really like to start this app from the beginning." While I was debugging, though, restarting usually wasn't what I wanted; I wanted the app to continue execution after the breakpoint.

 ✔ *Step over the line of code that the debugger is paused on.* Click this button to step through your program's source code one statement at a time. You will be executing your app statement by statement and you do this to watch what your app is doing at each step. This button is disabled if the app is executing.

 ✔ *Step into the line of code that the debugger is paused on.* Some lines of code are methods that your app calls, using objects to do work. Rather than step over one of these lines, you may find it useful to step *into* the code of the method. When you click this button, the debugger will go into and pause just before the first line within the method. Note that this is useful only for methods within your own code, and not code provided by Mac OS X. This button is disabled if the app is executing.

✔ *Step out of a method.* When you've stepped into an object's method from another method you've implemented, you'll eventually want to step out of the method and back up to the code that made the call. Once again, this button is disabled if the app is executing.

The Variables pane

When you've paused your app, the Variables pane displays a list of the variables that are available to the code at the place where the app is paused. You can choose to list the following items:

✔ *Local variables:* These variables are all the variables that the method can access. This includes the self variable as well as the _cmd variable which is the selector of the method.

This does not include member variables of the object.

✔ *Auto variables:* These variables are those that have been accessed up to this point in the code. This includes member variables as well as the self variable.

✔ *All variables:* Selecting All shows the local variables as well as the contents of the CPU registers.

I haven't needed to know what the CPU registers contain in my recent Mac programming efforts, but in the past, the information has proved to be useful, especially when I was using libraries developed by someone else.

The Console pane

You see information coming from the debugger posted in the Console pane while your app is running. In the section "Using the Macintosh Logger," I cover how you can send messages to this pane from within your code. When the app is paused, you can also issue commands to the gdb or LLDB debugger from within the Console pane.

The pop-up menu lets you switch among different types of output, but I recommend showing all of it.

You can copy all the contents from the Console pane and paste them in an empty file to search for specific messages. The Clear button clears the pane, and the three buttons on the right side let you control whether the Variables pane, the Console pane, or both are visible. (At least one is always displayed.)

Setting, deleting, and disabling breakpoints

In this section, I go over breakpoints in depth because they're very useful tools for figuring out what your code is up to.

A *breakpoint* is a location where Xcode places a flag that the debugger will detect while it's running your app. The debugger pauses your app just before it tries to execute that line of code. You use breakpoints to stop the operation of your app before it does something incorrect so that you can check the values of all the variables involved in upcoming operations and be sure of what should happen before your app makes it happen.

Objective-C will let you place multiple executable statements on one line. However, I prefer to keep each statement on its own line. When I set a breakpoint, and the debugger stops at it, I know exactly which statement is about to be executed.

Figure 11-7 shows you what the debugger window looks like when Xcode encounters a breakpoint during the execution of the app.

If your application is storing data in files and then retrieving that data later (for example) — but somehow the data that your app reads in from a file doesn't match the data that your app wrote out — you could set a pair of breakpoints: one in the code that writes the data and another in the code that reads it in. With your app stopped at either breakpoint, just before the read or the write operation takes place, you can step through each code statement and check the data at each step to make sure that everything is as it should be. If your app is doing something wrong, some part of the data at one of the steps won't be what you expect. At that moment, you can track down the code that's causing the problem.

Setting a breakpoint in your application is simple. Just follow these steps:

1. **Select a source file in Xcode.**

2. **Position the cursor over the left margin of the line you want to set a breakpoint on, and click the mouse.**

   A blue flag indicator appears, pointing to the line where you set the breakpoint.

Alternatively, you can choose Product⇨Debug⇨Add Breakpoint at Current Line. I find it easier to use the key combination ⌘-\ (backslash) to add or remove breakpoints.

Figure 11-7: Xcode has stopped running my app because I set a breakpoint at the first line of code to be executed when the user clicks the Calculate button.

One of the reasons I really like having the line numbers visible is because line numbers make it much easier to know exactly which line I'm placing a breakpoint on.

Breakpoints have evolved beyond the simple "stop when you get here" behavior that they're mostly used for. Here's how to see what Xcode provides for improving what you can do with breakpoints:

1. **Put a breakpoint at a line of code in a source file.**

2. **Right-click the breakpoint flag.**

   A menu appears, containing the elements shown in Figure 11-8.

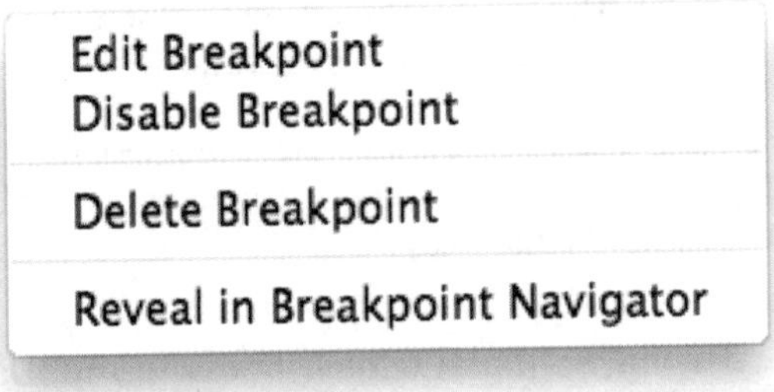

Edit Breakpoint
Disable Breakpoint

Delete Breakpoint

Reveal in Breakpoint Navigator

Figure 11-8: The list of operations you can use to modify the behavior of a breakpoint.

3. **Choose one of the items in this menu:**

- *Edit Breakpoint:* You can add actions to be executed when the debugger encounters a breakpoint. Your breakpoints can become *conditional*, meaning that the debugger will pause your app when the conditions attached to the breakpoint are true. I cover this topic in a later section of this chapter, "Setting conditional breakpoints."

- *Disable/Enable Breakpoint:* You can use this item to disable a breakpoint without removing it, such as to prevent a breakpoint from stopping your code while you're debugging it. When you're working with a large app, you may have dozens of breakpoints set for several bugs you're investigating. You can disable those that aren't directly related to a particular bug you're trying to fix right now and enable them again when you turn your attention to the next bug.

- *Delete Breakpoint:* You can delete a breakpoint from your code, such as when you've determined the cause of a bug and fixed it.

- *Reveal in Breakpoint Navigator:* Choosing this item displays the Breakpoint navigator and all the breakpoints you've set in your project, with the particular breakpoint from which you selected the menu item selected in the window.

You can also quickly deactivate all breakpoints in your code by clicking the Breakpoints button in the Project window toolbar. To reactivate all your breakpoints, click the button a second time.

Note that you can deactivate a disabled breakpoint and reactivate, but the breakpoint will still be disabled after reactivation.

In the following code, I've added some complications to the SimpleCocoa WindowApp since its debut in Chapter 3. The header file has two new methods, as shown in purple in Listing 11-1.

Listing 11-1: The new SimpleCocoaWindowAppAppDelegate.h

```
//
// SimpleCocoaWindowAppAppDelegate.h
// SimpleCocoaWindowApp
//
// Created by Karl Kowalski on 2/12/11
// Copyright 2011 Kowalski Software Enterprises. All rights reserved
//

#import <Cocoa/Cocoa.h>

@interface SimpleCocoaWindowAppAppDelegate : NSObject <NSApplicationDelegate>
{
    NSWindow *window;
    IBOutlet NSTextField* m_amount;
    IBOutlet NSTextField* m_tipPercent;
    IBOutlet NSButton* m_calculate;
    IBOutlet NSTextField* m_tipAmount;
}

@property (assign) IBOutlet NSWindow *window;

- (IBAction)calculateTip:(id)inSender;
- (double)retrieveAmount;
- (double)retrieveTipPercentage;

@end
```

The two new methods get the data that the user entered in the Amount and Tip Percentage fields. When Xcode compiles the SimpleCocoaWindow AppAppDelegate.m source module, it looks for these two methods. As you see in Listing 11-2, however, these two methods aren't implemented, and Xcode is unable to find them. It doesn't issue an error for missing methods, however, even though I'm lying about their existence. Xcode assumes that they'll show up somewhere. (Xcode is rather trusting sometimes.) The changes I made in the source module appear in purple.

Listing 11-2:   The modified source module, SimpleCocoaWindowApp AppDelegate.m

```
//
// SimpleCocoaWindowAppAppDelegate.m
// SimpleCocoaWindowApp
//
// Created by Karl Kowalski on 2/12/11
// Copyright 2011 Kowalski Software Enterprises. All rights reserved.
//

#import "SimpleCocoaWindowAppAppDelegate.h"

@implementation SimpleCocoaWindowAppAppDelegate

@synthesize window;

- (void)applicationDidFinishLaunching:(NSNotification*)aNotification
{
    // Insert code here to initialize your application
}


- (IBAction)calculateTip:(id)inSender
{
    NSString* amountValue = [m_amount stringValue];
    NSString* tipPercentage = [m_tipPercentage stringValue];
    //double amountValueD = [amountValue doubleValue];
    double amountValueD = [self retrieveAmount];
    //double tipPercentageD = [tipPercentage doubleValue];
    double tipPercentageD = [self retrieveTipPercentage];
    double tipAmount = amountValueD * tipPercentageD / 100.0;
    NSString* tipAmountString = [NSString stringWithFormat:@"%.2f", tipAmount];
    [m_tipAmount setStringValue:tipAmountString];
}

@end
```

The modifications to `SimpleCocoaWindowAppAppDelegate.m` are minor: instead of getting each of the input values from the text entry fields, the method `calculateTip:` calls the two methods mentioned in the header file. Because those methods haven't been implemented, of course, the debugger halts the app when it can't do what my code tells it to do.

Objective-C allows your app to declare and use methods that you have not implemented because it uses *dynamic typing* to determine what code to execute when your app is running. Dynamic typing allows your code to send a message to an object that does not have that message specified in its interface. This provides increased flexibility for your objects to respond to any message by forwarding the message to another object that can handle the message.

Viewing intentional errors in the debugger

In this section, you get to watch the code intentionally misbehave. Follow these steps:

1. **Make the changes to** `SimpleCocoaWindowAppAppDelgate.h` **and** `SimpleCocoaWindowAppAppDelegate.m` **shown in Listing 11-1 and Listing 11-2, earlier in this chapter.**

2. **Build the app.**

   Xcode displays warnings that some variables are unused and that the class is incomplete because of the missing methods.

3. **Set a breakpoint within the** `calculateTip:` **method at the first statement that will execute.**

4. **Set the Debug area to be visible.**

5. **Click the Run button.**

   `SimpleCocoaWindowApp` should launch with the screen in Figure 11-9.

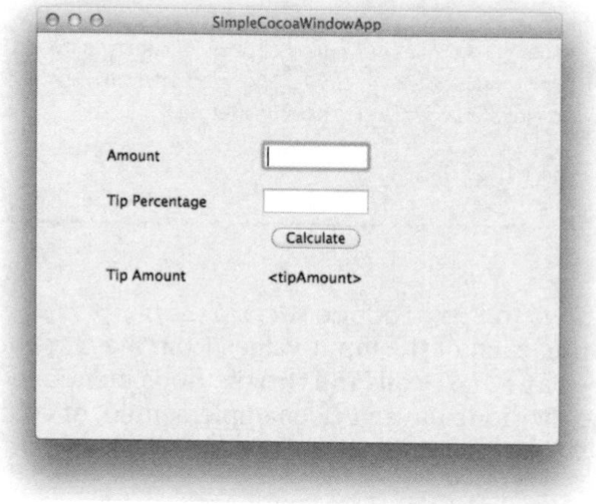

Figure 11-9: The application launches.

6. **Enter a value in each text entry field.**

   I prefer to use values that will make what I see in the debugger easy to understand, so my amount for this example is 100.00, and my tip percentage is 15.

7. **Click the Calculate button.**

   The debugger stops at the breakpoint you set, waiting to execute. Looking back at Figure 11-7, you see that the debugger stopped the app at the first line in the calculateTip: method; that's the green arrow on top of the blue breakpoint indicator in the left margin of the window. In addition, the gray bar highlighting the line that will be executed next is another reminder and is much easier to see. Finally, if all that weren't enough, the message Thread 1: Stopped at breakpoint 1 on the right side of the screen definitely tells you what's going on and what to do:

   - *Look at the Debug navigator,* which was displayed automatically in place of the Project navigator. There are two threads, but for this app, you're concerned only with Thread 1. The top item is item #0: [SimpleCocoaWindowAppAppDelegate calculateTip:]. This method is the one where the breakpoint is set, and the items below it are the call stack of Thread 1 — the list of methods and functions that have been called down to the method containing the breakpoint. Item #1, for example, [NSApplication sendAction:to:from:], is the method that called [Simple CocoaWindowAppAppDelegate calculateTip:].

   - *Look at the Variables pane.* This pane shows the variables that the current method is able to access. (I always want to know what my code's local variables are up to, as well as see the arguments passed in, so I always keep both the Variables and Console panes unfolded and visible.) Because the first line hasn't executed, only a few of the values have been set. The _cmd and the self variables, for example, have valid values (each set before the debugger stopped in this method), but all the others are random values. Even though tipPercentageD is set to 0, tipAmount is set to 465, and amountValueD is set to 135 because these variables are given places in memory that's being used as scratch space, and there's no telling what was there before the app was paused.

8. **Click the Step Over button.**

   Now amountValue gets set to the text representation of the value typed in the SimpleCocoaWindowApp main window. You also see the Variables pane change some of the elements to black from red, which is an indication that their values didn't change. The amountValue variable did receive a new value, and the Variables pane shows this modification by making both the Value and Summary fields red.

9. Click the Step Over button again.

The `amountValue` variable remains the same and is colored black, whereas the `tipPercentage` variable is modified to match the value typed in the main window. So far, so good. The red arrow is pointing to a line where the code will try to execute a method that doesn't exist.

10. Click the Step Over button once more.

The green arrow disappears, and the Console pane has a message for you, as shown in Figure 11-10.

```
All Output ≑                                                          Clear
GNU gdb 6.3.50-20050815 (Apple version gdb-1705) (Fri Jul  1 10:50:06 UTC 2011)
Copyright 2004 Free Software Foundation, Inc.
GDB is free software, covered by the GNU General Public License, and you are
welcome to change it and/or distribute copies of it under certain conditions.
Type "show copying" to see the conditions.
There is absolutely no warranty for GDB.  Type "show warranty" for details.
This GDB was configured as "x86_64-apple-darwin".tty /dev/ttys001
sharedlibrary apply-load-rules all
[Switching to process 8436 thread 0x0]
2011-08-13 14:33:41.360 SimpleCocoaWindowApp[8436:707] -[SimpleCocoaWindowAppAppDelegate retrieveAmount]: unrecognized selector
sent to instance 0x103219e10
2011-08-13 14:33:41.360 SimpleCocoaWindowApp[8436:707] -[SimpleCocoaWindowAppAppDelegate retrieveAmount]: unrecognized selector
sent to instance 0x103219e10
2011-08-13 14:33:41.420 SimpleCocoaWindowApp[8436:707] (
    0   CoreFoundation         0x00007fff8d42b986 __exceptionPreprocess + 198
    1   libobjc.A.dylib        0x00007fff8d792d5e objc_exception_throw + 43
    2   CoreFoundation         0x00007fff8d4b75ae -[NSObject doesNotRecognizeSelector:] + 190
    3   CoreFoundation         0x00007fff8d418883 ___forwarding___ + 371
    4   CoreFoundation         0x00007fff8d418618 _CF_forwarding_prep_0 + 232
    5   SimpleCocoaWindowApp    0x0000000100001166a -[SimpleCocoaWindowAppAppDelegate calculateTip:] + 138
    6   CoreFoundation         0x00007fff8d41b11d -[NSObject performSelector:withObject:] + 61
    7   AppKit                 0x00007fff9575d052 -[NSApplication sendAction:to:from:] + 139
    8   AppKit                 0x00007fff9575d784 -[NSControl sendAction:to:] + 88
    9   AppKit                 0x00007fff9575d6af -[NSCell _sendActionFrom:] + 137
    10  AppKit                 0x00007fff9575cb7a -[NSCell trackMouse:inRect:ofView:untilMouseUp:] + 2014
    11  AppKit                 0x00007fff9575dc57c -[NSButtonCell trackMouse:inRect:ofView:untilMouseUp:] + 489
    12  AppKit                 0x00007fff9575b786 -[NSControl mouseDown:] + 786
    13  AppKit                 0x00007fff9572666e -[NSWindow sendEvent:] + 6280
    14  AppKit                 0x00007fff956bef19 -[NSApplication sendEvent:] + 5665
    15  AppKit                 0x00007fff95655a42b -[NSApplication run] + 548
    16  AppKit                 0x00007fff9504d352a NSApplicationMain + 867
    17  SimpleCocoaWindowApp    0x000000010000015b2 main + 34
    18  SimpleCocoaWindowApp    0x000000010000001584 start + 52
    19  ???                    0x0000000000000001 0x0 + 1
)
```

Figure 11-10: The CPU is unable to find the method you told it to execute.

Because you know that the method is unimplemented, the message is easy to interpret: An *unrecognized selector* (the method named `retrieveAmount`) was sent to the `SimpleCocoaWindowAppApp Delegate` instance, which is a failure.

11. Click the Stop button to end the application.

There's no way to recover from this failure during debugging. The code will always fail when the CPU tries to execute this instruction.

As a consequence of Objective-C's dynamic typing, the result of an attempt to execute a method that doesn't exist does not cause your app to crash. Instead, while running within the debugger a message is delivered to the Console pane and the app continues as before. If you run this misbehaving app outside of the debugger, it simply fails silently.

Doing even more useful things with the debugger

Now that you know how the debugger can assist you in your efforts to track down problems in your code, this section shows you some other useful things that you can do with the debugger. Follow these steps:

1. **Select** `SimpleCocoaWindowAppAppDelegate.m` **to edit.**

2. **Modify the** `calculateTip:` **method so that it looks like the code in Listing 11-3.**

   You'll be removing some of the code that causes warnings.

3. **Add the two methods from the code shown in Listing 11-4.**

   You're implementing the code that the header file promised Xcode that you'd provide.

4. **Save your code changes.**

5. **Build your app.**

   This step makes sure that you didn't make any typing mistakes.

6. **Set a breakpoint at the first executable line in** `calculateTip:`.

   I have you stepping through the code again to see what happens for each line.

7. **Show the Debug area.**

   You won't need the Console pane, but you can show it if you want.

8. **Click Run.**

   The app should launch, ready for your input.

   Move the app's window out of the way of the debugger window so that you can see both at the same time.

9. **Enter values in the** `Amount` **and** `Tip Percentage` **fields, and click the Calculate button.**

   The Debugger window should display the first line of `calculateTip:`, ready for you to step through the code.

10. **Set a breakpoint within** `retrieveAmount` **at the first line of the method.**

    You can set breakpoints anywhere within your code while the app is paused, and the debugger will obey them.

11. Click the Continue button.

You can see the result in Figure 11-11: The Debugger paused the app before executing the first line of `retrieveAmount`. The program's call stack pane has updated to show that the method in which the debugger is paused is [`SimpleCocoaWindowAppAppDelegate retrieve Amount`], and the Variables pane has updated to show the local variables of this method.

Figure 11-11: Going deeper into the code to see what's happening.

12. Click Step Over twice.

This step takes you to the `return` statement after retrieving the text from the `Amount` field and converts it to a `double` value.

13. Click Step Out.

The debugger returns the green arrow to the first line of `calculate Tip:`. Even though that line has already executed, the assignment of the double value calculated in `retrieveAmount` hasn't happened; it's the last operation the CPU will make.

14. Click Step Over to move to the next statement.

The `amountValueD` variable has the value that was returned by the `retrieveAmount` method.

15. Click Step Into.

You've paused the debugger on the first line of the `retrieveTip Percentage` method.

16. Click Step Over twice to reach the `return` statement.

You're not happy with the tip that was entered, so you're going to change it.

17. Double-click the value for the `tipPercentage` in the Variables pane.

You can change that value to a better tip now. Figure 11-12 shows you what the Variables pane looks like when you change a variable's value.

18. Press the Return key on your keyboard to set the new value.

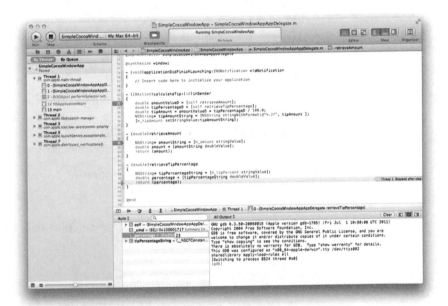

Figure 11-12: Editing the tipPercentage value while the app is running.

19. Click Step Out and then click Step Over to move to the next statement.

I assume that everything to this point has executed correctly (or at least as the app is programmed to do), that the tip percentage was retrieved successfully, and that the tip amount is ready to be calculated.

20. Click Step Over twice more to calculate the tip amount and create a string representation of the value; then click Continue.

The result of your tip calculations is displayed in the SimpleCocoa WindowApp. Figure 11-13 shows the final tip for a very expensive meal. You can see that the tip percentage hasn't changed, but the tip amount was calculated with a different value — the one you edited in the debugger.

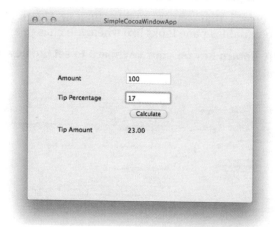

Figure 11-13: The tip amount of a much better tipper.

Listing 11-3:   The modified, warning-free calculateTip: method

```
- (IBAction)calculateTip:(id)inSender
{
    double amountValueD = [self retrieveAmount];
    double tipPercentageD = [self retrieveTipPercentage];
    double tipAmount = amountValueD * tipPercentageD / 100.0;
    NSString* tipAmountString = [NSString stringWithFormat:@"%.2f", tipAmount];
    [m_tipAmount setStringValue:tipAmountString];
}
```

Listing 11-4: **The two missing methods**

```
- (double)retrieveAmount
{
    NSString* amountString = [m_amount stringValue];
    double amount = [amountString doubleValue];
    return (amount);
}

- (double)retrieveTipPercentage
{
    NSString* tipPercentageString = [m_tipPercent stringValue];
    double tipPercentage = [tipPercentageString doubleValue];
    return (tipPercentage);
}
```

If you look closely at the two methods you added in Listing 11-4, you may notice that they look very similar. Here's a breakdown of what each one does, abstractly:

1. Get a string from a text field in the window.

2. Convert that string to a `double` value.

3. Return that `double` value to whatever called the method.

When you see a repeating pattern of behavior in your code, replace the repeating pattern with a method that can perform the same sequence of steps, but with a parameter passed in as an argument to the method. If you discover later that you want to improve the code for retrieving these values, you have to make changes in both the `retrieveAmount` method and the `retrieveTipPercentage` method. That process may seem fairly trivial for methods as simple as these, but as your apps become larger and the patterns repeat in more source files, you'll find it difficult to ensure that you've made all the changes you need to make in all the places where you need to make them.

Listing 11-5 shows a consolidation of the two retrieval methods and their uses.

Listing 11-5: **Collapsing two retrieval methods into one more-generic method**

```
- (double)retrieveValue:(NSTextField*)inField
{
    double value = 0.00;
    if (nil != inField)
    {
        value = [[inField stringValue] doubleValue];
    }
    return (value);
}

- (IBAction)calculateTip:(id)inSender
{
    double amountValueD = [self retrieveValue:m_amount];
    double tipPercentageD = [self retrieveValue:m_tipPercent];
    double tipAmount = amountValueD * tipPercentageD / 100.00;
    NSString* tipAmountString = [NSString stringWithFormat:@"%.2f", tipAmount];
    [m_tipAmount setStringValue:tipAmount];
}
```

As you'll note, the `retrieveValue:` method presumes that an `NSTextField` object was passed in as an argument. After checking to make sure the object is valid, the code extracts a `double` value from the string entered in the field and returns that value to the calling code.

Setting conditional breakpoints

Originally, breakpoints were stopping points. The debugger would stop when it encountered a breakpoint and wait for the programmer to tell it what to do next. As projects grew larger and apps became more complex, simply halting the app whenever the debugger encountered a breakpoint made software debugging somewhat unproductive, especially if only certain conditions were causing the problem. If a bug was triggered in a web-server application whenever some process attempted to download an image file larger than 1MB, for example, having the debugger stop the application when any size of image file was requested would elongate the session, because the programmer would have to tell the debugger to continue if the file was smaller than 1MB.

To assist your debugging efforts in this situation, Xcode provides conditional breakpoints. A *conditional breakpoint* is just like a normal breakpoint, but it comes with a condition: Use the values of variables available where the breakpoint is set to determine whether the debugger should halt. In the image-file-size example, you'd set a breakpoint after the size is determined and then place a condition on the breakpoint indicating that only if the size is larger than 1MB should the breakpoint pause the execution of the app.

To set a conditional breakpoint, follow these steps:

1. **Edit** `SimpleCocoaWindowAppAppDelegate.m` **in the project window.**

2. **Select the code at line 25 in the** `calculateTip:` **method, and set a breakpoint.**

    This line is where the calculated tip amount is converted to an `NSString` object.

3. **Right-click the breakpoint flag, and choose Edit Breakpoint.**

    You should see the message bubble shown in Figure 11-14.

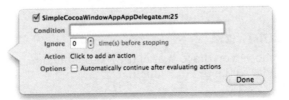

Figure 11-14: This breakpoint will pause the debugger only if the condition is true.

4. **Type** tipPercentageD > 10.0 **in the Condition field. Click the Done button in the message bubble.**

5. **Click the Build and Debug button.**

6. **Enter any tip amount, and enter a tip percentage greater than 10.0.**

7. **Click the Calculate button.**

    The debugger halts execution at the breakpoint you set, and the value of the variable `tipPercentageD` should be greater than `10.0`.

8. **Click the Continue button.**

    The tip is calculated correctly.

9. **In the SimpleCocoaWindowApp window, change the tip percentage to 9, and click the Calculate button.**

    The debugger doesn't halt the execution of the app this time, and the tip amount is calculated and updated onscreen.

Conditional breakpoints can make finding bugs much easier, because the debugger halts only for the specific conditions you set. By using conditional breakpoints, you're filtering the parameters of the situation you're trying to re-create, thereby reducing your investigation to just those scenarios you're interested in.

Using the Macintosh Logger

My favorite approach for debugging desktop apps involves printing text to a screen or, better still, a file. I call this approach *printf-debugging,* after the venerable C-language function printf. I realize that it's very retro, from a time before integrated development environments such as Xcode and before source-level debuggers. It's also very reliable, however, and it works with just about every programming language or development platform. Luckily for me, Xcode provides a way to support this debugging approach.

Introducing NSLog

Listing 11-6 shows you the format of the NSLog function. It's pretty simple and very similar to the printf function.

Listing 11-6:   The format of the NSLog function

```
void NSLog( NSString* messageString {,…} );
```

The NSLog function takes an NSString object as its first parameter, and optionally accepts more parameters that the contents of the NSString parameter can format — this is represented by the {,…} shown in the function format above.

Apple's documentation describes the function this way: "Logs an error message to the Apple System Log facility."

When the debugger encounters a call to NSLog, the NSString message is printed in Xcode's Console pane, even if the window isn't visible. Optionally, your code can also provide a variable number of parameters in addition to the NSString parameter, separated by commas. If you're going to add parameters to be included in the output to the Console pane, the NSString must contain formatting information to tell Xcode how to create the final textual result. You can use formatting parameters identical to those used in `printf`. In addition, you can use a special formatting character used specifically for `NSObject` objects, such as `NSString`.

Using NSLog

The next example demonstrates how to use `NSLog` and some formatting. Follow these steps:

1. **Select** `SimpleCocoaWindowAppAppDelegate.m` **for editing in the project window.**

   You may want to remove any breakpoints, because they won't be needed.

2. **Add the purple code shown in Listing 11-7 to the three separate methods.**

3. **Display the Console pane, and click the Clear Log button.**

   This step starts the log from a clean slate.

4. **Click the Build and Debug button to launch** `SimpleCocoaWindowApp`.

5. **Enter an amount and a tip percentage, and click the Calculate button.**

   The tip should be calculated correctly, and the Console pane should display the messages shown in Figure 11-15.

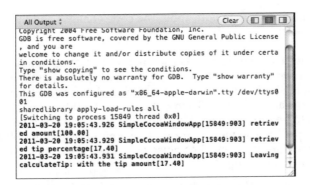

Figure 11-15: The Console pane writes out these messages when the app calls NSLog.

Listing 11-7:   Adding NSLog messages to be displayed during execution

```
- (IBAction)calculateTip:(id)inSender
{
    double amountValueD = [self retrieveAmount];
    double tipPercentageD = [self retrieveTipPercentage];
    double tipAmount = amountValueD * tipPercentageD / 100.0;
    NSString* tipAmountString = [NSString stringWithFormat:@"%.2f", tipAmount];
    [m_tipAmount setStringValue:tipAmountString];
    NSLog( @"Leaving calculateTip: with the tip amount[%@]", tipAmountString];
}

- (double)retrieveAmount
{
    NSString* amountString = [m_amount stringValue];
    double amount = [amountString doubleValue];
    NSLog( @"retrieved amount[%.2f]", amount );
    return (amount);
}

- (double)retrieveTipPercentage
{
    NSString* tipPercentageString = [m_tipPercent stringValue];
    double tipPercentage = [tipPercentageString doubleValue];
    NSLog( @"retrieved tip percentage[%.2f]", tipPercentage );
    return (tipPercentage);
}
```

Here are some points to note about the code changes and the results in the Console pane:

- ✏ The format character %@ is used to tell the NSLog function that it should call a specific method on the object that's passed in to be displayed. That method is description, which is defined for NSObject and returns an NSString. Then NSLog uses the NSString object as the text to be printed in the Console pane. You're not required to create a description method for each of your classes, but doing so can be helpful for displaying the values of an object's member variables while the app is running.

- ✏ I recommend that you place square brackets [ ] around any variable data that you plan to display, which helps define the space in which the information is displayed. It can be helpful to demonstrate that an NSString object that you believe to contain text actually contains nothing.

- ✏ The Console pane places a time stamp and your app's name ahead of every message.

Why use NSLog instead of the debugger and breakpoints?

For small apps, you can debug your app fairly easily by using the debugger and judicious placement of breakpoints. As apps get larger and perform a larger variety of different tasks, however, I've found that I'd rather generate information in many different places and have it logged to the Console pane, so that I can go back over the information and trace the flow during the app's entire execution.

Another time to use NSLog is when your application uses multiple threads to perform its tasks. You may have one thread handling the user's mouse clicks and key presses while another thread is searching a database and a third is off pulling data from a network connection. In a multiple-thread scenario, each thread may hit a breakpoint at a different time, which can make debugging confusing.

In general, I find it easier to review what's happening over the entire app rather than what's happening in one or two places at one particular moment during the app's execution. You'll find that each approach is better in some situations than in others and use a variety of methods to eliminate the misbehaving parts of your code.

Removing NSLog statements

NSLog is a useful tool for providing you with information while your app is running within the debugger. Each NSLog message is also sent to the Mac OS X system logs, and your app will send its messages into the users' system logs if you leave active NSLog statements in your app. This can be useful for providing your users with information about your app while it's running, but you may not want to deluge your users with too much information. You may want to remove the NSLog statements from your code before you publish it at the Mac App Store.

You can view the messages sent to the system logs using the Console app found in the Applications➪Utilities folder. Be warned: There are lots of messages sent into the logs *every minute* your Mac is powered on.

Here's one way to remove NSLog statements:

1. **Modify the code in the** retrieveAmount **method so that it matches Listing 11-8.**

   You're placing a test for the existence of a *preprocessor macro* (a standard C programming technique) around the call to NSLog. This test tells the compiler to check whether the macro named DEBUG has been defined and, if it has, to compile the code containing the NSLog function.

2. In the Project navigator, select the top item, `SimpleCocoaWindowApp`.

This step displays the settings for both the project and its individual targets, even though there's only one target for this project.

3. Select the `SimpleCocoaWindowApp` **item below the project listing, as shown in Figure 11-16.**

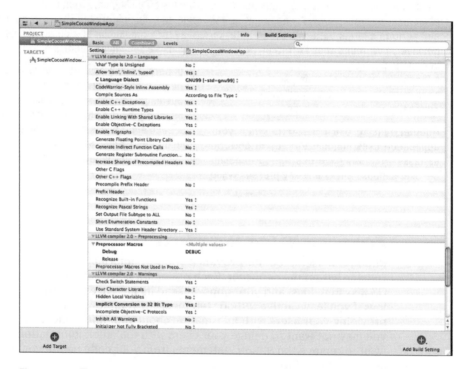

Figure 11-16: The project info screen displaying the build settings for a debug build.

4. Select the Build tab, and scroll down to the LLVM compiler 2.0 – Preprocessing set of information.

You can see that the Preprocessor Macros list shows one macro already defined for Debug builds: `DEBUG`. (This macro isn't set in release builds.)

5. Run your app.

The Console pane should still display the text from all the `NSLog` statements in debug mode.

If you change to a release scheme and run once more, the `NSLog` statements from `retrieveAmount` no longer appear. Also, your app's size is reduced, which can save a lot of space if you have many of these statements sprinkled throughout a large application.

Listing 11-8:   Using a preprocessor macro to conditionally include or exclude code

```
- (double)retrieveAmount
{
    NSString* amountString = [m_amount stringValue];
    double amount = [amountString doubleValue];
#ifdef DEBUG
    NSLog( @"retrieved amount[%.2f]", amount );
#endif
    return (amount);
}
```

Although I prefer to log messages to the Console pane as my main debugging approach, this method does have limitations. My primary concern about this method is performance. If I write information to the Xcode debugger's Console pane at every step of an app's execution, the app is going to slow down. For some applications, such as real-time games, this can adversely affect the app's behavior and operation while I'm trying to pin down the location of misbehaving code. Therefore, I use Console-pane logging to narrow the scope of examining my application's behavior, ideally drilling down to one method in one class, where I can heavily log events and inspect just that one area of my application. This method prolongs the debugging experience, as I have to create log statements, execute, review the log, and repeat until I've discovered and fixed the bad code.

Keeping Track of Bugs

Though it would be wonderful to write completely bug-free code, your app will eventually encounter a situation somewhere, on someone's Mac, that causes it to malfunction. Maybe your app refuses to run because the user updated his OS to the latest version automatically, and Apple pulled out some feature that your app was using, so now the OS can't execute your app because it can no longer find that OS code. Then again, the bug may be more subtle, executing only at noon on the first Friday of every month that has an *n* in its name and taking out the entire set of accumulated data at that moment, leaving you with some very unhappy users and an inability to reliably reproduce the error.

Small development efforts don't require a full-featured bug-tracking database to keep tabs on all the things that go wrong. The sooner you start taking app development seriously, however, the sooner you'll find yourself delivering high-quality apps. Serious development efforts require equally serious bug-maintenance efforts. The more apps you write and the more code you type, the more bugs you and your users will find. Although you may find it easier to list all the known issues of all your apps in a simple text file, at some point it's worth the effort to create a more structured repository to list all issues that you or your users encounter.

Identifying common solutions

I know several ways to manage the business of tracking bugs:

- **Purchase bug-tracking software from a reliable vendor.** You run this software on your own machines, and it keeps track of the bugs you enter in its own database. The major drawback to this approach is the cost, which may prohibit its use by a developer who's just starting out. Some free bug-tracking apps are available, so be sure to search them all.

- **Use an online bug-tracking service.** Both free and subscription services are available. The only drawback of this approach that I can think of (other than the cost of the paid services) is the fact that your bugs aren't completely under your control. If you're writing an app that needs to maintain some degree of secrecy — one that uses a new encryption algorithm, for example — this method may not be the best choice.

- **Use a web-based bug-tracking system.** Bugzilla (www.bugzilla.org) is my favorite option because I get to keep the information secure on my own machines and because it's free. The disadvantage is that you need to provide both a web-server application and a database application to support Bugzilla's operations. For more information, see the section "Using a bug-tracking program," later in this chapter.

The most important action you can take to keep track of your app's bugs is *writing everything down.* This sounds simple, but you'll find it very challenging to discipline yourself to do this when you're running your app and something unexpected happens.

Simple bugs are easy to reproduce, and they generally happen because of one particular set of circumstances that occurred at the last moment before your app did something that caused the bad thing to happen. This feature is what makes them easy to resolve. The more challenging bugs are subtle and may depend on a sequence of events that must occur in a specific order. You may not pick up on all the pieces of the sequence or their proper order when the bug causes your app to go wrong. Sometimes you see only the result and lose track of all the steps that were taken on the way to that result. Even worse, the subtle bugs typically show up only when you're trying to solve or see something else, and your focus is on something other than the problem that shows up. Nobody ever said this was going to be easy.

Here's a list of the information you'll want to record when you find an anomaly in your code:

- **Steps to reproduce:** This information is the most crucial piece of information you'll need for describing a bug. Recording the steps that reproduce an issue provides you two pieces of useful data: what it takes to cause the problem and how to know when the problem has been resolved.

- **OS version:** The application you write will be built to use a specific OS version. Normally, you can expect that your app will run in all the future revisions of that OS version. If you built your app to use OS X 10.6, for example, your app should run on 10.6.1 through 10.6.9. When running on OS X 10.7, however, your app may encounter challenges. Apple generally doesn't remove features without warning, and usually, you have one major OS release cycle in which to update your app. Apple may provide information indicating that a certain feature available in 10.6 is deprecated in 10.7 and will be completely removed in 10.8, for example.

Because an app can go wrong in so many ways, you want to establish the boundaries of the problem to "fence in" the bug's behavior. Following are a few common situations that bring bugs into existence:

- **Improper initialization of variables:** This situation is probably the biggest cause of bugs, and it happens more frequently than any other cause. In Objective-C, a member variable can be initialized in any method of the class. If a class has several member variables, you may want to provide an `initialize` method that handles setting all the member variables to a default value. When you're reviewing the variables and their values while debugging the code, anything assigned a default value clearly hasn't been set separately from the `initialize` method. As any member variable can be modified during the execution of any method in that class, however, you can restrict access to internal member variables through the disciplined use of getter and setter methods. This technique won't prevent invalid values, but you'll be able to find where your code is executing the methods to set and retrieve the values, such as by setting a breakpoint in a setter method.

- **Improper timing of threads:** You can avoid this error by avoiding the use of all threads, all the time. Still, if you use threads to perform background tasks, this error will happen eventually. This situation occurs when your app has multiple threads running at the same time (such as for retrieving multiple hotel-booking options over a network) and you haven't prepared for the possibility that the first thread to finish won't be the one you expected.

✔ **Failure to check an object for being `nil`:** This particular behavior was prevalent in the early days of the Macintosh, before OS X. Generally, this problem was caused by a lack of available memory: The OS would return a big 0 (zero) when you requested a new object from a framework API. In today's 64-bit-app world, this problem is less likely to occur as a result of a lack of memory, but it can still happen for other reasons. One cause in particular is forgetting to connect a member variable representing a control to its counterpart in Interface Builder. Because the stitching-together of the interface elements with the member variables happens during the build process, this lack of a connection may go unnoticed.

Using a bug-tracking program

Using a bug-tracking solution helps you solve the problem of keeping track of all the things that can go wrong with your applications. In addition, bug-tracking services enable you to track progress in fixing things. Ideally, your app will have hundreds of thousands of users stress-testing your app in a multitude of environments, which means that they'll start finding more bugs for you. Users are a lot like unpaid quality-assurance engineers: They'll exercise your application in ways you never considered.

As I mention earlier in this chapter, my favorite bug-tracking solution is Bugzilla. Getting it up and running is fairly easy, and if you do this on your development Macintosh, the web server is included as part of OS X. You may have to configure your Mac to get the web server operational; check your user guide for more information. You will have to download and install a database server such as MySQL (www.mysql.com) to support Bugzilla.

You can find documentation for setting up Bugzilla at its website, www.bugzilla.org. I like Bugzilla because it's free, fun to use, and supported by expert developers who like to keep it fun. Because Bugzilla is an open-source product, however, getting support for it can be a bit challenging. The support web page (www.bugzilla.org/support) provides a link to some Bugzilla consultants whom you can contact for paid support of the issues you encounter. Alternatively, you can visit the Bugzilla wiki (https://wiki.mozilla.org/Bugzilla) for more information.

You can get away without using a bug-tracking system for a while, but the more prolific you are, the more apps you develop, and the more users you sell to, the more necessary it is to get organized in this aspect of software development. Your development machine itself will suffice to support what Bugzilla needs to do its job.

Implementing a solution ahead of time and disciplining yourself to use it correctly is an investment in the future that will reward you in the end.

Chapter 12

Putting On the Finishing Touches

A t this point in your Mac app development, everything works. Your app has no known bugs; it does everything your users will make it do; and you've added all the nifty features you can think of to keep your users coming back for more. What's next?

In this chapter, I introduce some of the finishing touches you can apply to polish up your apps. These touches are some of the little things that users have come to expect, as well as the important items Apple will check to make sure that your app includes during the App Store submission review. You see how to add an application icon and file icons for any data files your app creates. You also create a custom About panel for your app, to add some flourish beyond the standard dialog that Xcode provides. In addition, I show you how to communicate with your users in their preferred language. Finally, I show you how to track down and plug those areas in your apps where memory is leaking away. You won't need to spend a lot of time or money incorporating the features in this chapter, but the more you include in your app, the more your users will appreciate the work you've done.

Working with Application and File Icons

I was hooked on the Mac when a colleague showed me how to double-click something that looked like a piece of paper with a picture on it, and the app that created this file was launched with that file open, ready to go. I was impressed because I'd no longer have to remember the correct spelling of the name of the app that created my `Whiz-Bang.kgk` file. Double-clicking the file would launch it for me, all by itself. Also, the picture on the file was related to the picture of the app's icon, so I'd always be able to tell which file was a Microsoft Word document and which one was my saved game of Space Invaders. This enchantment I felt about the use of icons for relating data files and the apps they came from led me on a quest to do the same for *my* apps. That was the first goal of writing my first Macintosh app: creating an icon for the app and one for its data files, and using the magic of the OS to bring the two together.

You'll find it much easier to do the same with your apps in the 21st century than ever before. Apple has continued its support of linking an app and its data files, and today's users can't imagine what using computers was like before this feature existed. Your app will have to give the users what they want: an icon that makes your app stand out visually on a user's Mac Desktop or is easy to find in the user's Dock or Launchpad. Most important, your app must provide an application icon for Apple to display on its Mac App Store page. An icon is one of the requirements for App Store submissions, so you have to add it to your app.

Painting a good picture

I freely admit that I'm not an artist. Creating an application icon is the last thing I do for my apps. Apple prides itself on creating very good looking icons for its own apps and expects you to put some time and effort into making yours visually appealing. You can look around the App Store for examples of the styles and displays of apps that Apple has accepted for sale. Figure 12-1 shows the Apple Staff Favorites on the date I started writing this chapter. You can see icons ranging from very simple shapes to very rich images.

Figure 12-1: Apple Staff Favorites apps.

Relax, and don't be daunted. Check out the productivity apps, and you'll find quite a few simpler app icons that are easy to put together. Your own app icons may be as simple as a few words on a colored background or a picture that represents the basic concept or theme of your app. You can even use a photograph or a collage.

For DiabeticPad, I wanted a high-quality app icon, so I engaged the services of a colleague who works with me and actually *is* an artist. I wanted to make sure that my app's first contact point was striking and impressive. If you can afford the expense, I highly recommend hiring a professional.

You can find artists of varying skill all around you if you keep your eyes and ears open. Your relatives, friends, and neighbors can recommend people whom they know. The more you network, the more you discover. A very inexpensive way to find an inexpensive artist is to visit a college that has an art school and post a flyer or two in the art school's main building, asking for art students who are interested in adding to their portfolio. These young adults are just starting in their art careers, and *everything* they work on is something they can add to the growing collection of their work.

You have to provide the following icons with your app when you submit it to the App Store:

> ✔ **A 512-pixels-wide-by-512-pixels-high icon:** This icon is the image that will be on display at the App Store.

> ✔ **A 128-pixels-wide-by-128-pixels-high icon:** This icon is the image that your app will display when it's installed on a user's Macintosh. You can make this icon a scaled-down version of the 512 x 512 icon.

You see some of the standard Apple apps' icons in Figure 12-2, and in Figure 12-3, you can see the different file icons that Xcode uses for the files it takes care of.

In addition, your icons must be files of one of the following types:

> ✔ JPEG or JPG
> ✔ PNG
> ✔ TIFF or TIF

You're free to use any tool you prefer on a Mac or other computer to generate your image files.

ZIP-compressed TIFF images are not supported.

Chess.app   Dashboard.app

Front Row.app   GarageBand.app

Figure 12-2: Icons for Apple apps.

DiabeticPad_CoreD   DiabeticPad_CoreD   DiabeticPad_CoreD   DPLogEntryArrayCo   DPLogEntryArrayCo
ata2.xcodeproj   ata2_Prefix.pch   ata2-Info.plist   ntroller.h   ntroller.m

main.m   MyDocument.h   MyDocument.m   MyDocument.xcdat
                                                                     amodel

Figure 12-3: Icons for different file types that Xcode uses.

Apple suggests keeping the icon files you supply as small as possible. I prefer to use PNG formats for my image files, but JPEG usually generates files that are smaller.

Apart from the preceding constraints, your creativity is unlimited when it comes to designing your app's icons. In the following section, I show you how to put an app icon and a file icon in an app.

Adding an application icon to your apps

I'm going to work with the `StockMarketer` app from Chapter 6. You can use that project also, or one of your own. If you already have your own application's icon, you can use it instead, or you can download the app icon available for this book at `www.dummies.com`.

To add an application icon to `StockMarketer`, follow these steps:

1. **Launch Icon Composer.**

   This app is installed with Xcode, and you can find it by choosing Developer⇨Applications⇨Utilities.

2. **Drag and drop your app icon file into the large rectangle.**

3. **Repeat Step 3 for all the other rectangles.**

   You see the Icon Composer window, shown in Figure 12-4.

   You can see that the smaller icons make the text impossible to read — and this is a good reason why you should avoid using text in your application icon. Apple provides suggestions for creating application icons at the Mac Developer Center website.

Figure 12-4: Icon Composer creates a file of type ICNS that provides scaled versions of your app icon.

4. **Save your changes.**

5. **Name the file** StockMarketerAppIcons.icns, **and save it to the folder that contains the** StockMarketer **Xcode project.**

6. **Launch Xcode, and open the** StockMarketer **project.**

7. **Select the** StockMarketer **project item at the top of the Project Navigator and click the StockMarketer target in the Project editor. Select the Summary tab.**

8. **Outside of Xcode, open a Finder window and navigate to show the** StockMarketerAppIcons.icns **file. Make sure you can see both the file in the Finder window and the Summary tab view in the Xcode project window.**

9. **Drag the** StockMarketerAppIcons.icns **file from the Finder window and drop it into the square labeled** App Icon **in the Xcode project editor. In the Xcode window, click Finish.**

   You should see the display shown in Figure 12-5, with the StockMarketer application icon.

10. **Choose Product⇨Clean.**

    This step removes all the compiled code files and all the other files used in building the app. You're ensuring that the new icon file will be used.

11. **Build your app.**

12. **Open the** Products **group in the Project Navigator, and select** StockMarketer.app.

    You should see a display similar to Figure 12-6.

13. **If you'd like to confirm the results, right-click the** StockMarketer. app **item in the Project Navigator, and choose Show in Finder from the contextual menu.**

    The Finder displays a window containing StockMarketer app with its new icon, just the way a user will see it.

Figure 12-5: Adding the app icon to the StockMarketer project.

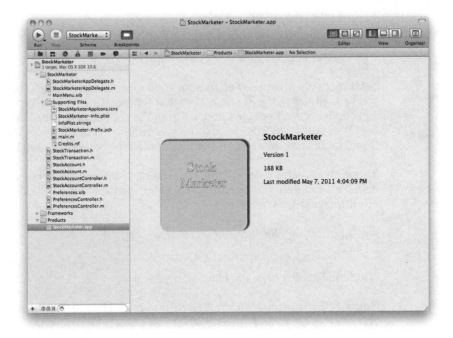

Figure 12-6: The StockMarketer app, displaying its icon.

That's all you need to do to add an icon to your app.

TIP

If you're curious, you can create different icons for the different sizes you find using Icon Composer. Then you'll see which icon is used when your app is displayed in the Finder. Using different icons can help you figure out which icon is being used and when, which can assist your understanding of why a particular icon display looks great, whereas another looks less good. OS X will perform some amount of scaling if the icon size that your user selected to display your app's icon isn't a perfect match.

Adding file icons to your apps

Your next step in rounding out the details of your Mac apps is adding icons that your app's files will display so that your users can tell those documents from the other documents they create. Figure 12-3 shows the different files that Xcode provides file icons for:

✓ The project file

✓ .h files (class headers)

- ✔ .m files (source modules)

- ✔ .pch files (precompiled headers)

- ✔ .xcdatamodel files (CoreData models)

Xcode actually provides icon files for even more file types. If you're curious, you can right-click the Xcode application (choose Developer⇨Applications) and choose Show Package Contents from the contextual menu. Drill down into the Contents⇨Resources folder, and you see the list of all the icns files contained in the app, as well as other files containing resources used by the app.

If your app creates data files for your users, you have to assign each kind of data file a different *file extension* (set of letters that follows the decimal point in a file's name), as follows:

- ✔ Application files have the extension .app.

- ✔ PNG files have the extension .png.

- ✔ Icon Set files have the extension .icns.

Figure 12-7 shows an icon of a StockMarketer data file. In the next exercise, you use this file to add file icons to the StockMarketer app.

Figure 12-7: The StockMarketer data file icon.

Here's what you need to do:

1. **Launch Icon Composer.**

2. **Drag the image file for your app's file icon into the 128-pixel size box.**

3. **Repeat Step 3 for the smaller sizes.**

   You should see something similar to Figure 12-8.

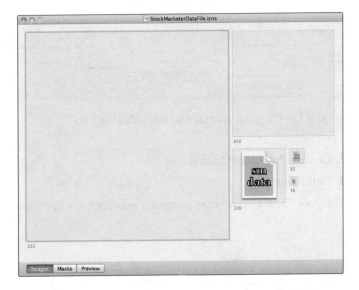

Figure 12-8: The StockMarketer data file icons. You need only the 128-pixel and smaller sizes.

4. **Save the file.**

   I called mine `StockMarketerDataFile.icns` and placed it next to the Xcode project file for `StockMarketer`.

5. **Launch Xcode, and open the** `StockMarketer` **app.**

6. **Add your new file-icon ICNS file to the project in the** `Supporting Files` **group.**

7. **Select the** `StockMarketer` **project item at the top of the Project Navigator. Select the StockMarketer target and Click the Info tab.**

   You're going to modify the Document Types and Exported UTIs properties.

8. **Click the drop-down triangle next to Document Types.**

9. **Click and hold the Add button in the lower-right corner of the Project editor and select Add Document Type from the pop-up menu.**

10. **Click the drop-down triangle next to the Untitled document type you just added.**

11. **Add the information shown in Figure 12-9.**

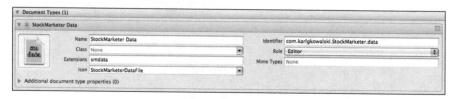

Figure 12-9: The Document Type for a StockMarketer data file.

12. **Choose Product⇨Clean.**

13. **Build your app.**

Figure 12-10 shows what a custom application's file icon looks like.

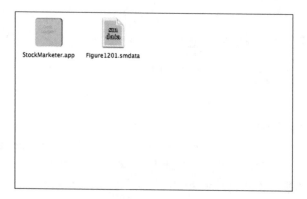

Figure 12-10: StockMarketer and a StockMarketer data file.

`StockMarketer` isn't written to create or read data files. To test the custom-file icon steps you just executed, you modify any data file's extension to match the extension you assigned to your app's data files. I used the PNG file that I created for Figure 12-1 in this chapter and changed its extension from

.png to .smdata. Double-clicking this file launches StockMarketer, but no file opens because StockMarketer isn't able to handle open-file requests from OS X. But OS X now associates the file extension .smdata with the StockMarketer app!

Creating Your Own About Panel

When you create a new project with Xcode, Xcode provides a really basic, boring About box for you. You can see StockMarketer's default About box in Figure 12-11. If this Xcode-created About box is all you want, you don't need to do anything more. You may want to modify the basic information in the About box, but that's pretty easy. Just follow these steps:

Figure 12-11: The standard Xcode-provided About box for StockMarketer.

1. **Launch Xcode, and open the StockMarketer project.**

2. **Open the Supporting Files folder, and select the Credits.rtf file in the Project Navigator.**

You see the same text you saw in the default About box. This file is what Xcode uses to populate the About box's scrollable text area. The file contains Rich Text Format text, so you can do some basic formatting of the text that you display.

3. **Modify the text to your satisfaction.**

4. **Select** `StockMarketer-Info.plist` **in the Project Navigator.**

5. **Change the value of the** `Bundle version string, short` **to** 2.0.

6. **Change the value of the** `Bundle version` **to** 2A001.

7. **Build and run the application.**

When you display the About box, you should see that the text has changed to the data you added in the `Credits.rtf` file. In addition, the version data should have changed to say `Version 2.0 (2A001)`, due to your modifications of the `Bundle` version data in `StockMarketer-Info.plist`. Through these two files you can create content for your About box, so long as your content is text-only.

Xcode 4 lets you change the `Bundle version` in the Project editor summary tab, but not the `Bundle versions string`.

An About box is a way of providing users information about your app and your business. You can put just about anything you want in the standard About box, but it's limited to text. What if you want something more? Simple: You create your own About panel, which contains an `NSView` that you can customize, and then add any content you choose. Here's how to do that:

1. **Launch Xcode, and open your project.**

Once more, I'm using `StockMarketer`.

2. **Right-click the** `StockMarketer` **folder, and choose New File from the contextual menu.**

3. **Select User Interface below Mac OS X.**

4. **Select the Window template, and click Next.**

5. **Name your new XIB file, and save it.**

I chose `AboutStockMarketer.xib`.

Xcode creates the new XIB file with an empty window inside and then opens the Interface Builder Editor with the XIB file's contents.

6. **Add a Custom View object to the window in your XIB file.**

7. **Change the Custom View's class to** `NSImageView` **using the Identity inspector.**

   You will be adding an image file to the project to display in your custom About window. You can find the image file I used at this book's website at `www.dummies.com`. I recommend setting the size of the `NSImageView` to the same size of the image in the file so that no scaling or stretching is involved.

8. **Add a copyright notice and some information about your business, using** `Label` **objects.**

   Figure 12-12 shows the new About panel.

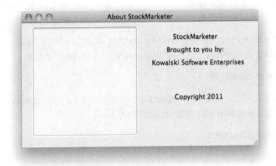

Figure 12-12: A custom About panel.

9. **Save your changes.**

10. **Right-click the** `StockMarketer` **folder, and choose New File from the contextual menu.**

11. **Create a new source module and header file for the About panel, and make the class a subclass of** `NSWindowController`.

    I named this class `AboutStockMarketerController`.

12. **Modify the** `AboutStockMarketerController` **header file to add the** `purple` **code shown in Listing 12-1.**

    The change is fairly simple: You're just adding a member variable to reference the `NSImageView` and a method that will be called when the OK button is clicked.

13. **Save your changes.**

14. **Select the** `AboutStockMarketer.xib` **file in the Project navigator to edit it in Interface Builder.**

15. **Select the top icon —** `File's Owner` **— in the Interface Builder Dock, and open the utilities view so that you can modify its parameters.**

16. **Show the Identity inspector, and select** `AboutStockMarketerController` **to be the** `File's Owner` **class.**

17. **Save your changes.**

18. **Control-drag from the** `File's Owner` **object to the** `NSImageView` **in the window and select the** `m_aboutImage` **IBOutlet to make the connection.**

19. **Control-drag from the** `File's Owner` **object to the window and select the** `window` **Outlet from the list.**

I find it easiest to Control-drag to the window's title so I don't accidentally make a connection to the wrong UI component.

20. **Save your changes.**

21. **Modify the** `AboutStockMarketerController` **source module to add the** `purple` **code shown in Listing 12-2.**

22. **Save your changes.**

23. **Modify the** `StockMarketerAppDelegate` **header file to add the** `purple` **code shown in Listing 12-3.**

You're adding a method for showing the new About panel and a member variable that will give the delegate a reference to the controller you just created.

24. **Save your changes.**

25. **Modify the** `StockMarketerAppDelegate` **source file to add the** `purple` **code shown in Listing 12-4.**

26. **Save your changes.**

27. **Select the** `MainMenu.xib` **file in the Project Navigator.**

28. **Connect the About StockMarketer menu item to the** `showAbout Window:` **in the** `StockMarketerAppDelegate` **object in the Dock.**

29. **Save your changes.**

30. **Build and run your app.**

`StockMarketer` launches, and if you choose StockMarketer⇨About StockMarketer, you see the customized About panel instead of the standard Xcode window.

Listing 12-1:   The contents of the header file for the class AboutStockMarketerController

```
//
//  AboutStockMarketerController.h
//  StockMarketer
//
//  Created by Karl Kowalski on 5/8/11.
//  Copyright 2011 Kowalski Software Enterprises. All rights reserved.
//

#import <Cocoa/Cocoa.h>


@interface AboutStockMarketerController : NSWindowController
{
    IBOutlet NSImageView* m_aboutImage;
@private

}


@end
```

Listing 12-2:   The contents of the source module for the class AboutStockMarketerController

```
//
//  AboutStockMarketerController.m
//  StockMarketer
//
//  Created by Karl Kowalski on 5/8/11.
//  Copyright 2011 Kowalski Software Enterprises. All rights reserved.
//

#import "AboutStockMarketerController.h"


@implementation AboutStockMarketerController

- (id)init
{
    if (nil == [super initWithWindowNibName:@"AboutStockMarketer"])
    {
        return (nil);
    }
    return (self);
}
```

(continued)

Listing 12-2 *(continued)*

```
- (id)initWithWindow:(NSWindow *)window
{
    self = [super initWithWindow:window];
    if (self)
    {
    }

    return self;
}

- (void)dealloc
{
    [super dealloc];
}

- (void)windowDidLoad
{
    [super windowDidLoad];

    // Implement this method to handle any initialization after your window
    // controller's window has been loaded from its nib file.
    // load NSImageView with proper image
    NSImage* stockGraphImage    =   [NSImage imageNamed:@"AboutBoxGraphic.png"];
    [m_aboutImage setImage:stockGraphImage];
    [m_aboutImage setNeedsDisplay:YES];
}

@end
```

Listing 12-3: Modifications to the StockMarketerAppDelegate header file

```
//
//  StockMarketerAppDelegate.h
//  StockMarketer
//
//  Created by Karl Kowalski on 4/24/11.
//  Copyright 2011 Kowalski Software Enterprises. All rights reserved.
//

#import <Cocoa/Cocoa.h>

#import "StockAccountController.h"
#import "PreferencesController.h"

@interface StockMarketerAppDelegate : NSObject <NSApplicationDelegate>
{
    IBOutlet PreferencesController* m_prefsController;
```

```
@private
    NSWindow *window;
}

@property (assign) IBOutlet NSWindow *window;

- (IBAction)showPreferences:(id)inSender;
- (IBAction)showAboutWindow:(id)inSender;

@end
```

Listing 12-4:   The updated StockMarketerAppDelegate source module, showing its own about window

```
//
//  StockMarketerAppDelegate.m
//  StockMarketer
//
//  Created by Karl Kowalski on 4/24/11.
//  Copyright 2011 Kowalski Software Enterprises. All rights reserved.
//

#import "StockMarketerAppDelegate.h"

@implementation StockMarketerAppDelegate

@synthesize window;

- (void)applicationDidFinishLaunching:(NSNotification *)aNotification
{
}

- (IBAction)showPreferences:(id)inSender
{
    if (nil == m_prefsController)
    {
        m_prefsController = [[PreferencesController alloc] init];
    }
    [[m_prefsController window] makeKeyAndOrderFront:self];
}

- (IBAction)showAboutWindow:(id)inSender
{
    AboutStockMarketerController* aboutController =
              [[AboutStockMarketerController alloc] init];
    [[aboutController window] makeKeyAndOrderFront:[self window]];
}
```

(continued)

Listing 12-4 *(continued)*

```
-   (void)dealloc
{
    [m_prefsController release];
    [super dealloc];
}

@end
```

If you've already gone through Chapter 6, you've probably noticed that displaying the About panel in this section is almost exactly like displaying the Preferences panel in that chapter. One key difference exists, however: The `AboutStockMarketerController` object is created and initialized in the `StockMarketerAppDelegate`, but the object is never released.

The `PreferencesController` object is created as a member variable maintained within the `StockMarketerAppDelegate` object and is created only if it doesn't already exist, but the `AboutStockMarketerController` object is created new every time the `showAboutWindow:` method is executed. Also, that method is executed every time you choose StockMarketer⇨About StockMarketer. This is an example of a *memory leak*, which happens when your app requests memory from OS X, but does not free up that memory when it no longer needs it. A memory leak isn't a flagrantly dangerous behavior, but you should do your best to avoid creating one where possible — which is the subject of the next section.

Tightening Your App's Memory

When your app creates a new object, it's requesting memory from the OS to store that object's information. When your app is done with that object, it makes a call to the OS to mark that object as no longer needed, which causes the OS to reclaim the memory at a future moment. But this situation forces your app to keep track of which objects are in use and which ones are no longer needed. Sometimes, your app leaks memory: It creates a new object and then misplaces the reference to that memory. Mistakes do happen, and you'll make some.

Here's the memory-leaking code from the custom About panel sample code in the preceding section:

```
AboutStockMarketerController* aboutController =
        [[AboutStockMarketerController alloc] init];
[[aboutController window] makeKeyAndOrderfront:[self window]];
```

The `AboutStockMarketerController` object is created from OS memory as a result of calling the `alloc` method, but it's a *local variable* — one that's not remembered outside the method that the code is contained within. When that method exits, the access to the local variable is lost. You have no way to find it or get it back. Because the `alloc` method automatically calls `retain` on the object that it returns, the OS considers that object to be still in use by your app, and because your code can't access that object again, your app can't call its `release` method to signal the OS you're no longer using the object.

Memory leaks such as this one can be very difficult to track down just by reading the source code. Apple has developed a tool that's included in Xcode to help keep track of your app's memory use, however. This tool is called Instruments, and you'll find it very helpful when you're looking for leaking memory while your application is running. Using Instruments is very simple. Just follow these steps:

1. **Launch Instruments.**

   You can find the app by choosing Developer⇨Applications. (Applications is the same folder where you find Xcode.)

2. **Select a template.**

3. **Select Memory below the Mac OS X heading.**

4. **Choose Leaks.**

   Figure 12-13 shows what you should see at this point.

5. **If your app is already running, choose Attach To Process from the Choose Target drop-down menu and then choose your app's name from the submenu that opens.**

   or

   If your app isn't running, choose Choose Target from the Choose Target drop-down menu, and navigate through the file system to find and select your app.

   You can see where it is in the Finder by opening the Products folder in the Project Navigator, right-clicking the app item, and choosing Show in Finder from the contextual menu.

6. **Click the Record button.**

   Instruments starts keeping track of all the memory allocations, retains, and releases during your app's execution. It monitors every piece of your app that you exercise and checks it for memory leaks. While Instruments is recording your app's memory use, you should exercise *every* part of your app.

Figure 12-13: Instruments will help you find leaks in your apps.

Write down the sequence of steps you will follow while exercising each part of your app so you can coordinate what you did with Instruments' recording of your app's responses.

7. **Click the Stop button.**

Instruments halts its recording of your app's memory manipulations. You'll be able to see all the items where Instruments detected a memory leak, as well as the analysis Instruments did to determine where the leaks occurred.

Using Instruments to track down memory leaks

In this section, I demonstrate how to use Instruments with a very simple Xcode project that simply leaks memory by allocating objects that never get released.

Xcode 3 would build the app for your project in a subfolder called Build inside your project's main folder. Xcode 4 puts the app in a new place: Navigate in the Finder to your Home directory and then choose Library⇨ Developer⇨Xcode⇨Derived Data⇨*{project_name}-{identifier}*⇨Build⇨ Products⇨*{Debug, Release, or some other scheme}*. In OS X 10.7 Lion, the Library folder in your home directory is now hidden, so you will need to select Go⇨Go To Folder . . . in the Finder menu and enter ~/Library to show this folder in a Finder window.

To get a good idea of how to track down memory leaks, follow these steps:

1. **Launch Xcode.**

2. **Create a new Mac OS X project, and call it** Leaker.

   Xcode creates a default window-based project. You won't need the frills of CoreData or a document-based app.

3. **Select** LeakerAppDelegate.h **in the Project navigator, and add the** purple **lines shown in Listing 12-5.**

4. **Select** MainMenu.xib **in the Project navigator, and add a button and four labels, as shown in Figure 12-14.**

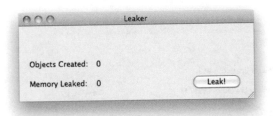

Figure 12-14: The Leaker main window. Each click of the button creates new objects and loses track of them all.

5. **Connect the** LeakerAppDelegate**'s** IBOutlet **variables to the two labels representing the number of objects created and the amount of memory leaked.**

6. **Connect the window's button to the** LeakerAppDelegate**'s** IBAction **method** leakObjects:.

7. **Save your changes.**

8. Select `LeakerAppDelegate.m` **in the Project navigator, and modify the source code to add the** `purple` **lines shown in Listing 12-6.**

You're implementing the code for the `leakObjects:` method and can leave everything else alone.

9. **Save your changes.**

10. **Build and run your app.**

Every time you click the Leak! button, a random number of 2KB memory allocations occurs. The window displays the current amount of memory that was allocated and leaked, as well as the total number of objects that were allocated.

11. **Launch Instruments, and create a session that will look for leaks.**

I find it easier to launch Leaker first and then tell Instruments to look for leaks in the running process.

12. **Click the Record button to start the Instruments memory-watch recording session.**

13. **Click the Leak! button several times in Leaker.**

Figure 12-15 shows that my session created almost 1,000 objects and leaked almost 2MB of memory.

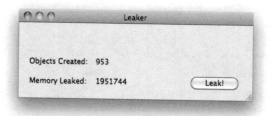

Figure 12-15: The Leaker main window after 953 leaks.

14. **Click the Stop button in Instruments.**

Figure 12-16 shows the result. The third line in the list of statistics in the Category column, Malloc 2.00KB, shows that 953 objects were allocated, which matches what Leaker said it had created. It also shows the total number of bytes allocated in the column titled Overall Bytes.

15. **In the Instruments pane, just below the Record button, Click the Leaks Instrument.**

You see one entry in the Leaked Blocks list, but you can click its drop-down triangle and get the full list of 2KB leaks. Each leak that Instruments has recorded is shown, and included in each item is the name of the object and its method where the leak occurred. Figure 12-17 shows the top portion of this list.

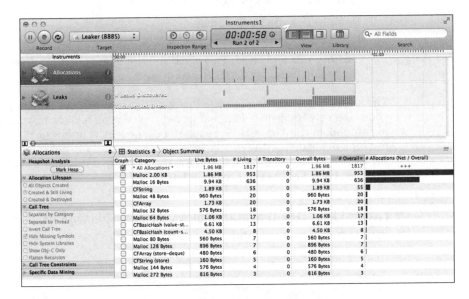

Figure 12-16: Instruments watching all the leaking going on in Leaker.

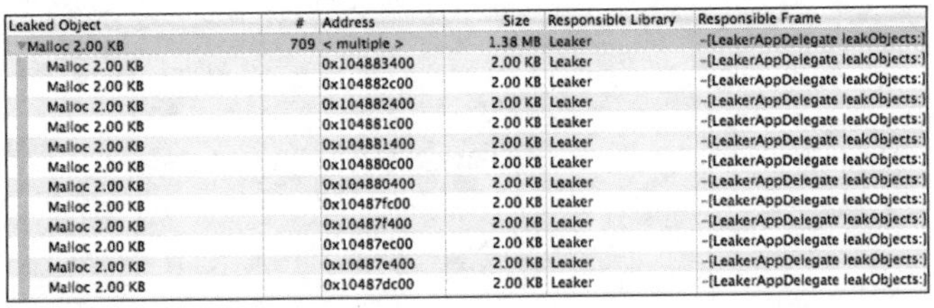

Figure 12-17: The list of leaks.

Viewing the line that created the leak

One useful feature of Instruments is that when you find a leak, and Instruments lists the class and method that caused the leak, you can jump right into the code to see the line that was executed to create the leak. To do this, follow these steps:

1. **In Instruments, with the list of leaked objects on display (refer to Figure 12-17), select one of the individual leak items.**

   In the Address column, you should see a circle with an arrow inside.

2. **Click the circled arrow.**

   Instruments shows you the leaked item.

3. **Double-click the leaked item.**

   Instruments displays the code within the object's method where the memory was allocated. This gives you a starting point for determining where and how leaks are created in your apps.

The location in your source code that Instruments displays may not show you why the leak is happening, but it gives you a place to start looking around. In the `leakObjects:` method, the leak is intentional, and Instruments is displaying precisely where the memory is being allocated: at the call to `malloc(2048L)` within the `while` loop. If this application were a real one, I'd definitely want to clean it up.

Listing 12-5:   The LeakerAppDelegate header file with its member variables and sole method

```
//
//  LeakerAppDelegate.h
//  Leaker
//
//  Created by Karl Kowalski on 5/8/11.
//  Copyright 2011 Kowalski Software Enterprises. All rights reserved.
//

#import <Cocoa/Cocoa.h>

@interface LeakerAppDelegate : NSObject <NSApplicationDelegate>
{
    IBOutlet NSTextField* m_objectsCreated;
    IBOutlet NSTextField* m_memoryLeaked;
@private
    NSWindow *window;
}

@property (assign) IBOutlet NSWindow *window;

- (IBAction)leakObjects:(id)inSender;

@end
```

Listing 12-6:   The LeakerAppDelegate source that will intentionally leak memory

```
//
//  LeakerAppDelegate.m
//  Leaker
//
//  Created by Karl Kowalski on 5/8/11.
//  Copyright 2011 Kowalski Software Enterprises. All rights reserved.
//

#import "LeakerAppDelegate.h"

#include <stdlib.h>

@implementation LeakerAppDelegate

@synthesize window;

- (void)applicationDidFinishLaunching:(NSNotification *)aNotification
{
    // Insert code here to initialize your application
}

- (IBAction)leakObjects:(id)inSender
{
    // generate a random number between 1 and 100
    long randomNumber = random() % 100 + 1;
    // make that many calls to malloc
    char* randomArray = 0L;
    NSUInteger  allocCount  =   0;
    NSUInteger  memCount = 0;
    while (randomNumber > 0)
    {
        randomNumber--;
        randomArray = malloc(2048L);
        allocCount++;
        memCount += 2048;
    }
    NSInteger currentObjectCount = [m_objectsCreated integerValue];
    currentObjectCount += allocCount;
    [m_objectsCreated setIntegerValue:currentObjectCount];
    NSInteger currentMemoryLeak = [m_memoryLeaked integerValue];
    currentMemoryLeak += memCount;
    [m_memoryLeaked setIntegerValue:currentMemoryLeak];
}

@end
```

Memory leaks are a nuisance in any app. When the app exits, all memory leaks disappear; your app is no longer running, so it has no memory to leak. You should make an effort to reduce all the memory leaks that your app creates to make sure you're not running your users out of memory. Small leaks may not have a great effect on your app's performance, but you really ought to clean them up, no matter how small they are.

The most important rules of memory management are these:

- Every call to `retain` should be matched to a call to `release`.

- Every call to `alloc` automatically calls `retain`.

- If a class needs to keep a reference to an input parameter, call `retain` on the incoming parameter and then call `release` on the previous reference.

- Convenience methods return objects that have had `autorelease` called on them. If you want to keep a reference to them, you must also call `retain`.

- Call `release` on all the member variables within an object's `dealloc` method.

Keeping these rules in mind while you're writing your apps will take you a long way toward reducing the memory leaks that creep up on you while you're not looking.

Localizing Your App

If you're planning to sell your app only to English-speaking users in the US, this section isn't for you. But if you're looking to increase your sales and your app's penetration among Mac users worldwide, you should seriously consider creating an app that speaks the native languages of your users.

For my previous Dummies book, *BlackBerry Application Development For Dummies,* I wrote a BlackBerry application and put it up for free at BlackBerry App World. Although the app is English-only and has enjoyed thousands of downloads throughout the BlackBerry realm, I can only imagine how many more downloads would have resulted if I'd simply added the native languages of the countries where large numbers of users live, such as France, Germany, and India. Although the users in these countries are comfortable using an English-only app, as I write more apps, the benefits of using a native-speaking app could make the difference between my app's being downloaded and a competitor's app being downloaded. If your app has limited displays of text — and especially if most of your app's text strings are in the user-interface sections of your app — you'll find that enabling your app to speak a foreign language is important, and it's easier than it seems.

During my years of public school and college education, I made several attempts to learn French and German. I don't know either language well enough to translate my apps into those languages. A couple of websites, however, can do translations of simple (and some not-so-simple) phrases and sentences for free:

```
www.babelfish.com
www.google.com/language_tools
```

I've experimented with both sites and found that each has advantages and drawbacks. For short phrases and single words that you might use for buttons, labels, and menu items, both sites offer fairly good translations. I recommend having a real person who knows the language review the results, but for the most part, you can trust that the translations done for your apps will be reasonably correct. Also, your users will be happy to correct Google's or BabelFish's grammatical mistakes, so be sure to pay attention to your e-mails, and review feedback.

You can also download the Language Translator Dashboard widget from Apple, which uses Google's language translation service.

Xcode makes it very easy to create a localized version of your XIB file where all your UI text resources reside. To get started, here's what you need to do:

1. **Launch Xcode, and open the project to which you want to add a new language.**

   I'll be working with Leaker, because I still have it open in Xcode, and it's pretty simple.

2. **Select** `MainMenu.xib` **in the Project navigator.**

   The main window of Leaker is displayed in the editor.

3. **Display Utilities view, if it's not already visible, and select the File Inspector.**

   You should see the display shown in Figure 12-18.

Figure 12-18: The File Inspector, showing the details of MainMenu.xib.

4. **Click the drop-down triangle in the Localization section to open it if it's closed.**

   English is the default language, and now you're going to add French.

5. **Click the + button at the bottom of the Localization section.**

   A menu pops up, displaying a basic set of foreign languages.

6. **Choose French from the menu to add French as an optional language.**

   Xcode copies the `MainMenu.xib` file from the English folder (`en.lproj`) in your project folder to the French folder (`fr.lproj`). Now your app is ready to support the display of French-language text in your user interface (UI) when your app is run on a French-language Macintosh. If you open your project's folder in the Finder, you see the folder `fr.lproj` and its contents: a copy of `MainMenu.xib`.

Xcode didn't translate any of the text in this alternative XIB file to French; it merely provided a separate file containing all the UI components in the original XIB file, which will be loaded instead of the English-language components when your app is launched on a French-speaking Mac.

When you want to modify this file's contents, here's what you do:

1. **In the Project Navigator, click the drop-down triangle next to** `MainMenu.xib`.

   This step should reveal the two language-specific files: `MainMenu.xib` (English) and `MainMenu.xib` (French).

2. **Select the** `MainMenu.xib` **(French) item in the Project navigator.**

   You're looking at the UI components that will be loaded, with their eventual French-language text, when this app is run on a French-speaking Mac. Now all you have to do is translate the window title, the button text, and the two labels.

   Figure 12-19 shows you my limited efforts toward achieving something that my high-school French teachers would fail me for.

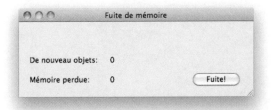

Figure 12-19: I'm not a native French speaker, but if it helps my users and encourages them to buy my apps, I'll make it happen.

You should clean your project and then build before running. In addition, to test your non-English-language UI, you need to choose Settings⇨Language & Text Setting so that the language you want to test is at the top of the list.

That's all there is to making a localized version of your app's UI. You need to do a little more work if your app generates text within its code, but for most projects, this won't be a problem. Your apps will soon speak your users' native languages — all the languages that a Mac can speak.

Part V
The Part of Tens

The 5th Wave   By Rich Tennant

In this part . . .

Mac app development can be filled with joy and frustration, sometimes only minutes apart. This part is filled with examples and tips to make your life as a Mac app developer somewhat more productive and less challenging. In addition, you'll find a list of tools that can make your development efforts more rewarding.

Chapter 13

Ten Useful Apple Sample Apps

1 began my adventures in programming when I was handed a book of source code, in the BASIC programming language, containing more than 100 games. This book was page after page of the computer instructions needed to program apps like roulette, blackjack, craps — apparently games of chance were a big hit — as well as mazes, puzzles, and other interesting and strange ways to explore what a computer program could do. The book did not go over theory, data structures, or anything remotely philosophical — object-oriented programming was still not mainstream. Most of the games worked as written, some required a workaround, and (of course) there was one that I never did get to run. But after reading through all the games, and trying to get them all to work, I learned the basics of programming from those examples. And so I learned the best lesson about programming: Sample Code.

Xcode does not come with code examples of the many different things you can implement within your apps. The Apple Developer website, however, provides hundreds of examples of sample Mac app code that you can download and get up and running on your development machine. When you search the Developer Library for Core Data, for example, your search will return Sample Code resources, in addition to Tutorials and Guides about Core Data. The website delivers a great deal of material on each sample app. You can look at all the code through web pages without having to download the app; this is helpful if you're only looking to see how a particular class is being used. You can also download the project and build the app. Each sample app is contained within a complete Xcode project. Most of the sample apps are small, and you'll find them focused on demonstrating one or two fundamental concepts. This chapter describes the ten sample apps that I find the most interesting and useful.

Apple is constantly adding improvements to its Macintosh OS, and consequently Apple is also constantly adding new sample apps to demonstrate the new features and functionality. As great as that is, you must keep in mind that some of the sample apps you find at the Apple Developer website may be out of date — and this can lead to some difficulties in getting an app to work. Like the games in the book that required me to find a workaround, you can learn a lot from downloading a sample app that was written for a version of OS X that's older than what you're running Xcode on. But stay calm, cool, and collected when the app doesn't build. You just might learn something new.

TIP

You can find all of the Apple Sample apps at the following URL:

```
https://developer.apple.com/library/mac/navigation/#section=Resource%20
                Types&topic=Sample%20Code
```

Figure 13-1 shows just the top lines of the result — note the "753 of 3085" documents in the list: you've got *lots* of sample apps to choose from, and it's a safe bet that somewhere in the full set is the example you're looking for. Make sure you pay attention to the Topic column in this list — while most of the samples are written in Objective-C, there are a few Java-based and AppleScript app projects as well.

Apple is constantly updating its sample code, so you may find an updated list of sample apps when you check out the URL above.

▼ Sample Code

Get hands-on familiarity with Mac OS X APIs by studying, building, and modifying Sample Code projects. Each Sample Code project consists of buildable and executable source code that illustrates how to accomplish one or more tasks with specific Apple technologies. Every project shows the correct sequence of API calls that you can modify for your specific needs.

Documents 753 of 3085

Title	Resource Type	Topic	Framework	Date
JAWTExample	Sample Code	Cross Platform Java		2011-03-09 Content Update
ImageBrowser	Sample Code	Graphics & Animation 3D Drawing	Quartz	2011-03-08 Content Update
ToolbarSample	Sample Code	User Experience Controls	AppKit	2011-03-01 Content Update
OpenCL Hello World Example	Sample Code	Performance	OpenCL	2011-03-01 Content Update
MyFirstJNIProject	Sample Code	Cross Platform Java		2011-03-01 Minor Change
IconCollection	Sample Code	User Experience Windows & Views	AppKit	2011-02-15 Content Update
HeightArray	Sample Code	Graphics & Animation 3D Drawing	OpenGL	2011-02-15 Content Update
GLEssentials	Sample Code	Graphics & Animation 3D Drawing	OpenGL	2011-02-08 Minor Change
OutputBinsPDE	Sample Code	Graphics & Animation Printing	ApplicationServices	2011-02-07 Content Update
QTCoreVideo101	Sample Code	Audio & Video Video	QuartzCore	2011-01-22 Content Update
NullAuthPlugin	Sample Code	Security	Security	2011-01-22 Minor Change
CustomMenus	Sample Code	User Experience Menus	AppKit	2011-01-19 Minor Change
DictionaryController	Sample Code	Data Management Data Types & Collections	AppKit	2011-01-13 Content Update
SimpleCocoaApp	Sample Code	General	AppKit	2011-01-12 Content Update

Figure 13-1: Some of the Sample Mac Apps added or updated in the beginning of 2011.

You'll also find Sample code as a result of a search — when you're looking for information on an Objective-C class such as NSTableView, the search results will show links to sample code, as shown in Figure 13-2. So always be on the lookout for the words "Sample Code" whenever you're looking through web pages at the Apple developer website.

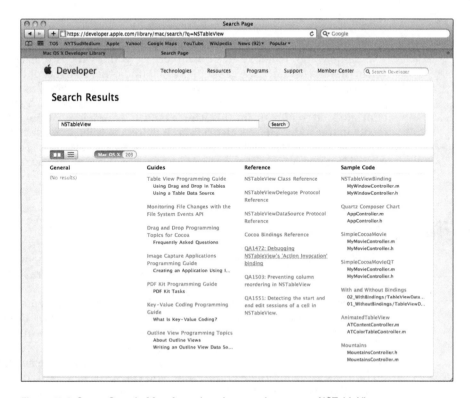

Figure 13-2: Seven Sample Mac Apps that show you how to use NSTableView.

No more preliminaries. Let's meet my favorite sample apps.

ToolbarSample

Many apps that you use today come with a toolbar. Toolbars are a great way to provide functionality that used to be contained within menus — your app still provides a multitude of menu items, but for those operations that users are using most frequently, your app can provide a toolbar button to perform the same task. You're likely to use all the toolbar buttons that Xcode provides for building, running, and debugging your apps. An app that displays an NSToolbar for its users must implement NSToolbarDelegate methods — and you'll find this done in the code, nicely separated out from the other methods in the Controller class implementation. I like this sample because it's small and focused on demonstrating how to provide toolbar features to your users — which is a great way to demonstrate your app takes your users' needs and expectations into consideration.

CustomMenus

This sample app demonstrates how to create your own customized menus. While that may sound overly simple, you'll find other nuggets of code within this app. You'll see how to create a pop-up menu that displays its own custom view for selecting from a set of images. I was surprised by the level of effort needed to implement this view; you can learn a lot just from the comments in the code. There's also a search field that will list image files available from the current folder when the user types a single letter. For an app named "CustomMenus", this sample app demonstrates not only menus but a whole lot more.

ButtonMadness

There's always something special about sample apps that come with "madness" in the name. And if you want to see buttons coded like crazy, this is the sample app for you. One of the best lessons you can learn from this app is that you don't have to use the Interface Builder Editor to create buttons and link them into your app. Apple recommends using Interface Builder as much as possible, but you can learn a lot about how to adjust your app's user interface while your code is running by creating connections in code. The ButtonMadness project demonstrates how to do both: you can see how to set up buttons using Interface Builder, and you can also see how to do the exact same things programmatically.

SimpleCocoaApp

Apple provides a simple app to demonstrate how to use Cocoa and Objective-C at a beginning level. It's great for reinforcing the ideas and concepts you learned in this book, and you can always find it online so you don't have to carry this book around with you everywhere. You'll discover that this sample app is really not so simple — you encounter some subtleties about the messages that one Objective-C object sends to another, including creating messages on the fly to be sent programmatically. You'll need to spend time reviewing both the code and the connections made through Interface Builder to come to a complete understanding of what's going on.

NSTableViewBinding

Sooner or later you'll create an app that displays collections of information using an NSTableView. I did so for one of my first Mac OS X products, and it was (as they say) a learning experience. This sample app was created to demonstrate how to use Cocoa Bindings with an NSTableView so that your app's data source — in the app, an NSArrayController using an NSMutableDictionary to hold the data — will be displayed as both rows of records in the NSTableView and as individual pieces when a row in the table is selected. As always, a lot of different aspects of Mac app programming are present in this sample app; I recommend you study it closely to see exactly how this app does what it does. The comments are especially helpful, so you should read them as well.

IconCollection

This sample app demonstrates interactions between several different XIB files in creating a window that displays icons. You'll see how to use an NSCollectionView for displaying the collection of icons — or anything, really — within the app. As always, Apple's sample app delivers far more than its name suggests. You'll see how an NSArrayController keeps track of all the icons, and you'll learn how to use an NSSortDescriptor to manipulate how the array of icons is sorted for display.

PictureSharing

Today's fast-paced users are *connected* users: They are using the Internet not simply on a daily basis but on a moment-to-moment basis. When I started learning how to program, I used a telephone to connect my dumb-terminal to a remote computer, using audible signals. Today users are communicating billions of bytes across electrical cables or through the air, thousands (or even millions) of times faster. These Apple sample apps — both a server and a client — will show you how to provide and access a network service using Bonjour, Apple's protocol for broadcasting, discovering, and interacting with services over a network. This sample provides a server app — PictureSharing — and a client app — PictureSharingBrowser. To see them in action, build and launch the server app, and then build and launch the client. The client will find the Bonjour services available on the network — which had better be the PictureSharing service! These sample apps also demonstrate the use of NSStream objects to move data across a network.

Squiggles

If you write only data-management-and-display apps, you'll be making use of standard components and Cocoa classes. But your app will stand above the crowd if you make use of the users' screens by displaying information in a more visual way — and that means creating custom NSView classes that draw their data in a different way. Squiggles is one such app; its display looks like those old Etch-a-Sketch™ toys, only you can draw in color and then rotate the colored lines you've drawn into a circular pattern that gets drawn again and again onto the screen. This sample app introduces you to creating a custom view that uses custom objects that contain information about how to draw themselves. In addition, you'll learn about applying visual transforms when drawing two-dimensional images; then you can rotate any particular drawing your apps do through 360 degrees.

Dictionary Controller

You will use many different collection classes in your Mac apps. The NSDictionary and NSMutableDictionary classes let you store objects in a key-value mechanism: each value object (a subclass of NSObject) is mapped to a key object, and this form of collection storage has a variety of uses. The DictionaryController sample app shows you how to use an NSDictionaryController object to manage the data your app stores in an NSDictionary or NSMutableDictionary so that your app's visual components can access and display the information contained within a collection. You'll find examples of Cocoa Bindings in this app as well.

Image Transition

The Apple iPhone brought animations to apps to wow the users. Apple gave its iOS developers some programmatic tools that made animation easy to add to their apps. And you can add similar animations to your Mac apps as well. ImageTransition shows the various animated transition types, applied to a view that changes one image to another via a transition animation. You'll also learn how to find out what animation types are available from the OS — these will change over time, but you can query the system

When I first used ImageTransition, before Xcode 4 was released, the app built and ran fine. After I installed Xcode 4, the build ran into a snag — Xcode 4 didn't get along with some setting in the build files for the Xcode 3 project — the problem was in the settings for the *machine architecture*, which reflects on the specifics of the Mac's CPU and the libraries for it. This is one of the most-likely problems with using older sample apps in a newer version of Xcode. In Figure 13-3, you can see the changes I made in the Xcode 4 display of Build Settings — which you display by clicking the top-level item in the left pane. In the Architectures group, I modified the following items:

Figure 13-3: Sometimes elderly sample apps need a few tweaks. This app was last updated in August 2010.

 ✓ **Architectures.** I set this value to *Native Architecture of Build Machine*. I wanted Xcode to build the app only for the machine on which Xcode was running. I didn't want Xcode to worry about coding for some other kind of machine.

 ✓ **Base SDK.** This value tells Xcode which SDK — which set of OS libraries — to use for the app. I set it to *Latest Mac OS X (Mac OS X 10.7)*. As with Architectures, I didn't want Xcode to go out of its way to accommodate a technology from the past that the app's users probably wouldn't be running.

 ✓ **Valid Architectures.** Since I knew there was only one machine architecture on which I would execute the sample app, I reset this value to *x86_64*.

Once these changes were made, the app built and executed just fine.

Chapter 14

Ten Macintosh Development Tips

*Y*ou'll discover that programming a Macintosh app is, in general, very similar to programming an app for any other type of computer. There are certain unique aspects to Mac programming with Cocoa that you'll need to keep in mind, however — and in this chapter, I point out and remind you of some of the most important ones.

I find that developing Mac apps provides a variety of challenges with each app I write. Sometimes these challenges are simple and easy to overcome; other times the challenges are difficult enough that I am forced to choose another approach for accomplishing my goals. Most development effort falls between these two extremes, and I think you'll find the information in this chapter helpful to move your own challenges from the Difficult end of the spectrum closer to the Easy side.

Keep Track of Memory

Your app is going to need to take system memory to do everything. Your app's windows require memory to keep track of their contents, where they're located and how big they appear on the screen. Every part of your app uses memory to perform the feats of application magic you've designed it to perform. Today's computers now come with billions of bytes of system memory — but today's users make their computers do ever more things. Your app should keep a tight rein on its memory requests; to get it to do this, you'll have to be careful about how you request memory, how you hold onto it, and how you send it back to the system. Chapter 4 provides a basic course in OS X memory handling, and I think this is important enough to remind you here of where you'll find that information quickly. Table 14-1 provides you with a quick-hit list of memory functions you'll use when your app creates Objective-C objects.

Table 14-1	Objective-C Memory Functions
Function Name	*When To Use It*
`retain`	When your app needs to use the `retained` object outside of the method in which it was created. A `retain` call is made automatically during an `alloc` call.
`release`	When your app is finished with a `retained` object and no longer requires access to it. Usually this happens during the `dealloc` method of a class.
`autorelease`	When your app needs an object to behave as if you had called `retain` on it, but which is scheduled to be `released` automatically at a future point. Cocoa classes that provide convenience methods such as `NSString` `stringWithString:` will call `autorelease` automatically before handing the object to your app.

When you create a setter method for a member variable object such as an `NSString`, always obey the following rules:

- ✓ Retain the incoming object first.
- ✓ Release the old object stored in the member variable second.
- ✓ Assign the incoming object to the member variable.

Memory leaks can cause problems and even lead to your app being rejected by Apple. Calling a method on an object that was released and whose memory was returned to the system will cause a crash — which will definitely get your app rejected by Apple if they discover it and will make your users unhappy with your app if it happens to them. Chapter 12 provides an introduction to the diagnostic tools such as Instruments that come with Xcode and can help you track down memory leaks.

Read Apple's Documentation

I know very few professional programmers, myself included, who go to the development documentation *first*. But although I wrote this book to assist in getting you *started* with Mac app programming, Apple's engineers have written thousands of pages of documentation — discussing every different class and OS function that your apps will use. Apple's documentation is *complete*, and is very good at explaining each class and the methods your apps can use in that class to achieve your apps' goals. Use that documentation.

When I started Macintosh programming, the documentation was all in book form, costing several hundred dollars for the complete set. Now you can access all the details over the Internet, for free. Apple's documentation can be challenging to understand (and that's another reason I wrote this book — to help you bypass some of the overwhelming details that Apple delivers and get right to the core information you need to get the job done). But Apple's documentation will always be the definitive answer for all Mac programming inquiries, and you'll get to know an invaluable resource by reading Apple's docs.

Apple's documentation is divided into multiple categories; the following are the ones I find to be the most useful:

- Reference, where you find the specifics of Cocoa classes, methods, and OS X functions.

- Guides where you can follow, step by step, how to use various aspects of the Cocoa frameworks — for instance, how to use Core Data for storing information in your application.

- Sample code, where you see how Apple's engineers used the Cocoa frameworks to perform specific tasks, and which you can use to build working apps that demonstrate how particular features can be implemented.

- Getting Started, where you learn how to start using different features of Mac OS X programming in your apps.

- Xcode Tasks, which gives you assistance in all the different things that you can do with Xcode.

Sometimes the sample code projects are not updated for the current version of either OS X or Xcode.

Apple's Macintosh programming online documentation sources can be found here:

```
http://developer.apple.com/library/mac/navigation/
```

Use Online Resources

In addition to Apple's online documentation, you will find a wealth of information online, both at Apple and spread all over the Internet. Apple provides Developer Forums where you can ask questions, answer questions, and find answers to your questions regarding all aspects of Macintosh development. Access to the Apple Developer Forums is free, and you should definitely take advantage of this. Remember, there are tens of thousands of developers just like you, writing Macintosh apps and hitting problems identical or similar to yours. Sometimes you'll be answered by Apple engineers. You should search through the forums before posting a question, to ensure that your particular challenge has not already been addressed.

You can reach the Apple Developer Forums here: `https://devforums. apple.com/index.jspa`. You will need to be logged into your registered developer account to access them.

In addition to Apple's Developer Forums, several other non-Apple forums have arisen on the Internet: the Internet is a great place for everyone to find information, and for everyone to share information they've encountered — especially solutions to challenging problems. Some of my favorite third-party Mac developer forums are

- Cocoa Builder: `www.cocoabuilder.com`
- Cocoa Dev: `www.cocoadev.com`
- Cocoa Dev Central: `www.cocoadevcentral.com`
- MacTech: `www.mactech.com`

Finally, you can find a large amount of information on individual developers' blogs and websites that are not specifically forums. You'll have to use your favorite search engine to find them, so you'll need to carefully select the proper words to define the problem you're looking to solve. The following sites offer the blogs of Mac developers who provide a great deal of information:

✔ Cocoa Is My Girlfriend: www.cimgf.com

✔ Theocacao: www.theocacao.com

✔ Domain of the Bored: www.boredzo.org/blog

Always Remember the Parent Class

Objective-C gives you an object-oriented way to develop Macintosh apps. Your apps and the classes you create for them get to take advantage of the code that Apple's engineers have written and tested and proven to work, without you having to write any of it. Every class in the Cocoa framework, with the sole exception of the NSObject class, is a subclass of some other class in the Cocoa framework. Consequently, every class has access to functionality and data that its parent (and grandparent, great-grandparent, and so on) classes provide. This feature of object-oriented languages, called *inheritance*, is a gift from the Apple engineers to you — and to all developers of Macintosh apps.

For example, the Cocoa UI class you would use to allow the user to enter or see text is usually the NSTextField class or the NSTextView class. Both are grandchildren of NSView, but they have different parent classes: NSTextView is a subclass of NSText, while NSTextField is a subclass of NSControl. Interestingly enough, neither of these two classes comes with a method for setting the text they each display. To find those, you have to move up one level to the respective parent classes for each class:

✔ NSText comes with the setString: method.

✔ NSControl provides the setStringValue: method.

If a class does not come with a method you want to use, make sure you check its parent class's methods. In Xcode, if you enable the Code Completion preferences, you'll be presented with a list of methods while you're entering the code, so you'll find all of a class's methods, including the methods of its parents, grandparents, great-grandparents, and so on back into time.

Look Beyond the Current Problem

I find it very easy to get focused on solving the immediate coding problem when I run into one. I will narrow the problem's scope, dream up an approach to getting the code to do what I want, and implement my solution, moving on to the next problem once the current one is fixed. While this works great for simple problems, you will find that complex problems generally require more thought, including looking outside the little circle of scope where the problem resides.

In addition to looking beyond where the current problem exists within your code, consider the future effects of your solution: Look outside the little circle of *time* where the problem exists. At some point in the future, you'll return to your code, either to fix a bug found by one of your users or to implement a feature you hadn't thought of when you first wrote the code.

Objective-C and the Cocoa framework will support you in your efforts to go beyond just solving the immediate problem. Objective-C's object-oriented feature of class inheritance enables you to maintain your existing classes while adding onto them in the future — you can modify your code incrementally by creating subclasses that do more.

You'll find it useful to take a few moments and just think about how you're solving a new problem instead of acting on it right away. This can be difficult if you're under pressure to release your app within a certain time period, but it's almost always better to consider options now rather than face them later when your code has been implemented and you've committed to a specific design.

Follow Interface Builder's Guidelines

Apple requires you to follow its Human Interface Guidelines (HIG) to develop your apps, and they're likely to reject your app submission if your app does not comply with the HIG. If you look through the online documentation of the HIG, you'll find rules that govern just about everything you're going to display in your app's windows. I cannot keep them all straight in my head, there are simply too many. Luckily, Interface Builder gives you some assistance when it comes to laying out your app's windows with the standard controls that Apple provides in Xcode: When you drag a control from the Interface Builder Editor's Object Library onto your window or view, you will see guides appear when you move the control to a boundary or position of interest within the HIG. These guides assist you in lining up controls and placing them within the HIG-preferred bounds of the window or view.

You're not required to obey these guides, but you really should. Apple takes their UI very seriously, and they have many rules about how your interface should work to deliver a positive and pleasant experience for users. Nothing stops you (technically, anyway) from ignoring or violating the guidelines that Apple has established and that Interface Builder indicates, but your users will be happier if you remain consistent with their experiences with other HIG-compliant apps. And Apple is more likely to accept your App Store submission because your app is well-behaved in its interface.

Reduce, Reuse, Recycle

Object-oriented software development was, in part, designed to help save you from having to reinvent the (code) wheel. Before you create a new class, one of the most important things you can do is to search the Apple documentation to see whether someone in Apple's engineer corps has already done it for you. And moving from one app to your next, you will encounter coding problems that you've encountered in the past. Your code in one of your apps can be reused in future apps, especially when Objective-C allows you to subclass to implement greater functionality to address the slightly different new problem you've just encountered. For example, if you create a class to manage access to users' contacts in their Address Book, you can use that manager class in every app you write that requires that access. This reduces the time you'd spend to re-implement the code.

It's easy to reuse class files; all you need to do is drag the class header file (.h) and source module (.m) from your old project into your new one, or just from the old project's folder in the Finder into the new project's Project navigator. And you can reuse XIB files exactly the same way.

Use Keyboard Shortcuts

Apple popularized the user interface for applications, giving users the ability to control their computers without having to memorize or type in an endless supply of text-based commands. But the engineers at Apple also were aware that the keyboard is still the primary means of commanding computers, because it is a consistent physical interface that nearly everyone who types regularly has memorized — including programmers. Because your programming hands are always on or near the keyboard, Apple has added keyboard shortcuts for the most familiar and well-used operations in Xcode. You'll speed up your development by pressing a set of keys instead of moving your hands from the keyboard to the mouse to engage in an operation, then back again to the keyboard.

Table 14-2 lists the keyboard shortcuts for the most frequently used operations.

Table 14-2	Highly Used Keyboard Shortcuts
Shortcut	*What it does*
⌘+S	Saves a file
⌘+O	Opens a file
⌘+M	Minimizes the project file to the Macintosh Dock or into Xcode's icon in the Dock
⌘+B	Builds the project's app
⌘+R	Launches the project's app after building it (if necessary)
⌘+Z	Undoes the previous change
Shift+⌘+Z	Redoes the previous change (undo the undo)
Shift+⌘+K	Cleans the project's binaries
⌘+,	Opens the Xcode preferences
Shift+⌘+Y	Shows or hides the debug area
Option+⌘+W	Closes the file displayed in the main editor window
Option+⌘+?	Displays the Organizer documentation screen
Shift+⌘+2	Displays the Organizer window

In addition to keyboard shortcuts, Xcode also has support for *gestures*. If you've used an iOS device such as an iPad, you're familiar with using a touchscreen interface to access your apps. Apple Mac laptops are already equipped with multi-touch trackpads, and the Magic Mouse and Magic Trackpad can be used with Mac desktops. All of these input devices allow users to perform certain operations that involve multiple fingers touching and moving on the device, and Xcode is set to support the following gestures:

✓ Two-finger swipe: Scrolls vertically for up/down motion, horizontally for left/right.

 This is very useful for large source files.

✓ Three-finger swipe: In the source editor, swaps a source file (.m) with its associated header file (.h).

✓ Two-finger tap: Opens a context menu, identical to right-clicking a mouse.

Gestures are only possible when using a multi-touch input device such as the Apple Magic Trackpad, Magic Mouse, and the trackpads on MacBooks made since 2009.

Set Xcode to Your Preferences

Xcode comes with nine categories of preferences — each of which comes with its own subset of modifications you can make to change the way Xcode does everything it does. You should look over all of these to make sure Xcode is behaving as you want it to behave, instead of just acting the way the Apple defaults want Xcode to behave. The little things you can do with Xcode's preferences can make your software development experience much better. I have my favorite formatting preferences all set to my proper specifications; I also make use of code coloring to give me the best display of my code. You should at least play around with the settings in Fonts & Colors to come up with your favorite: definitely cycle through the different *themes*, such as Presentation and Midnight. Presentation is starting to appeal to me personally, since my eyesight is getting incrementally worse. But Midnight looks pretty cool, too.

You'll find the preferences that suit your style and taste, and remember, you can change them as often (or as seldom) as you prefer. Xcode's preferences are for you to choose.

Stay Up to Date

Apple is changing things — often. The most important changes regarding your Macintosh apps will come within OS X, which seems to get a major upgrade approximately once every 18 months. These upgrades generally add new functionality that your apps can take advantage of. But sometimes the upgrades *remove* functionality, replacing it with something new and different. Thus your app written for (say) OS X Snow Leopard may use features that aren't available in OS X Lion. When your users upgrade their Mac OS X to Apple's newer version, your app may crash. The most important thing for you to do is make sure your currently-shipping app will run on the latest and greatest OS X. As a registered developer, you'll have access to early editions of the next version of OS X. You should take advantage of these early access editions where possible.

Minor upgrades happen several times in between the major upgrades. Usually these just fix bugs, so your app written for OS X 10.6.5 will run on OS X 10.6.6 without any changes. But it's good to check and make sure that your app runs on these minor upgrades — which is something you can inform your prospective users about on your app's App Store description.

Apple holds the Apple Worldwide Developers Conference (WWDC) every year in California. This is a great opportunity to learn about Mac OS X and iOS development. The conference this year was sold out very quickly, but as a registered developer you can access the session videos from the conference. As of this writing, the WWDC 2011 Session Videos are available at `https://developer.apple.com/videos/wwdc/2011/`.

Index

● *T* ●